The 33rd
an anthology

DREXEL UNIVERSITY
College of
Arts and Sciences

Editor	Gail Davida Rosen
Drexel Publishing Group Director	Scott Stein
Book Designer	Andrew Turner
Editorial Co-ops	Emma Zoe Polyak
	Lauren Walinski
Student Interns	Sophia Aitcadi
	Patrick Crane
	Michael Emmert
	Grace Fisher
	Sope Lartey
	Rohan Mathew
	Ilse Nunez
	Aamna Rehman
	Miriam Reid
	Michael Singleton
	Evan Smith
	Jeanna Stedman

Sponsors

Drexel University
The College of Arts and Sciences at Drexel University
The Department of English and Philosophy at Drexel University

Dr. Kelly Joyce, Interim Dean, College of Arts and Sciences, Drexel University
Dr. J. Roger Kurtz, Department Head, English and Philosophy,
Drexel University

The 33rd Volume 15
Drexel University
Department of English and Philosophy
3141 Chestnut Street
Philadelphia, PA 19104
drexelpublishing.com

Cover photo by Shraddha Pandya
Back Cover photo by Dylan Lam

The 33rd is published once a year.

Submissions are open in the spring, winter, and fall terms of each academic year. Manuscripts must be submitted as an e-mail attachment (MS Word). Visit drexelpublishing.com for submission guidelines.

ISBN 978-1-7324500-6-6

Thanks to: Dr. Kelly Joyce; Dr. J. Roger Kurtz; all the judges from the Drexel Publishing Group Creative Writing Contest (William Albertson, Jan Armon, Valerie Booth, Cassandra Hirsch, Henry Israeli, Gregory Jewell, Lynn Levin, Deirdre McMahon, Jill Moses, Karen Nulton, Margene Petersen, Maegan Poland, Don Riggs, Doreen Saar, Fred Siegel, Andrew Snover, and Scott Stein); the Drexel Publishing Group Essay Contest (Stacey Ake, Benjamin Barnett, Ronald Bishop, Valerie Booth, Anne Erickson, Valerie Fox, Jamie Ludwig, Craig McClure, Marilyn Gaye Piety, Don Riggs, Donna Rondolone, Doreen Saar, Fred Siegel, James Stieb, Monica Togna, Maria Volynsky, Fengqing (Zoe) Zhang); the First-Year Writing Contest (Jan Armon, Anthony Chatfield, Judy Curlee, Anne Erickson, Tim Fitts, Cassandra Hirsch, Roger Kurtz, Deirdre McMahon, Kathleen Volk Miller, Christopher Nielson, Karen Nulton, Gail Davida Rosen, Doreen Saar, Sheila Sandapen, Fred Siegel, Matt Smith, Scott Stein, Errol Sull, and Maria Volynsky); the Department of English and Philosophy, especially Liz Heenan; contest participants; and the Drexel Publishing Group staff.

17177 Laurel Park Drive
Suite 233
Livonia, MI 48152
800-562-2147
www.xanedu.com

Credits

Britton, Jennifer and Ottinger, Gwen. "Let's Start Crafting Environmental Policy with an Anti-Racist Lens" was published in *The Philadelphia Inquirer* on November 8, 2021.

Cohen, Paula Marantz. "The Seminar Course Can Save Civility" originally appeared in *The Wall Street Journal* op-ed page on December 1, 2019.

Fitts, Tim. "Gigi" appeared in Big Windows Review on August 13, 2021. "YMCA" appeared in *Eunoia Review* on June 2, 2021.

Fox, Valerie. "Belongings (in Six Boxes)" was published in the Flash Fiction Festival Anthology #4 from Ad Hoc Fiction (2021). "Your Intemperate Life" was published in *Reflex* (2021).

Israeli, Henry. "Survival Song" was published in *Michigan Quarterly Review* on 2019, Vol.58 (4).

Kotzin, Miriam. "116 Plan B" and "Lessons" were published in *Offcourse*, Issue 88, 2021. "A Scholar Flunks Romance" and "Penmanship" were published in *BlinkInk*, in December 2021. "Daylight" was published in *Five Minutes* on March 31, 2022.

Levin, Lynn. "Dr. Rieux, Meet Dr. Fauci: Seeing Albert Camus's The Plague with 2020 Vision" was published on *The Massachusetts Review* blog, October 22, 2020.

Mele-Bazaz, Leah. "Second Sight" was published in *Barren Magazine* in April 2021.

Riggs, Don. "Occasional Communities: Academic Conferences and Arthurian Romance" appeared at the 43rd International Conference on the Fantastic in the Arts, in Orlando, Florida, on March 18, 2022.

Rosen, Gail Davida. "Curtain Up: Teaching the Broadway Musical" was published in the Spring/Summer 2022 issue of *Honor Bound* on page 17: https://issuu.com/pennonihonorscollege2016/docs/full_1_.

Stein, Scott. "Excerpt from *The Great American Betrayal* (Chapter 1)" is an excerpt from *The Great American Betrayal* which was published by Tiny Fox Press in 2022.

Warnock, Scott. "Yes-More People" was originally published on August 4, 2021 on *When Falls the Coliseum*: http://whenfallsthecoliseum.com/2021/08/04/yes-more-people.

Zillmer, Eric A. "The Murderer: A Psychological Analysis" was presented as *What might this be? The Art and Science of Inkblots* (2022, July) at the XXIII Congress of the International Society of Rorschach & Projective Methods, Geneva, Switzerland.

Welcome

As the home of Drexel University's programs in the humanities, natural sciences and social sciences, the College of Arts and Sciences serves as the institution's foundation, educating students in disciplines that sit squarely at the core of higher education. As always, *The 33rd* offers creative proof of the value and importance of such foundational curricula.

In this year's edition of the annual anthology, you'll find numerous examples of the College's unique blend of interdisciplinary collaboration, field experience, and community engagement in the pursuit of knowledge, truth, and equity. Our students and faculty are a creative, engaged collection of scholars, teachers and learners, as you'll see in the pages that follow.

Congratulations to the writers and editors of this year's edition of *The 33rd*. I hope you enjoy their work as much as I do.

Kelly Joyce, Ph.D.
Interim Dean, College of Arts and Sciences

Preface

You are holding the fifteenth annual volume of *The 33rd*, a unique anthology of outstanding writing by students and faculty from across Drexel University.

This book celebrates good writing, which means that it celebrates good thinking. We all know that writing is far more than just learning and following rules of correctness. Writing is actually our best tool for doing a university's basic job, which is to discover, preserve, and disseminate human knowledge. Writing is an inherent part of inquiry, of forging connections, and of communication. It is organized thinking.

Writing is especially indispensable at a place like Drexel University, where we pride ourselves on making our academic endeavors relevant to student success and to making our world a better place.

Cultivating curiosity and creativity in a supportive environment is a hallmark of our work in the Department of English and Philosophy. Whether it's through our MFA in fiction writing, through our community-based learning courses that connect with organizations and institutions in greater Philadelphia, through our many internships, or through other initiatives from the Drexel Publishing Group like *The 33rd*, our students find multiple outlets for their writing to reach the world.

All the essays and stories in this collection are adjudicated through a competitive review process. After publication, we use this volume as a textbook in many of our writing classes. The result is different every year, with new and creative surprises each time. What remains constant is the way that *The 33rd* embodies our mission of promoting imaginative and effective writing, starting right here on the street that gives the publication its name, and reaching out into a world that is limited only by our creative imagination.

Enjoy!

J. Roger Kurtz, Ph.D.
Professor and Department Head
Department of English and Philosophy

Table of Contents
First-Year Writing

Drexel Publishing Group Essays

Drexel Publishing Group
Creative Writing

Writers Room

Faculty Writing

Contributors

Writings Arranged by Context

Argument

Covid-19

Education

Explanatory Writing

Exploratory Writing

Fiction

First-Year Writing

First-Year Writing Nominees

The following students were nominated for the
First-Year Writing Contest.

Congratulations to all!

Phoebe Adobamen	Ryan Ferguson
Jayda Alfred	Julian Garcia
Owen Alicandri	Hans Geiser
Chris Bahr	Veronica Giraldo
Emily Batori	Lorelei Goodall
Christian Beck	John Guilfoyle
Kallee Bernish-Good	Nyla Hernandez
Lexi Carretta	Lilly Hopwood
Amanda Chao	Hana Huang
Catherine Citsay	Brynn Hurley
Olivia Mae Coleman	Charlotte Ingram
Tamier Dashawn Colon-Dorsey	Emma Joseph
Kate Coyne	Devon Kahley
Alex Cruceru	Ariyan Karim
Pritom Das	Syed Khizar Kashif
Nicholas DeCola	Benjamin Kivaa
Eric Del Rosario	Madeline Keane
Serena Diliberto	Emily Kohn
Yuki Duncan	Isa Lagan
Lucas Duong	Abby Litonjua
Londyn Edwards	Allison Lord
Lillian Fenzil	Tanya Lulla

Nicole Marie

Joshua Martinez

Lily Meuninck

Pearl Miller

Victoria Miller

Savannah Mitchum

Kushagra Mittal

Ryan Munn

Gabby Olivares

Isaac Omotoso

Rhythm Osan

Medhavi Pandit

Ankita Patel

Khushi Patel

Marilyn Paul

Vivian Pham

Doris Phan

Katherine Polo

Angelina Prashad

John Purisima

Xhoana Qoshlli

Ben Roe

Philip Samson

Areha Satta

Ethan Shapiro

Georgia Shwaiko

Aspa Sideris

Zoë Sliwinski

Shea Smith

Autumn Sontag

Gavi Spellman

Nawal Syed

Emily Thompson

Yala Tippett

Isaac Toub

Amelia Vial del Solar

Julianne Wagner

Hailey Washington

Aidan Winkler

Storm Womack

Jennifer Wong

Sophie Yoon

Alex Zavalny

Theodore Zinn

Introduction

As the Director of the First-Year Writing Program, I work with over 60 dedicated instructors who coach, cajole, and mentor 2,500-3,000 incoming students who produce tens of thousands of pages of writing. One of the best parts of my job is working with Jill Moses, our Assistant Director, on the First-Year Writing Contest.

This section of *The 33rd* includes essays written by the winners, runners-up, and honorable mentions from the contest that ran in the 2021-2022 academic year. Here is how the essays get from the classroom into this book:

- Students work very hard in their classes to produce lively, engaging writing about themselves and the world around them. Their instructors work hard, too, giving advice and encouragement throughout the writing process.

- Towards the end of the fall, we ask instructors to invite no more than two students from each of their sections to submit their best work to the First-Year Writing Contest. Last year, we got 100 excellent entries.

- With the help of approximately 20 faculty members, we go through a two-step judging process. After much deliberation, the judges come up with a winner, a first runner-up, a second runner-up, and seven honorable mentions.

- During the spring term, the winners, runners-up, and honorable mentions are announced at the English Awards Ceremony, along with the winners of various other contests. Furthermore, our winners receive prizes supported by a very generous endowment from the Erika Guenther and Gertrud Daemmrich Memorial Prizes.

- Finally, the editors of *The 33rd* step in to get permissions, to edit, and to create the book you are holding.

So, here is *The 33rd.* Your instructors in the First-Year Writing Program will ask you to read essays that won prizes last year so you can discuss them, debate them, and learn from them.

Are you interested in writing? Will you be in this book next year? On behalf of the First-Year Writing Program, we cannot wait to read your work.

Fred Siegel, Ph.D.
Director of the First-Year Writing Program

Turn the class on to your passion by writing a persuasive essay incorporating three pieces of research.

—Professor Kathleen Volk Miller

Madeline Burger

Sexism in Snowboarding Media and its Impact on Female Snowboarders

Snowboarding first came into popularity at the tail end of the 20th century, appealing to a primarily young, white, male audience. It wasn't considered particularly suitable for women: the rates of injury were high, it was extremely physically demanding, and any true progression in skill required a dose of the reckless abandon characteristic of a young man. So, as the early culture surrounding the sport formed, there was no serious space created for women. Similar to what is found in most male-dominated arenas—for example, NASCAR or NFL—women in snowboarding media were portrayed in an overtly sexual manner or not at all; existing as male fantasies, not humans with agency. This imbalance has continued to impact the perception of female snowboarders to this day, often making the sport seem exclusive of women.

Snowboarding is generally framed through a male-serving lens in its mass media portrayal. Women are seen in terms of their relations to the men around them rather than as individuals: the default assumption is that "any girl on a board is either looking for a guy, there because her guy is, or trying to be one of the guys" (Thorpe 204). This restrictive categorization doesn't allow female snowboarders to easily create identities within the community based on their ability and passion alone, the way their male counterparts can. The majority of mainstream snowboarding media reinforces these stereotypes in its portrayal of women. In a series of interviews conducted with lifelong female snowboarders, "there [was] a consensus...that the snow industry was marketing an overall image of a passive woman, rather than an active woman" (Garlic Media). Women are shown as passive objects of the viewer's perception, often posing with a board or snowboarding in minimal clothing. Men, on the other hand, are shown as active participants in the sport, usually shown fully clothed and in the midst of a stunt or run down the mountain.

Despite the heavily stereotyped image of women in most snowboarding media, the majority of female snowboarders are genuinely interested in the sport, not male approval. However, regular exposure to media that "emphasize[s] female snowboarders' physical appearances [and] promote[s] responses that position female boarders as sex symbols" has created an unfortunate phenomenon: women who are serious about the sport believe that they are part of a minority (Thorpe 203). When being interviewed, "this sentiment that 'I am not a typical woman...snowboarder' was actually echoed by many" (Garlic Media). This sows division between female snowboarders. There are substantially fewer women than men on the mountain, so it is difficult to form an image of female snowboarders based on personal experience alone, making their media portrayal all the more impactful.

Gear marketing is a category of snowboarding media that especially highlights the differences between the portrayal of men and women. There is not men's gear and women's gear, but rather gear and women's gear. 'Male' is presented as a default characteristic of a snowboarder. "The majority of brands seem to have based most of their female-orientated products on slightly insulting and somewhat outdated stereotypes about women," featuring "pink, purple, cute animals, Aztec patterns and flowers" (Hardy). Women's gear is often marketed for its style rather than its practicality. In the majority of cases, "women model what the clothes look like, while men model what they can do" (Garlic Media). This fosters a perception of women caring more for looks than achievement, reinforcing the stereotype that they are not as serious about snowboarding as men.

Despite its harmful impact on the general perception of women in the sport, the over-sexualization of women in snowboarding media is not entirely denounced by female snowboarders. Some even seem to "accept 'sexist' representations of models in the snowboarding media and construct their snowboarding identities within these discursive limits" (Thorpe 216). They argue that women can be hot and skilled; the two are not mutually exclusive. By this logic, condemning snowboarding ads featuring women in provocative outfits and poses is actually detrimental to improving the perception of female snowboarders. Instead, we should work to reverse the outdated belief that attractive women are two-dimensional beings incapable of possessing skill. This is, of course, much easier said than done; men objectify these women and, therefore, view them as inherently inferior to themselves.

I am a female snowboarder—I have personally experienced the sexist undertones of the snowboarding community. I introduced two of my male friends to the sport, but people would assume that they had introduced me. Snowboarding is perceived as belonging to men; "the mass media tends to promote a discourse of heterosexual femininity in which women's participation is based solely on consumption and the search for male approval" (Thorpe 204). When a woman's hair is visibly coming out from her helmet, male snowboarders refer to it as her having "slut strands" out, implying that a woman's primary goal while snowboarding is to sexually appeal to men. Men aren't even secretive about using language of this nature—as they are in many other circles–because it is so widely viewed as acceptable within the culture. I have had men call the pieces of hair sticking out of my helmet "slut strands" to my face. There is a palpable power imbalance between the sexes on the mountain, but if a female snowboarder addresses it, she is ostracized for being dramatic and uptight, especially considering that one of the major pillars of snowboarding culture—similarly to skateboarding and surfing–is a 'chill' attitude.

The sexist structure of snowboarding culture creates a significantly less welcoming experience for female snowboarders than male snowboarders. There is a default perception that they are there for male validation or attention; they are unskilled until proven otherwise. Female snowboarders are not able to subscribe to the 'chill' mentality characteristic of the culture to the same extent that male snowboarders are. They must either constantly work to escape the stereotypes surrounding them in mainstream media or accept them and build their snowboarding identities within their limits. Either way, female snowboarders are not yet seen as equal to men within the sport–change is needed, and the first step is collectively acknowledging the problem.

Works Cited

Hardy, Chloe. "The Problem with Women's Snowboard Gear." *Whitelines Snowboarding*, Whitelines Snowboarding, 2014, https://whitelines.com/longform/problem-womens-snowboard-gear.

"Marketing to Women in the Snow Industry (Part I): A Disconnect between Style and Functionality." *Garlic Media*, Garlic Media Group, 13 Feb. 2017, https://garlicmediagroup.com/2017/02/13/marketing-women-snow-industry-style-functionality/.

Thorpe, Holly. "Foucault, Technologies of Self, and the Media." *Journal of Sport and Social Issues*, vol. 32, no. 2, May 2008, pp. 199–229. https://doi.org/10.1177/0193723508315206.

Describe how an abstract concept, a lesson that you did not know you were going to learn, arose out of your day-to-day living. Narrate a "click moment," which showed you the importance of this unexpected or implicit lesson. Narrate this stunning realization or turning moment in as much detail as possible, which helps your readers see things as they happened to you, and hence helps them see from your perspective. Be sure to reflect on the significance of the events of your narrative; connect the event to how you were thinking or feeling at the time and why you hope others will consider what you have to say. Commenting on changes in your perspective will help your audience see the significance of the event you describe. (This would be more like a memoir.)

—Dr. Deirdre McMahon

Claire Brown

Claire's

If you're in the D.C. area and looking for something to do, but hopelessly bored by the idea of learning about the origins of our nation and taking in the vibrant culture of the city, look no further than Tysons, Virginia, an edgeless edge city chock-full of upscale steakhouses and luxury apartments centered around a mall called the Tysons Corner Center, a leviathan monument to excess and consumerism. Like any teenager in one of the smaller suburbs surrounding Tysons, I enjoyed loitering around the Center, gorging myself on soft pretzels and overpaying for vinyl records at Barnes and Noble. But I really got attached to it once I started working at Lolli and Pops, a boutique candy store in the Center that, despite charging upwards of three dollars for a lollipop, manages to hemorrhage more and more money every year. I started work as a "Magic Maker" (read: Retail Worker) at Lolli and Pops around December, when Christmas was in full swing, evidenced by the fake snow on the tables that looked suspiciously like the fake cobwebs on the tables they put out during Halloween. It was a long and narrow store, designed to shove as much merchandise in your face as possible. Floors crowded by a litany of tables, shelves sagging from the weight of gummy bears, countless displays of international chocolates that dazzle our customers with their proclamations of Swiss identity (though the fine print revealed they were actually manufactured in the far-off land of Wisconsin). All of these made the stampede of customers desperately searching for last-minute stocking stuffers all the more overwhelming. Still, my job was pretty simple. I stood outside with a smile and held a tin of gummy bears, aggressively offering them to potential customers and luring them into our store. Every now and then, some wisecrack would grin and ask me,

"Do these have any THC in them?"

And I'd always respond,

"Ask me after my shift."

And this was always followed by a hearty laugh and another sale. (Nobody ever took me up on the offer, but if they did, I would've directed them to my red-eyed shift manager.) Eventually, I was promoted to a position in which I actually got to stand *inside* the store, where I discovered my natural talent in sales. I learned quickly that the most important skill in a Magic Maker's repertoire was lying; retail is a performance, the world's least-interesting improv show, and the trick to making it through is simply playing a character. In fact, I don't even like candy; I seldom used my employee discount, and I never snuck a free sample. Fortunately, you didn't have to know the products very well to sell them. You just had to know the customers. The teenagers could always be steered into buying Japanese candies by insisting they were *huge* on TikTok. The old women would melt when you asked if they were too young to remember a Charleston Chew. And it was easy to prey on couples by recommending the cheapest candy in the store to the man and watching him walk out with the most expensive box of chocolates he could find just to prove you wrong. My particular favorite song-and-dance was the one I did for the little kids looking to spend their parent's money on something sweet.

"Do you like sour things?" I'd ask.

"*Yeahhhh*," they'd respond, their eyes already glazing over at the sight of so much sugar.

"Well, lemme show you the sour section. We've got Sour Patch, and WarHeads, and my favorite, (this is where I point to a candy called Toxic Waste, and suddenly, my tone grows more serious), actually, never mind about those. They're too sour. They're not meant for little kids."

And that would move two or three cases of Toxic Waste every time. I had a lot of fun with that job, but outside of the Christmas season, the store was a ghost town (though Easter, Valentine's Day, and Halloween, all being candy-centric holidays, drew sizable crowds as well). I spent most of my time twiddling my thumbs behind the counter, playing paper football with my coworkers while we did our best to endure the playlist our corporate branch ordered we pipe through our store at a deafening volume. It was an offensively bland mix of Shawn Mendes, electro-swing, and Spotify ads. But every now and then, it would shuffle into Kate Bush's "Running Up That Hill." Well, it would shuffle into a shitty cover of "Running Up That Hill," all the rawness of the original scrubbed out and softened for the artificial world of the American shopping mall. But, it didn't matter much to me anyways, since I never heard it over the sound of me passionately singing in the faces of my coworkers, usually turning a pen into a microphone as I dramatically strutted around the cash register.

If I only could, I'd make a deal with God, and I'd get him to swap our places...

Lolli and Pops is located across from a cheap accessories store targeted towards little girls, a nausea-inducing swarm of bright pink and purple specializing in ear piercings, plastic jewelry, and emoji-themed-fucking-everything. Being a man, and a pretentious one with a fragile ego (wearing that dorky little bow-tie was torture enough), it wasn't a store I ever felt I was supposed to go into, but I used to stare into their doorway, watching all the customers trickle out around 8:30, clenching my fists as they dropped their gates thirty minutes earlier than us. I would've quit my job and moved across the hallway in a heartbeat, but the jewelry store wasn't hiring. Besides, I made more sense peddling knock-off Rice Krispie treats than imitation diamond necklaces. I had a big gut that implied that I was well-acquainted with candy, despite my lack of appetite for it. I didn't wear any jewelry, and my parents would've killed me if they ever saw me with a piercing. And, of course, I would've felt weird being a guy and working *there*, in some strawberry-scented den of commercialized femininity. Instead, I kept up the candy store gig, but I'd be damned if I wouldn't spend half of my time wistfully gazing across the hallway, coveting their early closing time.

One of our most frequent customers was a six-year-old girl named Charlotte, who loved to zip through the store while her parents were at work, selling crepes out of a kiosk down the hall. She never bought anything, but she didn't have to. She was simply too adorable to pay. What she lacked in money she made up for in *pleases* and *thank yous*, spontaneous ramblings in French (her parents were immigrants from the country), and a seemingly infinite supply of bouncy balls that frequently toppled the ornate displays I'd spent the entire day arranging. She had a habit of asking questions, the kind most six-year-olds love to ask, ordinary questions spawned only for the joy of taking up conversational space that manage to strike the most well-hidden nerves.

"Do you like working here?"

"It's alright."

"Are you gonna work here forever?"

"Christ, I hope not."

"Where do you wanna work?"

"I wish I worked across the hall."

"That store is for girls!"

"Yeah, I guess so."

After about a year of employment, I finally got a name tag, and I realized I liked my apron more without it. Being nameless felt special, and I missed that special feeling a little bit. I'd never liked my name much anyways. It was hard to pronounce and felt awkward coming out of my mouth; a lot of people misheard it as *Gwen*, which I always thought was a much cooler name. I'd been losing interest in my job by now, especially as COVID slowed the foot traffic to an unsustainable low, but I still carried on the same routine, lying about how much I loved certain candies, playing more paper football, waiting for that God-awful rendition of "Running Up That Hill" to come back on the radio.

Oh, come on angel, come on, come on, darling, let's exchange the experience...

Once while clearing the floors of foodstuff after Charlotte had torn out of the store, I found a plastic ring that I figured she must've dropped. It was a cheap little thing with a big yellow flower on it, and the band had cracked a little bit. Rather than leave my post to chase after her, I slipped it into my pocket, making a mental note to return it the next time she came around, and I continued sweeping. Without thinking, I stuck my free hand into my pocket and let my ring finger move in through the band. It felt like a pretty stupid thing to do; something embarrassing, something wrong, against some invisible rule established by the mall, or my family, or myself. Still, it made everything a little more bearable. And I never actually returned the ring. I kept in in the pocket of my work pants, and every time I dealt with some middle-aged mother screaming in my face over an unfulfilled order of macarons, or every time I lugged a mysteriously wet bag of garbage outside to the dumpster, or every time my manager yelled at me for failing to sign another victim up for our spam-filled email list, I would slip my hand in my pocket and secretly wear that ring for a little bit.

A few days later, when my manager clocked out early and left only me and my coworkers with the closing shift, I decided to wear the ring openly. It looked goofy on my giant, hairy finger, and after I left it on for too long it got kinda hard to take off, but it still felt nice. And I looked over at that jewelry store, the one that probably sold rings just like mine, and I realized I didn't care that they closed earlier than us. I wondered why I hadn't just fucking walked in there and bought myself a goddamn ring earlier. Because it was a *girl's* store? And I worked at a candy store. What an obviously imaginary rule, one as fragile and fake as the mall itself. So, the next day, before my shift, I went in there and bought myself a choker, one with a daisy on it, to match my stolen ring. And I looked down at my nametag, and I looked up at the sign that ran across the storefront in warm, soothing purple. And yes, that is where I got my name.

Second Runner-up—First-Year Writing

Write an essay incorporating primary research, such as interviews, surveys, or live observation.

—Professor Lynn Levin

Malea Troy

Attending a Predominantly White Institution as a Black Student

When choosing to apply to colleges, people categorize different aspects of the school and rank them accordingly, whether it be the strength of the program that they would like to major in, the school's party scene, their sports teams, how close it is to their home, or maybe even how good the dining hall food is. These factors and more all contribute, in one way or another, to one's happiness and success at a college. How these elements affect a student is immensely individualized, as one person's number one seller for the school could be another's red flag and can impact whether they even apply. Furthermore, some of these components are ones that some people would not even have thought to consider. One major factor that I had to note when I was applying to colleges was their diversity rates. I can speak for many Black and African American students when I say that the people you are surrounded by can significantly affect your experiences—especially when you are the odd one out. For Black and African American students, it can trigger various emotions and outcomes when choosing to attend a predominately white institution (PWI), such as Drexel University. For some, this may be all that they know and they do not feel affected by the lack of the same race around them. For others, it can be a struggle. Many Black students note enduring the cumulative effect of racial trauma in a myriad of microaggressions they feel occur daily attending a PWI. Though I have my perspective, I sought out others to decipher how Black students attending a predominately white institution, such as Drexel, feel affect campus culture and academic success.

Using the statistics that the Drexel University website promotes from the 2020 first-year student population, 48.5% of the incoming class identify as White. Following that was 23.2% identifying as Asian, the Hispanic population was 8.1%, and the Black or African American percentage was a mere 6.1%. This exemplifies a clear white majority within Drexel's student population; the dismal amount of Black students is apparent when walking around campus.

In order to gain perspective from a wide variety of opinions from Black and/or African American students attending this school, a survey was sent out that asked a few questions regarding how going to a predominately white institution affects their academic success and their overall experience on campus. The survey was sent out to 50 black students attending Drexel and 40 students replied. The survey began by asking what race they identified with using Drexel's same demographic labels for their data. 87.5% of the people that took the survey identify as Black and or African American, while the other 12.5% identify as one or more ethnicities. The following questions were asked to be scaled from 1 to 5. Answering 1 meant "not really, no," they "did not care," or they "did not feel it affected them." Five meant "yes, very much so" or "this is extremely important to me and holds significance." There was an additional free response area following each question to explain their answer further if they felt necessary. The first question asked: "Were schools' diversity rates a factor that you used when applying to colleges?" The average of the answer was a 3. While this average was closer to the middle, there were quite intriguing explanations. Someone wrote, "While I think diversity in a school is pretty important, it feels more like a want than a need. Other factors like the quality of my program and cost were way more important. I can suck it up for four years." There were many similar explanations to this one, but I feel this quote summarized them best. The next question asked: "Do you feel that attending a PWI affects the school's campus culture?" The responses leaned way more towards the higher end averaging around 4.7. One of the survey takers remarked, "There are not many people of color at this school, to begin with, then you wanna talk about how few black people there are. It can be very disheartening and frustrating knowing you are quite literally a black sheep." The third question asked "Do you feel the need to or ever 'code switch' when around your peers and professors either in or out of the classroom?" For those who might not be aware of the definition of code-switching, I iterated in a sub header of the survey the Britannica definition which states, "a process of shifting from one linguistic code (a language or dialect) to another, depending on the social context or conversational setting." Code-switching among African American students has been formally established since the 1970s. It derives from switching their speech patterns between formal American English and what is considered students' home dialect, African American Vernacular English (AAVE) or Ebonics. The usage of the AAVE or Ebonics dialect is widely known and marked with derogatory labels such as "ghetto" and seen as only "poor and broken English grammar" (Morrison). It is critical to understand the meanings behind code-switching, as many do not even comprehend that this is something that they might do. Speaking and/or acting in a particular way based on your observed audience is a hardship that some do not even realize Black Americans must partake in order to seem educated and articulate enough to be a part of the discussion. The survey takers' scores averaged 4.2 out of 5 for this question. "Whether there actually is an audience or not, the fear that someone is waiting for us to prove our lack of intelligence and our inadequacy based on our skin color is a demon I fight every time I walk into a classroom." Many Black students are likely to experience imposter syndrome or a fundamental skepticism of their own talents and capabilities. This brings up an important distinction that even if it is not with ill will from White peers, this mentality is engraved in everyone's mind that Ebonics is the talk of the uneducated, and it needs to be unlearned.

Many who are not people of color claim they value and want to embrace diversity and inclusion from different cultures and will strongly agree with it in the discussion, but do not actively engage in ways that support their notion. They do not actually go through their day-to-day living with those ideals. They make large claims in the classroom or in meetings without action outside the doors. Black people try to emulate and adapt their lifestyle to fit in and belong within the PWI culture, but others are unwilling to do the same. In my biology class, I was put into a group with a few other girls who were all white. My group members would only look towards the advice of each other and would never let me have any input about anything. I had similar if not better grades than all of them, and they knew that I excelled in the class. However, even with my best efforts to include myself, I always seemed to get brushed off or worse, the classic: Having another person reiterate precisely what I had said, yet somehow they are the genius who gets the credit. Heaven forbid I could contribute something valuable to "our," or should I say "their," discussion. I was viewed as invisible, as a shadow; my lack of value to them was crystal clear. This highlighted that some people even today believe that my thoughts and knowledge have no substance due to my skin complexion, and frankly, it sucked.

Though many African Americans and/or Black students face unnecessary hardships, there are positive aspects to attending a PWI that contribute to their character development and success. Students claimed they actively sought out some in-school organizations such as the African Student Association (ASA) and the Black Student Union (BSU), where they could bond with other students of their race who share everyday experiences. There they learned how to embrace their ethnicity further and how to face conflict with poise and professionalism. They've also pushed me further into the arms of those who can stand with me during trials. I have found allies outside of the Black community who are actively willing to educate themselves and advocate for change.

Overall, universities must assess how their institutional practices and policies disadvantage Black students, regardless of if institutions do so without malice or ill intent. In 2021, good intentions are no longer sufficient; it is critical to Black and other minority students that diversity and inclusion practices are created and implemented properly. Students of color can utilize their insight in the classroom, dispel stereotypes, and educate individuals who do not share their perspectives. These institutions must go beyond their staged gestures and implement antiracist policies to mitigate injustices and racial disparities while actively promoting an inclusive school atmosphere.

Works Cited

"First-Year Student Population Profile." *Drexel University Undergraduate Admissions*, Drexel University, 2021, https://drexel.edu/undergrad/apply/freshman-class/. Accessed 3 December 2021.

Morrison, Carlos D. "Code-Switching." *Encyclopædia Britannica*, Encyclopædia Britannica, Inc., 30 May 2017, https://www.britannica.com/topic/code-switching. Accessed 3 December 2021.

Table of First-Year Student Population Profile
(Racial Diversity of Incoming Freshman (2020))

Diversity	%
White	48.5
Asian	23.3
Hispanic	8.1
International	6.5
Black or African American	6.1
One or More Races	3.9
Race or Ethnicity Unknown	3.5
Native American	0.2
Pacific Islander	0

Interview a person for the story and significance of an event involving active participation. Share your draft, interviewing the person again for their critique. Include the story of the second interview in the final paper.

—Professor Jan Armon

Ebubechukwu Donatus Enwerem
The Story Behind the Concealed Scar

Wars. Are they necessary? Do they help us grow, or do they shatter us entirely? These are questions I ask myself. Fortunately, I have never experienced war. However, my father, Donatus Chukwumaeze Enwerem, was unfortunate to witness the Biafran war. It was one of those things that no one talked about in my house. The phrase that should not be mentioned. The past that should never be recalled. The scar that should be concealed.

There I was, on the 29th of September 2021, trying to get a peek of the pain my father's scar of the Biafran war held. I asked my father to tell me his story. His reply was "Call me again tomorrow, I will think about it" (Donatus Chukwumaeze Enwerem, personal interviews, 29 September 2021). I believed I had lost. "I will think about it" meant he would be in isolation with his thoughts, his memories, and the pain the experience brought him. "I will think about it" meant he was looking for a better way to say no. I would never hear my father's story. I had accepted that. He called me the next day and agreed to share his experience. This is his story.

It would be a crime for me to start Donatus' story without giving information about the Biafran war. It would be like giving you a Spanish novel without teaching you how to speak Spanish. The war was between citizens of southeastern Nigeria and the rest of Nigeria. The southeastern part of Nigeria departed from the union of Nigeria and formed their own country. They called this newly formed Union Biafra. However, the rest of Nigeria, especially the government, did not like this. A war erupted. This is all the information I will give regarding the war. This isn't a story about the Biafran War; this is the story of Donatus.

Sometime around late May 1968, Donatus was 17 years old living in the city of Port Harcourt. He lived in Port Harcourt with his father, Julius, and two younger brothers Clement and Okey. Okey was 15 years old, and Clement was barely 10. The other members of Donatus' family had moved deeper into the Biafran territory. At this time, the war had been going on for a year. The war had not impacted Donatus in a major way yet. The only way he was affected was that he could not attend school. That was the thing about Port Harcourt; it was a stronghold that fended off Nigeria's military advances. Donatus felt Port Harcourt was impregnable. So, on this day, he went out with Clement, to hunt a morning snack: lizards. This had become one of his favorite activities. One of those things that start to look interesting during times of turmoil. Clement was never good at catching lizards, so it was up to Donatus to catch enough for them both. There they were, two children bonded together by blood and war. The ideal representation of a perfect picture. "Boom!" A loud explosion followed. Time stopped for a while. Donatus could not comprehend the source of this noise. What could this be? Had someone impregnated the impregnable Port Harcourt? Donatus looked up and saw three airplanes with the Nigerian flag printed on them. It was an airstrike. More explosions followed and Donatus realized that Port Harcourt, his home for the last seventeen years, was about to be destroyed.

Donatus grabbed his brother and started running towards his home. That was what his father told him to do during times like these. This was his first time experiencing this, but his father, Julius, had taught him the routine. So he ran, stopping every few minutes to make sure Clement kept up with him. After running for a few minutes, he could finally see his house. Julius was getting the car ready for an evacuation. Donatus immediately remembered the new radio set he managed to buy. He wanted to run into the house to get it. "Where is Okey?" Julius asked. That was a good question. Where was Okey? Donatus was the oldest child, so naturally, he had the responsibility of taking care of his brothers. He now had a new quest: finding his brother Okey.

The airplanes kept coming. This meant more explosions happening, more buildings getting destroyed and more people wailing in pain. Donatus started his quest. He had to find Okey. Donatus knew Okey well. They had spent fifteen years together. He had a feeling Okey would be at the church's makeshift football field. Donatus began running there. His mind racing with negative thoughts. What if Okey had already been killed? What if he is not on the football field? A bomb landed on a house that belonged to a friend of his. No. He could not let this distract him. He had a job to do. He had to find his brother. On his way to the church, he saw many children running towards him. He kept praying Okey was one of them. Five people had passed him, no sight of Okey. Ten people had passed him. Twenty, thirty, and still he had not seen Okey. He was about to give up when he saw his brother running towards home. Donatus could feel himself get lighter. A huge weight had been lifted off his shoulders. Okey was alive. They did not have time to stop and exchange pleasantries, so they kept on running towards home. Two brothers, bonded by blood and fear.

On their way home, they saw their father's vehicle driving towards them. They flagged him down and got into the vehicle. Donatus could rest now. He achieved success. His younger brothers were okay. It was now his father's responsibility to drive them away from the strike zone. His father started driving. There was no location in mind. All he wanted to do was leave the airstrike zone. There were crowds of people running, mutilated bodies, and other vehicles along the road. Julius made sure he maneuvered every obstacle on the road.

After a while, the airstrike had ended. All the Nigerian planes had either been destroyed by an antiaircraft machine or had flown away. Julius had started driving towards Imo State, to meet up with the rest of the family. There were military checkpoints all over the road. Donatus finally had the opportunity to think about the event. To think about the friends he might have lost that day. To think about the new radio set he could not get. To think about the potential destruction his house had faced. This experience made Donatus lose hope in Biafra. He always believed in the Biafran cause. He believed Biafra would win the war. On this day, he realized that Biafra was no match for Nigeria. He understood that the next few years were going to be tough.

This is my father's story. This is what he went through. I believe the event played a huge role in shaping my father's present mentality. He hardly ties himself down to locations. He has lived in many places and is always ready to abandon them whenever he wants to. The event also made him become a strong advocate of the idea of building houses in villages. This is an idea that he has tried to teach all of his children. He tries to make us understand that our village will always be a haven. He makes us understand that we should always have a house in our village so we could retreat whenever we need to. He makes us understand that the only place worthy of being called home is our village. Every other place is just a house. Every other place is just a place for a temporary stay.

I asked my father to tell me how he feels the event has affected him. He told me that it has forever changed his view of wars. At the start of the war, he was enthusiastic. He dreamed of fighting in the war but could not because his father did not let him. He told me that seeing innocent people die and houses get destroyed that day made him realize that "in war, there is no good or bad, there is only bad and worse" (Donatus Chukwumaeze Enwerem, personal interviews, 16 October 2021).

I initiated a WhatsApp video call with my father to show him my draft. I emailed it to him and waited quietly as he read it. I realized he was done reading when he took off his glasses. Silence followed. I abhor communicating through phones. Mobile phones are criminals, stealthily stealing 80% of every interaction. They steal emotions, intonations, and facial expressions from most conversations. There I was with my father, trying to figure out how my draft made him feel. Unfortunately, my mobile phone had stolen all the emotions he displayed. After a while he began to talk. He talked about how reading about this event made him feel as if he was living through it again. He mentioned he liked how I was able to describe the emotions he felt perfectly. He said the house in Port Harcourt was not lost. After war, the Biafrans who retreated could still access their houses. The house in the story, which had later been renovated and rented off, is still standing strong today. He communicated how he disliked the fact that I could not talk more extensively about the war. I will now use the next paragraph to do that.

The Biafran War. At this point you know how it started, and you've seen a glance of it through Donatus' eyes. I will now try my best to make you live through it with a paragraph. The Nigerian army captured Biafran regions at a fast rate. They used airstrikes, to lower defense, then sent out armies to do everything else. The Nigerian army killed Biafrans. The Nigerian army's main weapon was hunger. Yes, hunger can be weaponized. Port Harcourt was Biafra's strongest access to outside aid. When it was captured, the Biafrans were like chickens in a coop. No, they were worse than that. Chickens in a coop are fed. The Biafrans were not. They were trapped in their region, waiting for the inevitable: death by hunger or attack and destruction of their homes by the

Nigerian army. Hunger killed Biafrans. Lack of food led to lack of motivation. Soldiers lost hope, but they could not show it. Soldiers who showed a hint of disobedience were labelled "saboteurs" and killed. Biafran officers who lost battles were killed as punishment. Biafrans killed Biafrans. The war ended on 14 January 1970. Biafra surrendered, and Nigeria won.

I ended my conversation with my father with him telling me how this assignment and my writing had made him more open to telling me about his experiences with the Biafran War. He said telling me his story and reading about it has made him feel lighter. In a way, you could say that it made him conquer his trauma. It took away the pain associated with the story behind the concealed scar.

Work Cited
Enwerem, Donatus Chukwumaeze. Personal Interviews. 29 September 2021, 16 October 2021.

Write a literacy narrative.

—Professor Daniel Featherston

Arthur Fink
White Girl Manuals

As a child, with all the time in the world, I loved to read.

"What's your favorite book?" I was regularly asked as a conversation starter by close friends or curious teachers.

"I can't pick a single favorite," I'd always say, "but I like the author Wendy Mass."

"What makes you like her books?" They sometimes asked next, if they particularly cared, and I would say, "I really like how realistic they feel. Like they are about real people and not just characters, you know?"

And they did, to an extent, feel like they were about real people. For those that aren't well versed in Books for Girls in the 2010s, Wendy Mass wrote some of the best preteen girl dramas. And she was good at giving her characters dimensionality, I'll give you that. These books had your typical preteen problem checklist: romance drama, friend drama, family drama, school drama, the works, through the angst-filled yet optimistic point of view of real average girls. Of course, "real average girl" and "anyone" meant any white girl.

It is apparent right now that I am not white *or* a girl. It was not so apparent back then.

I was a half-Asian didn't-know-I'm-trans kid trying my absolute best to become everything society wanted me to be—and everything I wasn't. My main goal, in everything I did, was to assimilate and be accepted as one of the White Girls.

I didn't *start* to feel this way because of books. That came from a lovely mix of my family upbringing; attempts at raising me in a "culturally neutral" way, based on whatever a Filipino mother and grandmother would know about whiteness, to avoid bullying; societal beauty standards and opinions on dark hair and dark hooded eyes; and your standard popular white-only friend groups that never wanted to accept me. But I noticed these differences between me and the characters I saw in books: shoes in their houses, attention from the popular boys, fights with their monolingual parents, and that sought-after blond hair and blue eyes; and I thought: this must be what normal (white) people act like. This is what I should act like, what I should *be*.

And so, these books, in addition to the genuine entertainment they did provide me, became my "White Girl Manuals." Most Asians I've met growing up, trans or otherwise, had their "white" phase; trying to blend in and assimilate. Whether or not their journeys with whiteness and fitting in were also fueled by gender dysphoria and these White Girl Manuals, I don't know. But I can definitely say for myself that during my White Phase, I held onto these books like a lifeline, basing my clothing choices, speech patterns, habits, *everything* on these white girls I read about. It never worked. I never fit in, but for years, I tried to keep doing it anyway.

I wish I could wax poetic on how my journey of understanding and accepting my own ethnic pride was influenced by more representative readings. But as it turned out, I had stopped reading for pleasure years before then for completely different reasons. Like many students my age, I found that school reading assignments completely extinguished my passions for reading. The more I had to read for school, the less and less I read on my own, until I realized I couldn't remember the last time I even picked up a book for myself. Every now and then, a decent school book would light a dim blink of that old love. But even then, outdated analyses, boring assignments, and formal essays would stomp on that spark before I could even try to cup my hands around it and let it grow into a warm flame again.

During this time, I resolved my identity crisis. I am a man, and I am Asian. These are facts of pride to me, not things I must hide. But by this point, reading books had nothing to do with my identity anymore. I was not without story altogether—*anime* and *donghua* with their depictions of normalized Asian living and fantasy became my go-to entertainment. I lived my life more richly, knowing who I am and being comfortable and proud of it. But I still felt, deep down, that I needed to mend my relationship with books. Logically, I still liked books. They share knowledge, tell stories, and do all sorts of other things that help people. But the relationship was not *personal* the way it used to be.

That was the dilemma I found myself with at beginning of quarantine. Time alone allowed me to reflect on myself in many new ways, and one of the things I did was try to get back into reading. But how could I find anything on the bestseller shelves, when I felt so distanced and put-off by overtold white stories?

The answer, as it turned out, was found in less "proper" literature. Just this summer, I've read probably close to five thousand pages worth of unprofessionally translated *danmei*, or Chinese gay novels. Compared to your dedicated bookworm it's not a lot, but that's probably as much as all the reading I've done put together since the sixth grade. I've been looking into other forms of Asian-made literature, and I found that the spark I had for reading was not entirely extinguished after all. Even now as I'm writing this, I'm excitedly waiting for my next book to come in the mail—a sci-fi mixing Chinese dynastic life and its misogynist impacts with *mecha* fighting. It's absurd, it's random, and it's everything I wish I had growing up. I'm excited about my new reading prospects. It feels like the sun rising in the Arctic after a winter entirely devoid of its light.

Just two years ago, I could not have said with certainty that I could mend my relationship with books. Even now, I don't know how long this book fever will last for me. But deep down, I know I love reading. And I like to think the small flame I'm holding close to me right now will, once again, develop into the blazing love I used to have—that I know it can become.

One of the goals of this course is for us to begin doing primary research. Use the processes described in Dana Lynn Driscoll's article to write an essay utilizing your primary research. In other words, you will be required to use interviews, surveys, or live observation to report on what you learned about the topic you have been exploring.

—Professor Anne K. Erickson

Tiffany Mai

The Effect of Media on College Students' Perception of Asian Stereotypes and Representation

Media has advanced tremendously in recent decades, acquiring influence along the way. Society places a great deal of faith in the media as a credible and reliable source to gain and learn information on current events, education, and entertainment. However, the media can be a harmful resource since stereotypes marked as entertainment can influence how society formulates opinions and beliefs about others, both correctly and incorrectly. I was a victim of being stereotyped due to the media portrayal of my Asian ethnicity.

On the first day of school of my sixth-grade year, I walked into my classroom and noticed the seating arrangement comprised of two seats placed next to each other. I searched around the classroom for a paper with my name on it. After finding my name tag, I sat down and peered at the blank sheet of paper on my desk that my teacher had warned us not to touch. Waiting for the rest of my classmates to arrive, I remained at my desk and anticipated what would be on the other side of the paper. After the bell rang, my teacher instructed our class to flip the paper around and ask our seating partner the questions on the paper.

Turning to my partner, I asked, "What is your favorite subject?"

"Science. I'm assuming your favorite subject is math because all Asians are good at it," responded my seating partner.

My eyes furrowed, and I awkwardly chuckled it off. "What are your hobbies?"

"I like to play baseball and tennis," my seating partner replied.

"Well, I like to do Taekwondo and..." I stopped talking as my partner interrupted my sentence with a laugh.

"I feel like all Asians do martial arts. I mean, Jackie Chan and Bruce Lee both practice martial arts. Name me one Asian celebrity that does not practice martial arts," he said.

I froze and became silent. Other than Jackie Chan and Bruce Lee, I could not think of any other Asian celebrities. I was perplexed as to why my race had not been shown in multiple portrayals by the media. As a result of that encounter, I felt compelled to seek out images of Asians that were not stereotypically depicted in movies and television shows. On YouTube, I discovered a range of Asian content creators, like Ryan Higa, Michelle Phan, OfflineTV, and Wong Fu Productions, portraying Asians in a new light.

To determine if Asian American college students had experienced a similar situation involving stereotypes and their opinions on the media, I issued a survey to a group of 30 Asian American college students. The majority of respondents ranked social media as having the biggest impact on today's society, with movies, television shows, and YouTube following shortly thereafter. The survey's finding supports a previously published study in which college students acknowledged that Asian Americans were stereotyped as karate masters, assassins, nerds, socially awkward, and professionals in high-paying fields, stemming from movies and television shows they have watched (Sun, et al). This study from Sun and his team demonstrates that the images and characters onscreen can extend beyond mere entertainment, indicating that racial bias can be imprinted onto members of society.

Moreover, when Asian American college students were asked how they felt Asians were reflected in the media, 42% of the respondents said Asians were reflected as slightly negative, while 22% felt Asians were reflected as slightly positive. This result from the survey suggests the idea that Asians have historically been depicted in negative, stereotypical ways by the media. However, some Asians can view their stereotypes as positive due to them frequently being depicted as the "model minority." The "model minority" can be referred to as the qualities of being quiet, naturally intelligent, overachievers, and highly successful (Zhang). The constant portrayal of Asians as the "model minority" implies to society that Asians are from a single, homogeneous group with the same characteristics and traits. These stereotypical images also can lead to society acknowledging and assuming how Asians are supposed to appear and behave.

Furthermore, the respondents were asked to rate how accurate they think the media represented Asians on a scale of 1 to 5, with 1 being not accurate, and 5 being absolutely accurate. 60% of the respondents gave a rating of 2, indicating that Asian Americans believe the media does not accurately represent Asians. Because of the lack of accurate representation of Asian Americans in the media, it can inhibit the perception of how Asian Americans should act and the ability of individuals to envision themselves doing anything else other than their limited media images (Iwamoto and William). As a result of the lack of representation, this can have a huge impact on Asian Americans' mental health and social identity. Asian Americans can suffer a decrease in their self-esteem and feel as if their future possibilities are limited, preventing them from the opportunity to explore a variety of identities. The absence of representation also leaves Asian Americans, such as myself, to resort to content creators online in an attempt to discover different images and have a role model to look up to.

The absence of Asian Americans in Hollywood also contributes to the stereotype that Asians are foreigners. The foreigner stereotype depicts Asians as exotic, non-American, and acting FOB (fresh off the boat), and are treated as if they do not belong in the United States due to common questions posed to Asian Americans during initial encounters like, "Do you speak English?" and, "Where are you really from?" (Zhang). Because Asian Americans are consistently seen as less American than other ethnicities, this can result in media corporations whitewashing roles intended for Asian characters. For example, Scarlett Johansson was cast as the Japanese protagonist of 2017's *Ghost in the Shell*, a film adapted to the Japanese manga of the same name (Loreck). Media corporations most likely whitewash characters in movies and television shows to boost revenue and popularity (Sun et al.). However, college students oppose the idea of whitewashing. From the survey, when asked if Asian American college students would watch a movie in which a Caucasian actor played a non-white character, roughly 65% were extremely unlikely to watch the film. This finding from the survey reveals that writers should avoid changing the ethnicity of a character and instead cast an actor who is appropriate for the role in order to include representation and maintain customer attraction.

Nevertheless, notable progress has been achieved in the past few years with the success of the movie, *Crazy Rich Asians*, featuring an all-Asian cast, and ABC's *Fresh Off the Boat*, becoming the first network television sitcom to feature a family of Asian Americans as main characters. BTS, a South Korean boy band, was the first Asian act to receive a Grammy nomination, while *Parasite*, a Korean film, won four Oscars in 2020. In addition, *Shang Chi and the Legend of the Ten Rings*, released in 2021, was the first Asian lead superhero movie. With these new breakthroughs and achievements from multiple celebrities, the Asian youth today have a diverse range of representations they could potentially be and role models to look up to. As of now, Asian Americans are being portrayed in Hollywood in a more authentic light than ever before.

However, media still has a long way to go to include a vast amount of diversities and ethnicities. A study by USC Annenberg Inclusion Initiative examined 1,300 top-grossing movies from 2007 to 2019 in which 5.9% of the characters were of Asian and Pacific Islander ethnicity (Yuen). This statistic reveals that there are not that many characters in the Asian media and provides evidence that the media is still lacking in representation for Asian Americans in the media. In addition, from the survey, 75% of Asian American college students believed there is a moderate amount of ethnicities within the media. This result indicates that college students today believe the media lacks a variety of ethnicities, indicating that there is potential for growth for more diversity to be incorporated in the future.

Hence, a lack of diverse representation in the media plays a contribution in reinforcing stereotypical attitudes and beliefs. More Asian representation may help overcome and possibly eliminate the ignorance and misperceptions generated by past media representations of stereotypes. Non-stereotypical images of Asian Americans and other minorities can benefit society as a whole by exposing individuals to Asians and other minorities in images they have not often been portrayed as. Through the exposure of portrayals that contradict stereotypes, society may be able to gain a better understanding of Asian Americans and other minorities.

Works Cited

Chao, Melody Manchi, et al. "The Model Minority as a Shared Reality and Its Implication for Interracial Perceptions." *Asian American Journal of Psychology*, vol. 4, no. 2, June 2013, pp. 84–92. EBSCOhost, doi:10.1037/a0028769.

Iwamoto, Derek Kenji, and William Ming Liu. "The impact of racial identity, ethnic identity, Asian values and race-related stress on Asian Americans and Asian international college students' psychological well-being." *Journal of Counseling Psychology* vol. 57,1 (2010): 79-91. doi:10.1037/a0017393

Loreck, Janice. "Race and stardom in Ghost in the Shell." *Science Fiction Film and Television*, vol. 11, no. 1, Apr. 2018, pp. 37+. Gale Academic OneFile, https://muse.jhu.edu/article/686933

Sun, Chyng, et al. "Shifting Receptions: Asian American Stereotypes and the Exploration of Comprehensive Media Literacy." *The Communication Review* (Yverdon, Switzerland), vol. 18, no. 4, Routledge, 2015, pp. 294–314, doi:10.1080/10714421.2015.1085778.

Yuen, Nancy Wang, et al. *The Prevalence and Portrayal of Asian and Pacific Islanders across 1,300 Popular Films*. Annenberg Inclusion Initiative, May 2021, https://assets.uscannenberg.org/docs/aii_aapi-representation-across-films-2021-05-18.pdf

Zhang, Qin. "Asian Americans Beyond the Model Minority Stereotype: The Nerdy and the Left Out." *Journal of International & Intercultural Communication*, vol. 3, no. 1, Feb. 2010, pp. 20–37. EBSCOhost, doi:10.1080/17513050903428109.

For this assignment, you will write in a new (for you) genre: Literacy Narrative. Write a story exploring your previous experiences with reading and/or writing that changed you/your world view/your lifestyle/your attitude about reading, writing, or anything else.

—Professor Maria Volynsky

Iris Nguyen Ho

The New Spectacles

If you have ever experienced myopia, you know the excitement of wearing a new pair of spectacles. Although it might be blurry and uncomfortable incipiently, the feeling when everything appears more clearly, or the ability to discern distant objects that you could not previously see, brings a unique satisfaction that plain words can not convey. Believe it or not, the influence that emerges after reading a book is just as wonderful as the feeling of putting on the new specs. With the power of a new language and belief, such influence will even be amplified, adding depth and dimensions to the worldview that you had been attaching to since birth.

I was born a Vietnamese, and from the beginning of life, I have been rooted in the beauty of my first language. Despite having learned other languages, my mother tongue was the foundation of my worldview: it shaped the way I think, observe, and evaluate the world around me. I was also born an atheist, and my "religion" nurtured my mind differently from how other religions affect its believers; instead of putting faith in the unseen, my belief appeared at the limitation of sight and science. These factors naturally formed the lens of my mind, shaping the way I reflected on the world until I read an English Bible for the first time.

At the age of 15, I left home to pursue education in the US. With a certain knowledge in English that I had been building for years, I expected my time spent in high school to be filled with roses. However, reality turned me down from heaven to earth. For some reason, I happened to be in a Christian high school which requires students to take at least one Bible class every school year. This policy, despite the frustrations it brought to the Vietnamese atheist me, gifted the new spectacles through which my worldview significantly changed.

As I recall exactly, it was during the New Testament class. My teacher was introducing the "Finished Promise" project, which was about how God fulfilled His promise through Jesus Christ, before he gave us permission to work on it. Although he said many things, most of them turned into the fallen leaves on the ground, which did not hesitate to fly away. All that remained in my memory was the importance of the Bible as the fundamental resource and standard to every point we could present in this assignment. These pieces of instruction brought little help if not nothing to resolve my problems as a new student who had never read the Bible in English!

Although I had been learning English for many years and collected many awards for my performance in this language, it was beyond my ability to at least guess the point of a short passage in the English Bible. Lofty ideas, unfamiliar vocabulary, and parable images in such a book all make reading a desperate battle. However, this battle against these "giants" was not the only source of my tension—the rattling and dissonant sound from the keyboards, the rustle from hastily turned pages, and the sensation of high concentration from my fellow classmates dramatically added to my stress at this very moment. These sensations that touched my brain told me that I was the only one among the experienced hunters who was totally lost in the adventure to seek the untold treasure. I could feel the beat of my heart getting stronger and stronger as if it was struggling to get out of this swampland of anxiety, or the consternation of isolation and disorientation.

Everyone's attention was put on their laptop screens, but I vividly felt the pressure of someone's sharp gaze stabbing me, observing my actions, reading my thoughts, and assessing my incompetence. Terrifyingly, I realized this sense of judgment derived from no one but myself. If only it came from someone else, these feelings would merely be worthless opinions whose reliability had not yet been confirmed. However, because it was me who made these valuations, it felt like a death sentence for my self-esteem and the confidence that took me time and effort to build.

This feeling of insecurity, disappointment, and disorientation had been existing in my consciousness for a long time, and the awareness of incapability tortured my mind throughout the course. One day, the desperation got so bad that it had me questioning the root of this frustration; were there any problems with the English Bible, or was I not "enough" to win such a battle? No! There was nothing wrong with this sacred writing, for there are countless people who have accomplished its message and been inspired by that. Also, the efforts I had put in were more than just "enough" to pay off the price it takes to read such an abstract book in another language. It was, however, because of the sunglasses I wore in the darkness that hindered my vision while hunting for the treasure of reading.

Looking back at my journey reading this English Bible, I was seeking the message conveyed through the specs of a Vietnamese girl instead of that of a person who strives to learn this language. I was constantly using the mindset of my mother tongue to shape the English ideas into Vietnamese concepts, and although it successfully brought good grades in my English homework, I missed the exquisiteness of depth and complexity hidden in English itself.

As my first language has its own beauty, English and other languages all have a rich history and complex culture that contributes to their existence. Therefore to actually comprehend writing written in a specific language, I had to approach the text the way it is without any transformations, allowing the language to lead my thinking process freely as it will. As 3-D spectacles are required to fully perceive the striking motions of a 3-D movie, just mere eyes without suitable lenses can never bring the same extraordinary feeling. Similarly, in order to apprehend the magnificence of ideas written in English, my identity as a Vietnamese should be smashed into pieces while establishing my new identity as an English-book reader.

You might ask why go through such hassles when I can just read any books in my first language, but let me tell you that only with the involvement of English that the ideas in the Bible appear to be more multi-dimensional and profound. Because ideas in the Bible are very complicated, especially when it is translated from ancient languages to the languages we use today, the ability to read it in different languages is a great tool to compare the potential points of a passage and analyze their meaning to the fullest. There were terms in a Vietnamese version that can not be clarified without the use of multiple translations, and English indeed derives more shades of the Biblical ideas than what Vietnamese can represent. Reading in English also provides me the access to approach a Biblical message in a different way, resulting in the development of new thoughts and connections that can not be drawn just by reading in my mother language. By that, the ability to read in English creates the novel lens to make the unseen revealed and creates a depth for my worldview, given different aspects of thoughts available to be considered.

Not only does reading in a new language affect my thinking process, but it also contributes to my growth as a person through the realization of "self." Throughout the process of reading an English Bible, the unfamiliarity of a foreign language and belief make my familiar self stand out by challenging the frame of my mind. The reflection derived from it has emphasized who I was in the past, questioned who I am in the present, and affected who I will be in the future for the past three years. At this point, I am not just myself but moreover, a result of the changes in me, and my reading has a big contribution to that. Moreover, as I strive to acquire its core values, I find reading is means by which the ability to understand oneself and others is revealed visually, by the beauty of words, and in the depth of language.

If a new language and faith are metaphorically compared to the spectacles, reading will be a frame that connects them together. At the point at which these specs are put alongside each other, there is a marvelous scene of wonder that enriches and deepens my inner world. With that being said, reading is not just any mere habit, but it is an insightful process of change and nurture of a precious soul inside each individual.

Final research project—What is a question that you want to explore about deception and yourself?

—Dr. Karen Nulton

Sarah Phan
Love as a Pessimist

Serotonin, endorphins, heart palpitations, butterflies in the stomach; what exactly do these all mean? Frankly, to me, they all mean fear. As someone who grew up only seeing the worst in the relationships around me, love was never something I understood as more than unattainable, something to keep the human imagination thriving. Love is not as magical as they make it seem in Hollywood—with cinematic effects and emotional music, and with tear-jerking moments that make viewers feel a secondhand sense of longing for two non-existent characters to come together. To this day I still cannot believe how famous of a story *Romeo and Juliet* is (Trigger warning: Shakespeare slander—like come on, two minors failing an attempt to elope and then ending their own lives?). My fear comes from the fact that I have already accepted love to be not as intense and moving as it is dreamed to be. The brutal truth is that love is a lie. It is something that we keep in our imagination for our sanity to grasp onto as a goal to keep us going.

But it has not been long since I have started feeling unexplainable things, things akin to what Google calls, "signs that you like someone." *Gross*, was my first thought in approaching the idea that my unusual behavior meant I was developing feelings for someone. Me accepting these feelings would go against the ideology I had built around myself. It would mean that I have fallen victim to the Hallmark agenda. It would mean that I am regressing to that naive 12-year-old self who believed I would be able to meet the Percy Jackson to my Annabeth Chase and be swept into a world of fighting gods and monsters alongside the love of my life. As if being a nerd wasn't critical enough for my image. *Oh dear.* As we approach the holiday season, I realize that I seem to have stored all of my romantic, dream-like emotions into the spirit of Christmas, which is great as I can focus on practical, real-world things during the rest of the year (the downside is being one of the world's biggest Christmas enthusiasts, i.e. looking like a lunatic), but it all comes crashing down on me during the winter and can become terribly overwhelming. This research project comes in perfect time with what is going on at the moment. It is almost like a sign that I am due for addressing what I may have tried to suppress for years due to disappointment and embarrassment. I have become a stranger to my own feelings as a result of it. The following is what I've discovered on my journey to finding the answer to my big question: What the heck is love and why is it doing this to me? As we go through the research I've done on this impossibly broad concept, we will have to bear through how much of a dunce I am in discovering what seems to be the most commonly known ideas that I was never exposed to before.

How the Professionals Explain it

Of course, we must look into science if we want to do some real research. It turns out that there are a plethora of theories behind why humans have a common behavior when feeling affection towards someone. The keyword "theory" had already told me that I wasn't going to be able to find a straightforward answer. Most of these concepts base themselves on what is called the *Triangular Theory of Love*. Developed by American Psychologist Robert Sternberg, it describes three main components that present themselves in different levels together to form an interpersonal relationship between two humans. These three components are passion, intimacy, and commitment. It's like a customizable and adjustable concept that can fit anyone's situation. I never thought of it in that way, honestly. It is like I could make my own smoothie with a decent amount of intimacy, a pinch of commitment, and a truckload full of passion. It is love in the way that I see it. To start to understand something that had previously felt muddled for so long is such a satisfying feeling.

Another theory that had caught my attention is called "Lee's styles of love." This theory details six different and common styles of love using Greek names (which is why it caught my attention as a mythology geek). There was the passionate lover, Eros, that we see in movies. There was the heartbreaker, Ludus, who treated relationships like a game. Storge and Agape are similar in their selfless, committed personalities. I could see myself currently being Pragma, a logical lover who approaches such a dangerous concept with delicate footsteps. But the more I succumb to embracing these obnoxious feelings, I feel I am leaning more towards the Mania, the one who is infatuated. I admit that I have grown an obsession with the idea of love. As I uncover more about it, I feel I am breaking through the cracks and discovering more about myself, while leaving behind the person I once was.

Katherine Wu from Harvard University shares the chemical perspective of love using witty puns in reference to iconic love songs from American discography such as "Total Eclipse of the Brain" or "Let's Get Chemical" (I personally think she is a genius). It is explained that love to the brain means three things: lust, attraction, and attachment; and there are different hormones that respond to each category. Lust entails testosterone and estrogen; attraction coincides with dopamine, norepinephrine, and serotonin; and attachment goes along with oxytocin and vasopressin. Now, I am not going to sit here and pretend that I understand what this means as someone who almost failed chemistry, but it does tell me that part of what I feel has a biological aspect. In other words, it is something that I cannot control. And in other *other* words, I have something to blame other than myself for this pain. What intrigued me most from this source is the last section titled, "Love Hurts." This section didn't actually talk about love as a physically painful experience, but it did remind me of the times my chest would flare up in pain or when my head hurt from feeling overwhelmed by my emotions.

After a quick search of "Can love actually be painful?"—expecting to be met with more confusing science lingo—I came across an article by Eric Jaffe on *Psychology Science*, who titles his work "Why Love Literally Hurts." You know that moment when you realize that something you've been doing most of your life may have been detrimental to your health and now you have that "well crap" moment while you regret your life decisions? Like how that habit of biting your nails now leaves your fingers permanently crooked and stubby, or staying up to read manga all night instead of sleeping apparently causes you to lose years of your life? That was me while finding out that you can actually *die* from being heartbroken. No less than a decade ago a rare condition was discovered called *stress cardiomyopathy*, or more widely-known as "broken-heart syndrome." This gave me some things to think about, to say the least. First was: "Wow, and I thought *I* was making it deep." Second was: "Wow, so I can actually die from this! How fun!" Of course, this was a dramatic first response as broken-heart syndrome is something very uncommon and I have only seen it one time in a Chinese romance drama. But I could not help feeling more guarded towards these intense emotions.

What was the use of putting myself through this internal crisis when there were so many external things to worry about? Why was figuring out my emotions such an important thing to me? What was the expected endgame to this research? I was hoping to come to some sort of resolve by the end of it.

Love Languages

Continuing on with the theme of Christmas, I was giving out candy canes this week for the holiday season. It reminded me that gift giving is a love language. I took a test to determine what my personal love language was, and it turns out to be 33% of quality time with words of affirmation following closely after. Thinking of the person I may (or may not) have feelings for, I would not say this makes much sense. I don't feel a strong need to spend time with this person nor do I want him to tell me he loves me or misses me. In fact, it makes me feel uncomfortable whenever he does say those things as it ironically makes me doubt my feelings even more. Gift-giving is simple and conveys the message that I care about the person and that I am thinking about them. Either this test must be very inaccurate, or I am deceiving myself.

Lost in Translation

Earlier this week, I came across a video that described a word: *Onsra*. As part of the Boro language of India, it means "the bittersweet feeling when you know a love won't last." I took it upon myself to find out if there were other words from different languages that describe feelings that could not be explained in the languages I knew. *Thoughts Catalog* had a list of "23 Untranslatable Foreign Words That Describe Love Better Than You Ever Thought." This was definitely something for me as someone who struggled with alexithymia. *Kilig*, in Tagalog describes a "sublime rush" that one may experience when something good happens, like hearing someone tell you that they love you for the first time. *La douleur exquise* in French means "the heartbreaking pain of wanting someone you can't have." *Yuanfen* in Chinese describes a union planned by destiny.

So many of these terms were personally relatable and in that way had validated some of the thoughts that have been going through my mind about this one specific person. Maybe my feelings are so confusing not because they are weird or nonrealistic. Maybe it is because until now there have been no words to my knowledge that could explain what has been going on with me.

However, the irony I've found in trying to search for the correct words is that I have started to question why there is a need for me to.

A Wonder Story

Before I delve into this section, I will first say a precursor apology to the person I admire most in this world, the person who practically raised me, my rock and my role model, my sister Christine. I am about to expose her love life.

Prior to meeting her boyfriend of now 6 years and ongoing, Christine was in college struggling around campus on crutches from a broken ankle due to her first time trying yoga. She really owned those crutches though, to the point of catching the attention of her classmate at the time, now boyfriend. Christine would always tell me, "I know you. You're like me. I always thought I would be living a single life forever, because there was no one out there for me." She was right, but she had a more pragmatic view of the world and didn't need a significant other in her life to validate her existence.

Christine says she doesn't believe in universal red or green flags, that "everyone is going to have their own opinion on what is okay and not okay in a relationship." As an example, she and her boyfriend are currently competing to see who can get rich first. She calls it a "win-win" because the winner will have the bragging rights while the loser gets to freeload off of the winner's success. She tells me that someone is bound to stick their two feet in and protest that it's bad to be a dependent person, but she doesn't see why it is a problem for her to spend the rest of her life being a cat-mom and getting to spend money at virtually no cost to herself. As long as the people in the relationship are happy with what is going on, then there is no issue. She makes it make sense.

Along with being amazed that she always knows exactly what she wants and does not want, my biggest takeaway is the idea of validating my own desires and thoughts because that is what makes me feel like me. I feel that I've always been unconsciously influenced to be embarrassed or to silence my emotions because they are too much of a burden for others.

I secretly am a dependent person. That may seem completely bogus as my anxiety allows me to carry myself in a way that feels distant to others. The scariest part is that while I don't know what I want, I don't even know what I don't want. And that goes for my relationships, my future, and my happiness. Love is just one of the murky swims of life that I drown in.

What now?

I'm sure that anyone who reads this will feel the sense of confusion I had when writing this. Every section was finished with me asking myself, "So what is it? Is love a yes now? Or a no?" In the simplest terms, for people like our beloved Romeo and Juliet, it is still a no. For the people like Noah and Allie in *The Notebook* (my favorite film), it is a yes, but for a different reason now. I still find love to be quite alien and deceptive. There are just so many takes on it that a simpleton like me finds it hard to validate such an existence. Out of all of my research, I found my sit-down with Christine the most personal and valuable. Affirming the Triangular Theory of Love, she says that love is what I *want* it to be, because it is *my* love. I need to be sure that I am happy first and foremost, as it would be embarrassing to die from a broken heart. I need to really think about what makes me happy, rather than what other people think should make me happy. Maybe the truth is that I've been the one deceiving myself all this time. Maybe this new love is helping me realize that I am not as pragmatic as I think I am or wish to be. There are times that I wish for a love that consumes me, that sweeps me off my feet, like the ones that took the lives of Romeo and Juliet. I sure do judge their recklessness harshly for someone who is jealous that they would die for each other without any regrets. (Here I am again, going back and forth on my thoughts.) In the end, the knowledge and advice I've acquired in this project has not helped me solve my problems. But all of it, even the sources I did not decide to include here have taken away the pressure of trying to. And right now, that is all I need to calm this turmoil in me.

Sources

Cherry, Kendra. "5 Ways That Theories of Psychology Explain Love." *Verywell Mind*, Verywell Mind, 21 Nov. 2019, www.verywellmind.com/theories-of-love-2795341. Accessed 05 November 2021.

Emamzadeh, Arash. "What Is Romantic Love?" *Psychology Today*, Sussex Publishers, 9 Feb. 2020, www.psychologytoday.com/us/blog/finding-new-home/202002/what-is-romantic-love. Accessed 05 November 2021.

Jaffe, Eric. "Why Love Literally Hurts." *Association for Psychological Science – APS*, 30 Jan. 2013, https://www.psychologicalscience.org/observer/why-love-literally-hurts.

Milligan, Tony. "Love." Routledge, Taylor, Francis. 2014. *Drexel University Libraries*. ebookcentral-proquest-com.ezproxy2.library.drexel.edu/lib/drexel-ebooks/reader.action?docID=1815516. Accessed 28 October 2021.

Neelis, Koty. "23 Untranslatable Foreign Words That Describe Love Better than You Ever Thought." *Thought Catalog*, 18 Nov. 2014, https://thoughtcatalog.com/koty-neelis/2014/11/23-untranslatable-foreign-words-that-describe-love-better-than-you-ever-thought/.

Oghia, Michael J. "The Theory of Love Pt. 1: Lee's 6 Love Styles." *The Theory of Love Pt. 1: Lee's 6 Love Styles*, 13 Sept. 2011, www.loveanon.org/2011/09/theory-of-love-pt-1-lees-6-love-styles.html. Accessed 06 November 2021.

Sternberg, Robert J. "Love." *Robert J. Sternberg*, http://www.robertjsternberg.com/love. Accessed 06 November 2021.

"The Love Language™ Quiz." *Discover Your Love Language - The 5 Love Languages®*, https://www.5lovelanguages.com/quizzes/love-language. Accessed 28 October 2021.

Wu, Katherine. "Love, Actually: The Science behind Lust, Attraction, and Companionship." *Science in the News*, 19 June 2020, sitn.hms.harvard.edu/flash/2017/love-actually-science-behind-lust-attraction-companionship/. Accessed 07 November 2021.

What is a question that you want to explore about deception and yourself? We'll talk about how to navigate good questions. This could also include a question about deception and your major/future career.

—Dr. Karen Nulton

Roger Vitek
Addiction and Locus of Control

Humans struggle with addiction. From social media, to food, to tics such as fingernail biting, to drugs that specifically target receptors in our brain— addiction can present itself in a variety of facets throughout our lives. We humans have it difficult with such an egregious number of temptations. Why do we become addicted to things, and how can there also be free will at the same time? How can two completely opposite phenomena coexist? Locus of control plays a significant role in the development and continuation of addictive behavior. In order to understand addiction and how theories of free will exist, locus of control, biological factors, and perceptions of addiction must be discussed.

In psychological theory, locus of control is the degree that an individual believes outcomes and events in their life can be controlled or influenced by their own actions (Rotter 1966). Whether conscious about it or not, we all harbor a locus of control ranging from internal (I am in control) to external (outside forces are in control). As a classic and potentially overused example, let's say I fail this paper miserably. When I see the grade next week, will I blame myself for not writing a good enough paper? Or will I blame Dr. Nulton, believing she hates me as a student? Whether or not one outcome is necessarily truer than the other, the former response would be a complete internal locus of control, while the latter a complete external locus of control. While this example serves to define the meaning between the two, it's important to remember that the locus of control exists on a spectrum (Tyler, Heffernan, Fortune 2020). Our day-to-day life consists of a series of decision-making. Some decisions are small (what color socks should I put on?), while some are larger (should I lie and call in sick to have the day off?). People approach some of these decisions internally, and some externally. Stressful, heavier decisions are likely to be approached with more of an external mentality, to remove self-blame beforehand, in case the outcome is undesirable (Tyler, Heffernan, Fortune 2020). The way these decisions are approached influences our behavior and habit-forming, leading to a locus of control that reliably leans more to one side of the spectrum than the other. This is important in the case of addiction treatment. Developing an internal locus of control through positive internal decision-making can help lead to better habits and routines that don't involve addiction as a driving force in life.

From a neurological perspective, locus of control can be severely affected by addictive behavior, and vice versa. Certain things become addictive to humans because our complex neural reward pathways, in combination with repetition, form habits. These reward-system driven habits range from healthy to detrimental, depending on the behavior that's been latched on to (Weinberg 2013). The reward system in our brains is extremely primal—it gives priority to certain behaviors that prolong life only momentarily. French fries taste better to me than boiled potatoes because deep frying something in hot oil makes it significantly more caloric. As a starving neanderthal, the energy and sustenance gained from deep frying would have been extremely beneficial to prolonging my life. I would be more likely to get eaten by a bear, or starve to death, than live long enough to worry about type 2 diabetes. As a human living in 2021, the dopamine let loose in my brain from eating greasy, calorie dense food, is useless to me as I'm at no risk of starvation. In fact, for the 29 million Americans living with some form of an eating disorder (Deloitte 2020), this instant-gratification centered reward pathway, has played a part in significantly reducing their health and quality of life. The addictive cycle of instant-gratification in our reward pathway, can lead those who have developed negative habits to also develop an external locus of control.

The nature vs. nurture debate is an important topic relating to addiction as well. Can addictive tendencies be hereditary? Can people really have an "addictive personality?" Or are we all subject to free will and choice, barring external influences (peers, environment etc.)? According to the National Institute of Health, certain gene expressions can represent 40-60 percent of an individual's risk of addiction (Bevilacqua & Goldman 2009). However, in most cases, there must be some form of an environmental influence present for addictive behavior to begin. Learned behavior can come from a friend or close family member—hence why an addiction such as alcoholism might not be hereditary if you had an alcoholic parent, but can be behavior that's learned and normalized throughout your development as a child (Kelley 2018). People may not have an "addictive personality" per se but can develop and worsen an external locus of control through poor environment and influences. We are all subject to free will, however some of us are more subject to temptation based on genetic and environmental triggers.

In a world of nicotine and social media-addicted youth, addiction seems more and more prevalent and normalized socially. Biology can only explain so much—the rest relies on our collective ability to understand the effects and consequences of an addicted society. The prevalent questions about pathology and behavior mean nothing without a solid response to *why should I care?*

My family has a history of addiction. My grandfather was a non-functioning alcoholic but apparently a decent character; sadly I never got to meet him as he passed away a year before I was born due to illnesses from alcoholism. My mom's side of the family is all nicotine addicted in some form or another, except for her, thankfully. She quit decades ago. My sister struggles with illicit substances, seeing herself in and out of mental hospitals and rehab centers seemingly endlessly. The struggle and suffering of addiction treads deep, affecting many more people than just the addict themselves. My relationship with my sister was effectively ruined for 4 years because of her addiction, and just recently I'm cautiously getting to know her again. For every addict who struggles through the cycle of substance abuse, there's a family member or close friend struggling through the cycle of destruction, and hastily rebuilding a relationship with that person. After experiencing this for a few years, it took a toll on me mentally, and I began to see it affecting my ability to build relationships with people in other areas of my life. This was when I became curious about the causalities and psychology involved with addictive behavior.

Years ago, when I cut off contact with my sister because of the emotional damage her addiction was causing, I remember her telling me "It's okay, we can have a relationship again when I'm sober." I remember thinking to myself, *so never then*? Luckily, I was wrong, at least for the time being. She's been sober for a few months now, but a part of me is always anticipating a phone call that she's been readmitted to the hospital. I asked her about her experiences with addiction recently, and she stated that "picking up the pipe was the worst decision I made in my life." While she wouldn't hesitate to admit this, she tends to downplay the affects her addiction has had on her own family. However, through rehabilitation and support groups, I believe she's been able to shift her locus of control internally. The biggest message behind rehabilitation is the idea that an individual *does* have autonomy over their life (Heidari & Ghodusi 2016). Whether or not they decide to internalize this message, is why some people spend their whole life in and out of rehab centers, never able to create any change.

The tax on my mental health from having family members struggling with addiction was huge. As a young teenager still trying to understand my own emotions and responses, the baggage from having a family torn apart by addiction caused me to become a distant and emotionally removed person. I did not feel in control or have any sense of free will—I felt as if my family was cursed, and my locus of control became extremely external. According to a 2009 correlational study on addiction and free will, making people feel as if they have less free will than they feel at their baseline, can lead to less interaction between the individuals, and even aggression (Baumeister & Vohs, 2009). When my free will was weakened due to unpredictable events, this aspect of feeling emotionally removed was very difficult to overcome.

While addiction has definite emotional and social costs, it has an immense economic cost as well. In 2019, drug abuse and addiction cost the United States an estimated 820 billion dollars (Gateway 2019). This includes the combined costs of drug use, treatment, criminal prosecution, healthcare, and estimated lost productivity. The issue with sustaining an addiction, is it requires a constant flow of money to be maintained. If the source of that money is cut off—or if the addict is unable to sustain themselves because they fell too deep into addiction, their situation only gets worse. Addicts can resort to stealing, which not only costs money in theft, but in judicial process and jail time as well. They may go through intense withdrawals, putting unnecessary strain on the healthcare system as well as leaving the individual with an inhumane amount of medical debt. Addiction is an unnecessary, preventable disease to society.

Realistically, struggling with a drug addiction is likely to leave a person in a much worser state of mental health than before. Degrading socioeconomic status, as well as neurological factors of the dopamine reward system in the brain, are bound to keep an addict scraping by, rather than making an attempt to enter rehabilitation. With more than 1/3 of Americans currently battling some form of substance use disorder (Thomas, et al, 2021), reframing the way rehabilitation is viewed in society is a task long overdue. Rather than rehabilitation centers being viewed as a resource for low-class, impoverished people down on their luck, they need to be viewed and funded as a respected community resource that saves lives—like a hospital. After all, addiction affects people from all levels of economic status. In fact, a 2012 study finds that drug and alcohol abuse may be correlated with higher socioeconomic status (Patrick, Wightman, Schoeni, Schulenberg 2012).

I have previously struggled with addiction as well. Besides the usual offenders of nicotine and alcohol, I spent a lot of time abusing Adderall in high school to get through the day. Back then, the effects of feeling sharp and confident were worth the depressing comedown, even if it was nearly every single day. I was less addicted to the mental effects—the focus everyone talks about; the false perception of doing higher quality work—but more addicted to the way it made me view myself. As an angsty, emotionally stunted teenager, the ability to feel confident in any situation with just the pop of a pill was exhilarating, while simultaneously mentally degrading. Rather than spend the time and effort to better my self-perception and confidence for the long term, I constantly took the short term, instantly gratifying capsule of powdered courage. However, nobody warned me about the comedown. The depression, self-hatred, and inability to sleep eventually turned me to seek healthier alternatives. As of 2020, the amount of 12th graders who had abused Adderall within the previous year was nearly 5% and growing (Elflein 2021). While not as big of an epidemic as other drugs such as nicotine have become in recent years, the number of high schoolers who have abused a Schedule II amphetamine, is concerning. I believe with more education on the importance of mental health and self-confidence, while emphasizing free-will and internal locus' of control in adolescents, will lead to a society built on a foundation of acceptance and support for one another.

Locus of control is a significant factor in our ability to reduce and shorten the cycle of addiction. Conclusively, an internal locus of control, and the feeling of having free will and direction in life, can be directly affected by positive mental health practices, education, and access to resources. We may be all subject to addiction at some point in our lives—the importance is in how we respond. To realize we carry our own torch and can make choices that point in the right direction, in order to paint a better, healthier future for ourselves, without the prevalence of addiction.

References

Bevilacqua, L., & Goldman, D. (2009). "Genes and Addictions." *Clinical Pharmacology andTtherapeutics*, 85(4), Point/Counterpoint, 359–361. https://doi.org/10.1038/clpt.2009.6

Heidari, M., & Ghodusi, M. (2016). "Relationship of Assess Self-Esteem and Locus of Control with Quality of Life During Treatment Stages in Patients Referring to Drug Addiction Rehabilitation Centers." *Materia Socio-medica*, 28(4), 263–267. https://doi.org/10.5455/msm.2016.28.263-267

Kelley, T. L. (2021, January 29). "Is Addiction Hereditary?" *Willingway*. Retrieved November 22, 2021, from https://willingway.com/is-addiction-hereditary/.

Patrick, M. E., Wightman, P., Schoeni, R. F., & Schulenberg, J. E. (2012). "Socioeconomic status and substance use among young adults: a comparison across constructs and drugs." *Journal of Studies on Alcohol and Drugs*, 73(5), 772–782. https://doi.org/10.15288/jsad.2012.73.772

"Report: Economic Costs of Eating Disorders." *STRIPED*. (2021, September 27). Retrieved November 22, 2021, from https://www.hsph.harvard.edu/striped/report-economic-costs-of-eating-disorders/.

Rotter, J. B. (1966). "Generalized Expectancies for Internal Versus External Control of Reinforcement." *Psychological Monographs: General and Applied*, 80(1), 1–28. https://doi.org/10.1037/h0092976

"The Cost of Drug Abuse & Addiction Treatment: Gateway Foundation." *Gateway*. (2021, October 4). Retrieved November 22, 2021, from https://www.gatewayfoundation.org/addiction-blog/cost-of-drug-addiction/.

Thomas, S. Et al. (2021, November 19). "Addiction Statistics: Drug & Substance Abuse Statistics." *American Addiction Centers*. Retrieved November 22, 2021, from https://americanaddictioncenters.org/rehab-guide/addiction-statistics.

Tyler, N., Heffernan, R., & Fortune, C.-A. (1AD, January 1). "Reorienting Locus of Control in Individuals Who Have Offended through Strengths-Based Interventions: Personal Agency and the Good Lives Model." *Frontiers*. Retrieved November 22, 2021, from https://www.frontiersin.org/articles/10.3389/fpsyg.2020.553240/full.

Vitek, R. O. (2021, November 19). Talking to my sister. personal.

Vohs, K. D., & Baumeister, R. F. (2009). "Addiction and Free Will." *Addiction Research & Theory*, 17(3), 231–235. https://doi.org/10.1080/16066350802567103

Weinberg, D. (2013). "Post-Humanism, Addiction and the Loss of Self-Control: Reflections on the Missing Core in Addiction Science." *International Journal of Drug Policy*, 24(3), 173–181. https://doi.org/10.1016/j.drugpo.2013.01.009

Research Log

11/8 – Researched NIH sources on addiction/locus of control at my desk in the PROD studio.

11/9 – Did some more research into NIH articles because I find the abstract sections are pretty quick and interesting. Worked at home.

11/12 – Realized abstract/discussion sections usually have most useful information. Sometimes read methodology for context but it can get confusing quickly. Keeping a list of all references I will use in the paper. Worked at home.

11/15 – Started writing paper for probably 30-40 min, did a short introduction after putting it off too long, I find mustering up the courage to start writing is always the hardest part. Worked at my desk in the PROD studio.

11/19 – Continued writing for about an hour, did first page. Working at home for the rest of the weekend.

11/20 – Wrote for about 5-6 hours, I have a really slow drawn out thought process and writing research papers can take me a *really* long time. Getting into the zone is kind of relaxing though. Tried to strike a balance between factual research, my analysis/opinion, and sections about my personal life.

11/21 – Wrote for 5 ½ hours and finished. Forgot some contextual citations and spent a while going back to find them online which was frustrating. References page took about an hour to sort out. Done!

What is a question that you want to explore about deception and yourself? We'll talk about how to navigate good questions. This could also include a question about deception and your major/future career.

—Dr. Karen Nulton

Maddie White

D1 Athletes' Mental Health Through Covid-19

What does it mean to be a Division 1 student-athlete? If you had asked me this question a year ago as a freshman, I wouldn't have been able to tell you. I spent the first half of my college lacrosse experience at home. Since Drexel wasn't housing any students in dorms for the fall of 2020, freshmen student-athletes would have to wait to live on campus. The rest of my team, the upperclassmen, were stuck on an empty, desolate campus being forced to follow an unimaginable number of rules in the name of health safety. At least they got to play lacrosse in the fall. Meanwhile, the seven other girls in my freshman lacrosse class and I were dying to get out of our houses and finally start our college experience. The upperclassmen on the team would occasionally text to check in and see how we were doing at home. They told us we weren't missing much and sometimes gave little complaints about the rules they had to follow. Apparently, an empty campus was no fun. I didn't believe them.

All I wanted to do was get on campus and play. I was sick of things being taken from me: my last high school lacrosse season, my graduation, senior prom, senior week, fall of my freshman year of college, my first fall ball games. The list went on and felt like it wouldn't end—so, sorry if I didn't think that having to follow some Covid rules would be that big of a deal. As long as I was on campus and able to play my sport, I didn't care what rules I had to follow to be there. I would do anything to get my college lacrosse experience started.

My wish finally came true when we got word that freshman student athletes would be allowed to live on campus for winter term. January was also the start of lacrosse preseason, so the timing was perfect to move back on campus. Before moving in, we joined a few zoom calls with our coaches going over the rules of living on campus. There were a lot of rules to follow, but I felt like it would all be worth it if I got to have my season. Little did I know that nothing would prepare me for the negative toll that this would take on my mental health.

Upon moving in, we were to have no contact with anyone outside of our direct roommate for two weeks. After the two weeks, we would start lacrosse preseason in pods within our team. The team was broken up into five pods and every two weeks, pods would combine until the entire team was allowed to practice together. While that was going on, we weren't allowed to hang out with anyone outside of our pods. This rule was kind of hard to follow considering our roommates were all in different pods, so that didn't make sense. On top of all of that, we also weren't allowed to hang out with anyone that wasn't a part of our team for the entire season. To recap it all, I basically would have to survive my freshman year without being allowed to make any new friends. Failure to follow these rules would result in player suspensions and possibly force the entire team to forfeit games.

To make matters even more confusing and burdensome, the rules we had to follow as athletes were different from the rules that regular students had to follow, and the consequences were worse if rules were broken. If we broke a Covid rule that Drexel put in place for all students, not only would we get in trouble with the school, but we'd also get in trouble with our coaches and the athletic department. Two rounds of punishment would be allotted to us. If we followed the normal school code of conduct that was sent to all students, we could easily be breaking athletic protocol. This contradiction in rule books made things very unclear and stressful to navigate, especially as freshmen that were new to the school. We received no adjustment period at all for this impossible set of standards.

As the season went on, the mental health of my team declined. We were mentally drained from navigating the rules and making sure we didn't test positive for Covid. Every Covid test was a threat to whether we would be able to play in our game or not and would determine if our sacrifices were worth it. I would hear stories of positive tests on other teams causing them to shut down for two weeks. Some things were completely out of our control and that was the scary part of it all. The worst part was feeling like we were doing everything we could to keep our season, but it was somehow still not good enough. We were deprived of normal social interactions, including eating in the cafeteria with other students, and it started to make me feel depressed. Take note, the feelings of depression and sadness I experienced were coming from someone who has never had past struggles with mental health. After looking into research done about the mental health effects of Covid-19 on college students and athletes, I could confirm that we weren't the only ones experiencing those feelings.

According to a case study done at Old Dominion University by Pease (2021):

> This health pandemic crisis was unmatched to anything the country and college student-athletes have collectively faced in recent decades. COVID-19 has thrown college athletics curve balls and significant obstacles. Student-athletes were at the forefront of these challenges and had to manage the daily protocols COVID-19 was presenting (14).

This case study focused on the effects the pandemic had on college athletes and specifically followed the Old Dominion University Men's and Women's Basketball teams. The theme observed across the country with this pandemic has been that college student-athletes are one of the groups that has been hit the hardest with changes. The case study done by Shannon Pease (2021) makes the point that a lot of changes were being made quickly without the thought of ramifications that these decisions would have on student-athletes (2). The abrupt changes uprooted the structured lifestyle student-athletes are so accustomed to and put them into a world of uncertainty. These findings aligned with my own experience at Drexel as well. In an interview I had with a fellow Drexel athlete, the structure of the student-athlete lifestyle was addressed, "...as student-athletes we are so used to a routine. Our routine was completely messed up with the pandemic." This drastic change seemed to have overwhelmed student-athletes. It is essential to stick to a schedule in order to handle the workload of being a student, an athlete, and maintaining a social life. In my past experience, I have always relied on planning ahead to excel in each of these areas. With all of the uncertainty related to the pandemic, planning ahead did not always work. Plans could change at any moment with a positive Covid test, or the suspension of games. The case study by Pease (2021) referred to this.

> Also, COVID-19 removed the student-athletes from their strict student-athletes routines and daily structure, they felt a lack of support from the overall university, and their mental health and overall wellbeing was challenged during this trying time (p.v).

This helped me realize that not being able to rely on a structured, planned lifestyle created a large mental hurdle that many athletes weren't prepared for. This was one factor that hurt the mental health of college athletes across the country.

Not only did the athletes not know how to handle this change, schools also did not give the support needed to help. The athletic departments were dealing with a crisis of their own as they attempted to navigate planning seasons in the midst of a pandemic. In a peer reviewed article by Kevin Kleps, the thoughts of many athletic directors across the country were highlighted when asked how they dealt with scheduling seasons. Kleps (2020) featured one athletic program stating, "The Yeomen, who compete in the Westlake-based North Coast Athletic Conference, spent five months plotting out potential calendars once the pandemic hit. They arrived at the same spot at which so many other institutions are: a standstill," (p.1). It took extensive planning from universities to figure out how to get their athletes back on the field in a safe manner, while following all NCAA Covid protocol, and staying within a reasonable budget. It was a logistical nightmare for athletic departments. This issue is understandable, however, with all the focus on scheduling, the mental health concerns of the student-athletes were forgotten. Although the various NCAA protocols and extensive number of rules were necessary for the safe return of students, they placed a burden on the schools that distracted them from thinking about mental health needs.

The world essentially abandoned helping mental health at the start of the pandemic. A situation like this has never happened in our lifetime. As a society, we are learning how to deal with a worldwide pandemic, and in dealing with this crisis people are going to make mistakes. In my opinion, the biggest mistake was neglecting the mental health issue that was already a big problem before Covid. In the article *Impacts of the Covid-19 Pandemic on the Health of University Students*, the author Laura Ihm (2021) makes the case that, "The mental health of the student population has been a major concern for several years and the pandemic has certainly exacerbated this problem" (p.1). This piece of evidence reveals that the mental health crisis was already an issue, and now that crisis is exposed because we have shifted all resources to helping physical health. According to Abbott (2021), the number of US adults reporting symptoms of anxiety or depression went from 11 percent before the pandemic to 42 percent during it (p.1). The odds were stacked against student-athletes, and in addition to the little help they were receiving, prevalent were feelings of loneliness and isolation. Abott (2021) continues and says:

> Studies and surveys conducted so far in the pandemic consistently show that young people, rather than older people, are most vulnerable to increased psychological distress, perhaps because their need for social interactions are stronger (p.1).

Students were deprived of vital social interaction for an extensive period of time. It is not natural for students in their college years to be forced to not interact with others. I would go as far as to say that it is detrimental to their health and dangerous. Isolation causes feelings of loneliness which snowballs into social anxiety and depression. I know because I experienced it first-hand last winter and spring. Students on college campuses everywhere felt the exact same way I did. This was a realization I didn't come to until researching this topic. I felt isolated and felt alone in my struggles because I did not have anyone to talk to about it. I would have no way of knowing that others were also struggling because everything felt very individual. Most students kept to themselves about the way they were feeling because they didn't know others were feeling the same way which points back to the lack of help with regards to mental health during those challenging times.

This brings me to the main question: Is it okay to sacrifice mental health in the name of physical health? If the university athletic departments didn't act in the way they did, then so many more student-athletes would have contracted the virus. The rules were put in place to protect us from a worldwide pandemic. However, the evidence I found in many pieces of research corroborates everything I was feeling. Mental health aid, specifically for college athletes, was completely abandoned during their greatest time of need. Athletes were struggling and deprived of social interaction for too long. I believe most of the rules were effective, but there were a lot of extra, unnecessary rules that were put in place too. Schools were dealing with their own scheduling crisis as they needed to prove to the NCAA that they were being safe enough to return to play. As a result, they came up with an encyclopedia-sized number of rules that contradicted each other, causing confusion and stress for many athletes. This created a mental health crisis for those trying to navigate the variety of stresses that were put on them. I, along with others, went through tough times last year, but I can honestly say that I have come out stronger on the other side. No matter the mistakes that were made, I hope that we can all reflect on them and handle situations like this one better in the future.

References

Abbott, Alison. "Covid's Mental-Health Toll: How Scientists Are Tracking a Surge in Depression." Nature News, *Nature Publishing Group*, 3 Feb. 2021, https://www.nature.com/articles/d41586-021-00175-z.

Ihm, L. & Zhang, H. & Waugh, M.G. (2021). "Impacts of the Covid-19 Pandemic on the Health of University Students." *The International Journal of Health Planning and Management*, vol. 36, no. 3, Wiley Subscription Services, Inc, pp. 618–27, https://doi.org/10.1002/hpm.3145.

Kleps, Kevin. "PLAYING (OR NOT PLAYING) THROUGH Pandemic Pain: From COVID Testing to Scheduling Dilemmas and Mental Health, Athletic Departments Attempt to Tackle the Unknown." *Crain's Cleveland Business*, vol. 41, no. 32, 31 Aug. 2020, p. 10.

"Transitional Impact of COVID--19 on Division I Men's and Women's Basketball Student-Athletes: A Case Study." *ProQuest Dissertations & Theses Global*, ProQuest Dissertations Publishing.https://www.proquest.com/openview/9d3073ec4869d40f1fe4d3aaa92ae2e8/1?pq-origsite=gscholar&cbl=18750&diss=y.

Drexel Publishing Group

Essays

Introduction

The following essays were selected from student submissions to the Drexel Publishing Group Essay Contest. The contest was judged by faculty from a wide range of disciplines in the College of Arts and Sciences. This was a very competitive contest that required two rounds of judging. The essays in this section of *The 33rd* explore diverse topics such as gender roles, identity, education, and literature. These student writers demonstrate their fine research skills in a variety of disciplines in the arts and sciences, and do so with originality, nuance, and passion.

To honor the stylistic requirements of each field, we have reproduced the essays and articles in their original forms.

—*The Editors*

Grace Fisher

Marian Virtue in *Sir Gawain and the Green Knight*

"Mary said, 'Behold, I am the handmaid of the Lord. May it be done to me according to your word.' Then the angel departed from her" (*NABRE*, Luke 1:38).

To the anonymous author of the 14th century poem *Sir Gawain and the Green Knight*, Gawain was arguably the most gallant knight of the Arthurian court. But the deeds by which he proves himself are not stereotypically masculine feats of strength or courage in battle, or even action at all. His noblest moments—resisting the advances of Lady Bertilak, and the acceptance of a deathblow from the Green Knight—require chastity and a passive bravery of surrender to God's will, both virtues historically associated with the feminine, and specifically the Virgin Mary, who is ever-chaste and, next to Christ, is the principal example in Catholic tradition of obedience to God (*CCC* 494-507). Mary features throughout the poem as Gawain's protector and object of devotion, which explicitly reinforces her importance and that of the so-called feminine virtues, in direct and deliberate contrast to the poem's patriarchal world of active and courageous "Knights for Christ," a world which must not "waste its strength in idleness" but rather display "its usefulness by carrying [out] war against [infidels]" (Moeller). Instead, by positioning Gawain as a Marian figure, the poet critiques the hypermasculine interpretation of Christianity common in Medieval England and underscores the importance of the feminine aspects of the religion.

The reader's attention is gently drawn towards Mary from the opening of *Sir Gawain*, which, as well as most of the action, occurs during Christmastide, a holiday almost as concerned with Mary as with Christ because of her willing role in the Incarnation. However, at this point Gawain is less obviously her narrative counterpart, as he commits a significant act of violence, partaking in the beheading game of the Green Knight, which can be viewed nobly, but not admirably worthy of Gawain, as attested to by his later acts in "battle" which are made unimportant by the status of his opponents and by their relegation to a mere few lines in stanza 31: "Here he scraps with serpents and snarling wolves,/here he tangles with wodwos causing trouble in the crags,/or with bulls and bears and the odd wild boar" (720-22). In contrast, Gawain's non-violent deeds—his stay at the castle and second meeting with the Green Knight—make up the bulk of the poem and are what he is explicitly praised for by Bertilak and, implicitly, by the author, because these deeds are deemed worthy enough to be presented in detail for thousands of lines throughout the tale. It is in response to Gawain's resistance to Lady Bertilak that the narrator in the voice of Bertilak calls Gawain, "the most faultless fellow on earth" (2363).

As Gawain prepares to depart Camelot, his status as a Marian figure begins to materialize in FITT ii when readers peruse the description of his shield and its pentangle, which is "appropriate to that prince" (623), and, more subtly, in his apparent submission to God's will: "I must set out tomorrow . . . and let God be my guide" (548-49). Gawain's shield, a symbol of his virtue against evil, is doubly associated with Mary. Her image adorns the inside, taking the place perhaps of a lady's favor, "so by catching her eye his courage would not crack" (650). Mary's image is also significant politically. Phillipa Hardman, a Reader in Medieval English Literature (retired) at the University of Reading, discusses religious controversy in *Sir Gawain* and notes that at the time of the poem's composition, the Lollards, precursors of Protestant reformers, protested the use of holy images, and so "readiness to venerate images [came to be known as] as the corresponding proof of orthodoxy" (5). The *Gawain* poet, though critical of his society's interpretation of Christianity in other ways, as this paper will argue, here aligns himself and positions Gawain within orthodox traditions, perhaps as a shield against the accusation of heresy or at least unorthodoxy.

The shield is also decorated on the front with the image of a pentangle, one of the five meanings of which is the five joys of Mary. The most significant is the Annunciation, when Mary issues her "fiat," or yes, to God's request that she conceive a child by the Holy Spirit, although if found guilty of adultery she would have faced being stoned to death. Her trust in God and bravery in passive acceptance rather than action are mirrored in Gawain's surrender to the Green Knight's axe.

Naturally, the reflection is imperfect, as Gawain, unlike the Blessed Mother, bears the stain of original sin. Mary's surrender is complete. Her faith is not that God will save her from death or disgrace, but that neither one matters if she serves His will. Of course, Gawain divides his trust between God and the girdle (a symbolic counterpart to Gawain's shield as an object of faith), but more than this, even that part of his faith which is in God is somewhat self-concerned, not as absolute and self-giving as Mary's. He is still concerned with his own fate, telling the servant guiding him to the green chapel that "those who strive to serve / our Lord, our Lord will save" (2138-39). But this is to be expected. Although Gawain is heroic, he is fallible as all men are.

When the revealed Bertilak praises Gawain, it is not for the climactic moment of awaiting his axe, but for resisting seduction from Lady Bertilak: "I sent her to test you...As a pearl is more prized than a pea which is white / in good faith, so is Gawain amongst gallant knights" (2362-64). Mary is of course a symbol of sexual purity, but Gawain's enduring chastity is also explicitly credited to her: "They talk with tenderness / and pride, and yet their plight / is perilous unless / sweet Mary minds her knight" (1766-69). Together Gawain's chastity and acceptance of God's will position him as a Marian figure within *Sir Gawain*.

An argument could be made that Gawain is not so much of a Marian figure as a Christ figure, since chastity and surrender to God's will—specifically to the point of death—are also attributes of Christ. But from a Christian viewpoint *all* the virtues are fulfilled completely in Christ, as would be expected, and Christ fulfills the role not only of willing victim but also of royal host in heaven and powerful judge at the end of time. In fact, a far more fitting Christ figure is

Bertilak, who takes on each of these roles in turn: martyr in the opening scene[1]; host when Gawain stays at his castle; and judge at the green chapel.

Gawain's Christian chastity and passivity rather than active bravery, as well as his Marian role and all the Marian references throughout, are an implicit critique of a Medieval society that viewed masculine bravery, action, and honor as central to Christianity and did not see combat as incongruous to the religion. The *Gawain* poet does not criticize these things in themselves (after all, Gawain does chop off a man's head), but he does challenge their being raised above the somewhat less glamorous virtues of chastity, obedience, and surrender to God. Gawain is the perfect vehicle for these virtues: the greatest knight of King Arthur's court, heroic, admirable, and unimpeachably masculine. He allows the poet's urging of feminine virtues to become universal in a way that would be impossible were the main character a woman. The poet's nods to orthodoxy, specifically the positive representations of religious imagery, may have served to protect him in this gentle critique of Medieval Christianity.

Works Cited

Catholic Church. *Catechism of the Catholic Church*. 2nd ed. Doubleday, New York, 1995. Print.

Hardman, Phillipa. "Gawain's Practice of Piety in *Sir Gawain and the Green Knight*." *Medium Aevum*, vol. 68, no. 2, 1999, pp. 247-67. ProQuest, http://ezproxy2.library.drexel.edu/login?url=https://www.proquest.com/scholarly-journals/gawains-practice-piety-sir-gawain-green-knight/docview/194190807/se-2?accountid=10559.

Moeller, Charles. "Order of the Knights of Christ." *The Catholic Encyclopedia*. Vol. 3. New York: Robert Appleton Company, 1908, http://www.newadvent.org/cathen/03698b.htm.

The New American Bible: Including the Revised New Testament and Psalms Translated from the Original Languages with Critical Use of All the Ancient Sources. Ed. Jean M. Hiesberger.   New York: Oxford UP, 2007. Print.

Sir Gawain and the Green Knight. Trans. Simon Armitage. *The Norton Anthology of English Literature. Vol. A: The Middle Ages*. 10th ed. New York: Norton, 2018. 204-56. Print.

---

1   His resurrection is of course also reminiscent of Christ, and the holly he carries is a symbol of the Prince of Peace.

Lily DeSimone
They Transcends Language Barriers

They. A pronoun with powerful significance in just four simple letters. They can be used to describe people or things, and most recently, a singular person of unknown or unspecified gender. This pronoun gained popularity for many LGBTQ+ people in recent years due to the inclusivity it provided for those who do not identify as a particular gender, or who identify as many genders. However, this change did not occur easily and many in the community faced backlash for the use of their pronouns because previously only he/him and she/her were accepted for a singular person. But what happens when a person does not identify as male or female? What are the gender roles that are inherently associated with the use of gendered pronouns? How does the use of these pronouns imply that there are only two genders? Is gender just a social construct? These are all questions that ruminated through my mind as I began my search for the political implications for the use of they/them pronouns. They/them are acceptable pronouns for singular use to identify a person whose gender is unidentified because it allows for gender inclusivity by giving those in the LGBTQ+ community freedom with their gender expression. Unfortunately, this seems to only be widely accepted in English, but not in other languages such as romance languages. Many romance languages are inherently gendered with verbs, nouns, and adjectives ending in a way that identifies a person to a specific gender; the only options are male or female, masculine or feminine. However, recently there have been some developments toward being more inclusive like English, which allows for gender expression and identity.

To approach this, I first had an interview discussing they/them pronouns on November 15, 2021—Yes, the date is important. This essay explores why the pronouns are more inclusive, and I had the opportunity to interview Kennedy Henricks and Koda Tousignant, students at Rhode Island School of Design, to discuss their take on their own gender expression. Koda's first language is French, which is an inherently gendered language, so I asked if they feel they have the same freedom for gender expression in French as they do in English, to which Koda replied with a hard no: "I am unable to come out to most of my family at home because of the lack of gender-neutral terms in French." At home, Koda will use he/him pronouns with their sister because "anything is better than she/her," and he/him provides some comfort in French. However, Koda still feels as though they are unable to fully express their gender identity at home because they speak in French. This is not the fault of the family's understanding of gender, but of the French language itself, because Koda cannot simply explain their gender expression with words that do not exist and with concepts that do not exist in French. Therefore, it is important to acknowledge that they/them pronouns in English allow for the inclusivity of those, like Koda, who do not wish to identify as male or female. They have the ability to express themselves in a way that they feel free to because the language itself allows for this inclusion.

Just two weeks after our interview, an article in the *New York Times* was published about the use of a gender-neutral pronoun in French. Even two weeks prior, it seemed nearly impossible, and although this new pronoun has been created, that doesn't necessarily mean it will be implemented without difficulty. Brigitte Macron, wife of French president Emmanuel Macron, spoke against "*iel*" as a pronoun: "There are two pronouns: he and she," she declared. "Our language is beautiful. And two pronouns are appropriate" (Gallois and Cohen). It is important to note that various languages are inherently gendered, especially romance languages such as French. Certain words end in a way that makes them masculine or feminine or even collective nouns take a masculine or feminine stance. To incorporate gender neutral terminology, it may require some languages to be entirely rewritten, which is why gendered language may persist outside of English (which will be discussed further later). Listen, I'm not saying the French language isn't beautiful with two pronouns. I don't even speak French, so I'll have to take her word for it. However, would it not be a more beautiful language if it were inclusive for all those who speak it? How can someone find a language and culture rooted within that beauty if they cannot identify in it or if they are outcasted by their own language because of their identity? To be honest, that is not a question I can answer myself since I use she/her pronouns in English, a language that has always accepted the way that I identify. That is why they/them pronouns have sparked interest among English speakers; these pronouns are inclusive to both the person and culture within the language, without having to create a new pronoun that people would refuse to use.

Also, during November of 2021, I had the opportunity to take a Grammar class at Drexel University that explored the various aspects of why modern uses and structures of grammar in English are formatted the way they are. For this class we read many guides for the use of grammar, some of which included Strunk and White's *The Elements Of Style*, Emmy Favilla's *A World Without Whom*, Patricia T. O'Connor's *Woe Is I*, and Lynne Truss' *Eats, Shoots, and Leaves* (which is actually a book on punctuation, but the point remains that I read a lot about the structure of the English language). In Emmy Favilla's *A World Without Whom*, she explores the various struggles of gendered terminology and how companies such as BuzzFeed attempt to be more inclusive. In the "Gender inclusivity and the singular they" section, Favilla remarks that she supports the use of they as a singular pronoun. Emmy Favilla writes, "I'm staunchly in favor of singular *they*, not least because it's too much of an elegant catchall to resist...but also because it's obviously the more respectful choice, taking into consideration a spectrum of gender identities," (219) that to use "they" is not only easier than writing "he or she," but that it is inclusive to those who do not wish to use the pronouns he/him or she/her. To be fair, it is quite annoying to have to write "he or she said" when I could just write "they said," so the use of these pronouns includes a person who identifies as either male or female without the hassle of having to write more. This is also validating to a person who is non-binary because they feel that they do not have to conform to the gendered pronouns of he/him or she/her. The use of "they" allows the grammatical representation of one's gender identity, which is crucial to validate those who may identify as non-binary.

In addition to Favilla, Patricia T. O'Connor expresses that "they" can refer to someone whose gender is unknown or to be inclusive of individuals who may not wish to specify. A chapter titled "The Living Dead" discusses the use of they as a singular pronoun and how the stigma surrounding the singular use is something of the past—a topic she previously opposed in an earlier edition of her grammar guide. O'Connor states, "Today, the best authorities agree that this usage is not only neutral but grammatically correct" (251), that the singular usage permits neutrality for those of all genders. She argues a similar point to Favilla that it can also be a nuisance to have to write "his or her" when someone could just say "they," regardless that it is not inclusive when specifying just "his or her." O'Connor even goes so far as to label this section " TOMBSTONE" (251), to state just how dead this stigmatization surrounding the singular use of they/them is, sigh, if only it were truly that easy. It has become outdated to perceive the pronouns as such due to the influence of the pronouns in the LGBTQ+ community. To reiterate, these pronouns are giving inclusivity and freedom from unnecessary labeling for members of this community.

To further what Favilla and O'Connor have stated, I also dove into a bit of a linguistical approach to why pronouns are important and useful identifiers in language. Now I would like to preface this with the fact that I am certainly no expert in linguistics, but I will demonstrate my understanding of what I have read in my research. The novel written by Horst J. Simon and Heike Wiese, *Pronouns: Grammar and Representation*, contains a section titled "Grammatical properties of pronouns and their representation," which explores exactly that: grammatically, the properties that identify a pronoun and why they are important to use. They write, "From a cross-linguistic point of view, person and number appear to be the basic pronominal categories that are involved here. Universally, paradigms of personal pronouns seem to distinguish at least some speech act roles and to give at least some indication of whether one or more than one entity is involved" (Simon and Wiese 3), that linguistically pronouns are important to identify a subject and the number of that subject. So now we are getting into how we can examine the structure of the English language, because the purpose of pronouns, as stated by Simon and Wiese, is for identity. If the purpose of a pronoun is for such quantitative purposes, then the literal name of said pronoun in use is not the issue, but rather its association to a quantity serving to identify said subject.

So, what this tells us about they/them pronouns is that the hesitance surrounding them isn't necessarily the sound of the pronoun itself, but people's idea that they/them pronouns only signify something of a quantity of more than one. Although, if this is true, how can we explain people's willingness to use they/them, if, for example, they spot a stranger across the street? For example:

- They have a very nice sense of style.

- They look like a student athlete.

- Did you bring it to them?

If people truly only struggled with associating the quantity of a subject with a pronoun, phrases to identify strangers such as these would not exist because people would say "he or she" instead of they in such cases. And you could argue, if you are an avid linguist, that over time people accepted the use of they/them in cases such as these out of ease and misuse of he or she. Sure, that argument could work, but I would also argue that people do not struggle with conceptualizing using they as singular because it is done all the time in English (this is not done in other languages which will also be mentioned later). What they *do* struggle with is the association of this pronoun when it comes to gender and identity. Because not all people can relate to identifying with pronouns such as they/them for their gender expression, it may cause a disturbance in the way they associate the patterns of pronouns and quantities because the social construct of gender disrupts this rule entirely. This whole idea also directly relates to what I have previously discussed regarding the pronoun usage in French compared to English with Koda Tousignant and Brigitte Macron; both are examples of how users of the French language may struggle to associate "they" as a singular quantity because the pronoun is not used in such a way in French and would cause confusion in the way people associate the rules of their language. Not to mention the concept of gender neutrality is also foreign, which is why English is one of the few languages that allows for this singular use.

I also had the opportunity to speak with Professor Pia Broncaccio, an Art History Professor at Drexel University. Professor Broncaccio is originally from Naples, Italy, so as you can guess, she is a non-native English speaker. Coming from a background speaking Italian and then learning other languages such as English, German, and French, I wanted to hear her thoughts on they/them pronouns and gendered language. Not only because of the political and social issues surrounding this, but because of the logistics forming the grammar and usage of other languages and how difficult that may be for a non-native speaker. To my surprise, some answers were not what I expected. I asked, "Was it difficult to learn how to use pronouns, or refer to someone by their pronouns in English?" To which she replied, "Not difficult, and not difficult to use. Romance languages have a tougher pronoun scheme," that she found the use of pronouns *easier* in English. Naturally, I then asked, is it confusing that they/them pronouns can be singular or plural? Broncaccio says that it is confusing, not because of someone's gender expression, but because of the agreement between the pronoun and the verb; in Italian there are no gender-neutral pronouns, so this was a new concept to learn. Broncaccio seemed to express what I had discovered after learning about pronoun use in French, that some of the difficulty with this concept is the principle that the language must associate a singular person with a singular pronoun, whereas in English that rule does not always apply.

I received a miniature lesson in Italian during our session in which she explained her confusion of usage of collective nouns: What are your thoughts on addressing with collective nouns that refer to a group? She says, "Always, English is tricky with collective nouns," that English is difficult because of some collective nouns that seem plural or singular, which aren't. As an example:

- Hair plural vs. singular
- "Hair they are black" should be "hair is black"

- *Capello*- hair singular (o masculine singular Italian)

- *Capelli*- hair plural (i masculine plural Italian)

In Italian, it is clear whether a collective noun is singular or plural due to the masculine or feminine ending. This was also a struggle when using pronouns and collective nouns together because it was confusing which ending and pronouns correlate in English. She also says that because of the way that we form collective nouns in English, it is much better than in Italian. In Italian, the vowel defines the gender at the end of the word, and we do not have that sound in English, so English words are more inclusive among various gender expressions. In turn, this also makes the concept of gender as a societal construction easier to understand in English because English users associate singular nouns with plural pronouns all the time, whereas Italian speakers may not.

Circling back to the interview that I had with Kennedy and Koda, I had also asked them their thoughts on more masculine collective nouns to address a group of people such as "guys," "dudes," "y'all," and others. As trans masculine people they find comfort in this address, but they also state that it could be invalidating to someone who may want to present more feminine. They suggested using "y'all," "folks," "people," or others similar, to avoid misgendering. Now, it appears as though my question relates to the defining difference between English, Italian and French: gendered addressing. Gallois and Cohen state, "It is broadly an attempt to wean the French language of its male bias, including the rule that when it comes to the choice of pronouns for groups of women and men, the male form takes precedence over the female; and when it comes to adjectives describing mixed gatherings, they take the masculine form," that in French masculine nouns and adjectives always take preference in group settings, and Broncaccio agreed that similar rules apply when speaking in Italian. While this may have been true in the past for English, many people agree with Kennedy and Koda that we should turn to other ways to address people. There are also greetings that have neither masculine nor feminine implications such as "y'all," which French and Italian do not have. To Kennedy and Koda's point, the lack of inclusivity when it comes to a group in romance languages may leave people feeling trapped with their gender expression, and that they lack the freedom to move freely with their identity because the language decides for them how they should express themselves.

To elaborate on the claim that gender is a social construct and the hesitance to pronoun use stems from this in the structure of languages such as English, we can also examine how it does so in romantic ones in general. Simon and Wise further mention how other languages use paradigms, "Many languages manifest further distinctions in their paradigms: Most notably gender (correlated with sex or with other conceptual or non-conceptual classifications), but also distinctions according to, for example, considerations of politeness" (Simon and Wiese 3). These authors discuss how many romantic languages create paradigms related to that of gender and sex, which is done some in English, but not quite to that extent. In English, we would first associate an adjective to a particular person's gender rather than creating one adjective and then changing the ending to make it masculine or feminine.

For an example in English, typically women are described as "beautiful" and men as "handsome," or other words of the like. Compared to a language such as Spanish for example where it would appropriate to call a woman or man "pretty," "*bello*" as masculine or "*bella*" as feminine. This creates issues in both structures of these types of languages: English speakers struggle to associate gender identity with an adjective that is not considered typical and romantic languages struggle to separate gender from the adjective that it is associated with. So, it appears that the struggle with English users is not so much the gendered language but more so the misunderstanding of gender as a social construct, whereas romantic languages tend to struggle with both concepts because gender is woven into the very nature of the use of said language, so it is then even more difficult to understand how to deconstruct the stigma surrounding gender expression because that is directly tied into the language.

Taking this further, it is important to note this when it comes to the use of pronouns in all languages, but to simplify we can keep examining Spanish and English. As mentioned, gender is woven into the very nature of the Spanish language by creating masculine and feminine endings. The same applies when it comes to pronouns in this language, unlike English which will associate a new pronoun entirely. Let's examine the following:

- *el/le* vs. he/him
- *ella/la* vs. she/her
- *ellos/ellas* vs. they/them

As shown above the pronouns for he/him in Spanish take the masculine ending "o" and the pronouns for she/her take the feminine ending "a," unlike English where the pronouns have no gender associated with them unless considering that of the one society has constructed. What becomes complicated within the structure of the Spanish language is that pronouns like they/them in English really fail to exist, or rather, in the sense that it may be used for a gender-neutral pronoun. In Spanish, the equivalent of identifying a singular person as "they" breaks the rules and structure of the language, and even if it were to be done it still associates gender in a masculine or feminine way. So, these pronouns will not aid in the development of deconstructing how some may view gender in language because the terms quite literally do not exist, just as mentioned before when analyzing Italian and French. There is no neutral pronoun in Spanish because "they" will only exist as a plural, not as a gender-neutral identifier for a singular person such as it could in English. Although I think English is an amazing language, it most certainly has its own issues when it comes to gender and identity, and an example would be the very reason that they/them gained use in the first place: due to the rejection of a new pronoun that allowed for gender neutrality. However, my argument in this case would be that the structure of the English language does allow for more gender expression grammatically, whereas languages such as Spanish, Italian, and French do not.

It is also important to note the use of the term "Latinx," which many attempt to use to try and provide gender inclusivity. Although it is well intended by Spanish speakers, it mainly occurs with those who are bilingual with Spanish and English. In an article written for the *Washington Post*, Jose A. Del Real writes that the term has not gained popularity among Latin Americans: "But the label has not won wide adoption among the 61 million people of Latin American descent living in the United States. Only about 1 in 4 Latinos in the United States are familiar with the term, according to an August Pew Research Center survey. Just 3 percent identify themselves that way." Del Real states that this term has been unsuccessful in gaining popularity and there are multiple reasons as to why this may be true. For one, this term is mainly used among only those who are of Latin American descent because it is an adaptation to the Spanish language taken from that of English. As discussed earlier, Spanish historically only has two endings of "o" and "a," so the ending "x" is a derivative of English to create a gender-neutral ending to adjectives and other identifiers in Spanish. Secondly, because this concept does not exist outside of speakers who are Latin American, it is not a global adaptation. The Internet has made some success in spreading this term, but overall, it remains unpopular to those outside the United States. To the rest of the Spanish speaking community this concept does not exist, so the inclusive ending of "x" fails to persist outside of those who may be native to both Spanish and English. While the intent is genuine, the adaptation of Spanish language would be difficult because it uproots the engrained idea of gender in the language and the culture associated with the language users, which is why it may only be those who also speak English that would use this term because they have a different cultural identity tied to gender expression. The English language and culture associated with it allows to be more adaptive, which is what those who are bilingual are attempting to do with Spanish.

So, I guess so what, right? Why should we care about what other languages use? Why bother comparing other languages to English? Because, how could we not conceptually see things differently based on the language that we speak? As a native English speaker myself, I could not possibly have the same view of the French or Italian languages as those native to it would. The concept that no gender-neutral pronoun exists is something I cannot understand, and vice versa. The very fact that in English we have the ability within the foundation of our language to allow for gender expression is a fundamental concept for all English speakers, but entirely new to those who are not native speakers. For other languages, the very creation of a pronoun that sounds plural but is used as a single identifier is a threat to the language entirely. It disrupts the way the language works and the foundational rules for how to speak and write in it. While many who are native speakers to these romance languages believe that it is unnecessary to create more inclusive terminology due to the disruption it may cause to the language, a closer look reveals that in turn many people feel exiled by their native culture and language and feel as though they cannot truly express themselves within their language because there literally- yes literally- aren't words to express themselves.

This is not in any way to say that English is a superior language, in fact, I think that we still have a long journey ahead of us as native English speakers toward being more inclusive. They/them pronouns and neutral terminology is just the first step toward accomplishing this, and by no means is it an end goal. We have a duty as English speakers to create; create new words just as we would with anything else when it comes to slang or emphasis in our language. This is no different. It just so happens that we may be leading this journey due to the structure of our language. We do not have the masculine and feminine obstacles that other languages may encounter, but that doesn't mean we cannot aid in how they may restructure or include. Who knows, maybe we can create a term used universally, or used by more than just English. A term that can make others feel accepted by their language. We have the opportunity within the structure of our language to be inclusive, whereas others may not, so we must use the opportunity that we have as English speakers and users to be adaptive. After all, we cannot say that we are inclusive if the very thing we use every day, such as our language, leaves some stranded because there is no place to describe them and their gender expression.

Works Cited

Broncaccio, Pia. Interview. Conducted by Lily DeSimone, 23 November 2021.

Del Real, Jose A. "'Latinx' Hasn't Even Caught on among Latinos. It Never Will.: The Term Is an English-Language Contrivance, Not a Real Gesture at Gender Inclusivity." *Washington Post*, WP Company LLC, 18 Dec. 2020, https://www.proquest.com/docview/2471094386?parentSessionId=biiVLd8sDEn cpVzKdB0FXMcVBliypD9o5%2F%2F3kGW4cVE%3D&pq-origsite=primo&accountid=10559.

Favilla, Emmy J. *World without Whom: The Evolution of Language in the Buzzfeed Age*. Bloomsbury, 2017.

Gallois, Léontine, and Roger Cohen. "A French Dictionary Added a Nonbinary Pronoun. Havoc Ensued." *ProQuest*, *New York Times Company*, 30 Nov. 2021, https://www.proquest.com/.

Heinricks, Kennedy, and Koda Tousignant. Interview. Conducted by Lily DeSimone, 15 November 2021.

O'Conner, Patricia T. *Woe Is I: The Grammarphobe's Guide to Better English in Plain English*. Riverhead Books, 2019.

Simon, Horst J., and Heike Wiese. *Pronouns Grammar and Representation*. Vol. 52, J. Benjamins, 2002. *ProQuest*, https://ebookcentral-proquest-com.ezproxy2.library.drexel.edu/lib/drexel-ebooks/ reader.action?docID=623014. Accessed 10 Apr. 2022.

Grace Carson
A Deep Dive into "Evening Primrose":
Charles' Philosophical Reformation

"Evening Primrose" by John Collier and its musical film adaptation of the same name by Stephen Sondheim are about a man's journey from materialism to idealism brought about by his desire for love. Though the two works have some differences, both share themes of materialism and idealism supported by setting, characterization, and symbolism.

The initial reflection of the theme of materialism is the setting, which is established at the very start. Both the short story and the film open in a department store. This setting and the scene involving Charles ecstatically rejoicing his freedom brought about by "food, wine, the soft furniture of my couch, and a natty smoking jacket" is the moment the theme of materialism is introduced in the short story (Collier 193). The filmmakers' decision to portray this same scene of Charles finding his "nirvana" (Greene 11) among merchandise in "If You Can Find Me I'm Here," supports their intent to drive home the theme of materialism in the film (Goldman and Sondheim). While the short story takes place in "Bracey's Giant Emporium," (Collier 192-193,196) the filmmakers deliberately filmed the musical in a real department store called "Stern Brothers," to preserve and stay true to this theme of materialism in the short story (Puccio 13). Because a department store is a structure erected for the very purpose of buying and selling material goods, the department store's role in both the book and the film is to serve as a persistent symbol of materialism.

The theme of idealism comes into play with the introduction of Ella's character consistently expressing a strong desire to experience the outside world, which she can only describe through merchandise (Puccio 15). It can be certain that Ella's characterization is crucial to the short story and the film, because her backstory is kept unchanged between the two. In both works, Ella is a static character and a steadfast symbol of idealism, because she is the only character that never chose to come to the store in the first place. Though at the beginning, Charles envisions his dream life among merchandise, signs of his affinity for abstract pleasures are revealed on his first encounter with Ella remarking, "She's beautiful and I'm a poet. Poets have deep feelings for what's beautiful" (Goldman and Sondheim). This is consistent with the short story, in which Charles describes her beauty as "a living flower in a French cemetery, or a mermaid among polyps" (Collier 196). Charles' appreciation for abstract beauty opens up the possibility for him being a dynamic character capable of adopting idealist values, and his ability to understand Ella's dreams communicated in "I Remember" further supports this in the film (Goldman and Sondheim).

The occurrence of Charles falling in love with Ella in both the film and the short story marks the beginning of his transition from a materialist to idealist outlook, as love is an abstract and intangible experience. The extent of this love is communicated in the short story—as him not being able to eat, sleep, or write without thinking of her (Collier 202) and in the song "When," where Charles repeatedly inquires about the next time he can be alone with her (Goldman and Sondheim). However, the specific moment marking Charles' turning point from materialism to idealism is different between the short story and the film. In the short story, though Ella does not return Charles' love, his decision to risk his life with the watchman to save her is when he made his final commitment to idealism (Collier 200). In the film, the same thing can be said, but Charles' specific turning point from materialism to idealism happens in the duet "Take Me to the World," when he finally agrees to leave the store with Ella after initially trying to demand they stay (Goldman and Sondheim). In both the short story and film, it was his desire for love and his new ability to see the world in Ella's perspective of idealism that drove him to make that decision (Greene 11). Charles' choice to pursue Ella in both the film and the movie, even if it means risking his life, signifies his abandonment of materialism for idealism in the form of love.

As Charles' own materialistic tendencies are what brought him to the store, subtle signs of his appreciation for idealism can be seen in his character from the start. It is Ella's characterization that serves as the catalyst needed to bring out this side of him and ultimately pull him over to an idealist mindset. She serves as a persistent symbol of idealism being forced to exist in a world of materialism, represented by the setting of the department store. The elements of fiction pulling at Charles as a dynamic character sets the theme of materialism versus idealism. Even being enveloped in a world of materialism, Charles' decisions indicate that idealism is ultimately what he pursues when he realizes he desires love.

Works Cited

Collier, John. *The John Collier Reader*, "Evening Primrose." Alfred A. Knopf, 1972.

Evening Primrose. Written by James Goldman and Stephen Sondheim, performances by Anthony Perkins, Dorothy Stickney, Larry Gates, and Charmian Carr, Entertainment One Ltd., 1966.

Greene, Frank. "A Talent Not to be Denied: *Evening Primrose* was a Memorable Step in Sondheim's Career." *The Sondheim Review*, vol. 21, no. 4, Fall, 2015,pp.11.ProQuest,http://ezproxy2.library.drexel.edu/login?url=https://www.proquest.com/magazines/talentnot-be-denied-evening-primrose-was/docview/1789382287/se-2?accountid=10559.

Puccio, Paul M. "Such a Lovely World: Adapting the 'Elegant Macabre' of John Collier's 'Evening Primrose.'" *The Sondheim Review*, vol. 22, no. 2, Spring, 2016, pp. 13, 15. ProQuest,http://ezproxy2.library.drexel.edu/login?url=https://www.proquest.com/magazines/such-l ovely-world-adapting-elegant-macabre-john/docview/1806014422/se-2?accountid=10559

Kathleen R. Grillo

Dante's *Inferno* as a Personally Biased Satire in the Juvenalian Style as a Critique of the Politics, Religion, and Class Divide of His Society

Dante Alighieri's *Divine Comedy* is one of the most prominent texts found in the western canon. It has impacted generations of literature since its publication in thirteenth century Italy, even shaping the modern idea of Heaven and Hell, previously known as concepts, rather than physical places. Not only has the *Divine Comedy* influenced our ideas of literature and religion, the first book of the trio, *Inferno,* challenged knowledge of Italian society at the time. Considered one of the greatest poetic comedies, *Inferno* describes the journey of a man, Dante, who travels through the circles of Hell with the Roman poet Virgil acting as tour guide. As they descend through the circles, the punishments and crimes of the souls within become increasingly more horrific. In the epic conclusion, Dante and Virgil face a powerful scene that displays the last circle of Hell with a special brutality. Dante uses his era's own beliefs, politics, and religion in addition to biases from his own life throughout *Inferno,* classifying this work as a personal satire. With a biographical lens, Dante's life and beliefs clearly influenced *Inferno.* Dante's heritage as a middle-class Italian, which led to an advanced education and political involvement as a White Guelph, are prevalent elements in the poem, seen by the placement of certain figures within the different levels of Hell; thus, proving that *Inferno* is a work molded by Dante's personal bias.

More specifically, Dante's *Inferno* is a satire in the Juvenalian style. These satires are those that use "any bitter and ironic criticism of contemporary persons and institutions that is filled with personal invective, angry moral indignation, and pessimism" ("Juvenalian Satire"). The name stems from first century satirist Juvenal, who criticized Roman society, specifically criticizing the balance of power and money and cautioning against city life. Much like Juvenal, Dante uses *Inferno* as a criticism of his society, especially within the political and religious spheres where Dante was a prominent figure. Dante's voice impacted both communities of his society. Not only does *Inferno* use dark humor, the entirety of it taking place in the depths of Hell, where the main character interacts with respected figures of Dante's life as they are being punished for sins Dante deems the severity of; it is also a criticism of his society. Unlike other types of satire that mock humor, Dante's use of satire came from anger. And, most importantly, Dante wished for *Inferno* to be a call to action for change.

To accept Dante's argument and his use of satire, specifically as a personal bias through a biographical lens, understanding his background is crucial. Dante was born to a wealthy family in thirteenth century Italy and exposed to a large background of knowledge in his education.

Through his studies, he understood a wide range of ideals in history, literature, religion, and eventually, politics. Examples of these are littered throughout *Inferno*, from literary figures, religious deities, and mythological creatures. Only later in life did Dante become politically active. Exiled by the Black Guelphs, this period of time marked the most artistic time of Dante's life. These enemies, as Dante saw it, were members of the Florentine government, so Dante wrote a diatribe against them and was promptly included on a list of those permanently banned from the city. Around this time, he began writing his most famous work, *The Divine Comedy* (Dante). He put his opinions on the page, in the form of *Inferno*. Largely targeting the Black Guelphs, those in favor with Pope Boniface VIII, Dante's anger is littered throughout *Inferno*, as are his opinions of this group.

Much of Dante's dislike towards those who cast him out of his home appears in *Inferno*, as the poem was written in the years after Dante's exile. The first instance of politics leaking into *Inferno* is seen as Dante and Virgil descend into the Third Circle, that of gluttony. As the reader, and Dante, delve deeper into the circles, the division between sin and forgiveness blurs. It is easier for Dante to interact with the people he sees and interacts with in this circle, as he has yet to meet his enemies. Instead, he meets Ciacco, the first notable politician Dante interacts with. They talk of the future of Florentine politics, including the taking over of the White Guelphs and reinstatement of Black Guelph power, leading Dante to ask about the whereabouts of his political enemies. This is the first time Dante not only asks about his political rivals but expects them as well. When asked, Ciacco responds with, "they are amongst the blackest sinners, booted into deeper pits, for darker crimes" (Dante, Canto VI Lines 85-87). This expectation alone is a play at Juvenalian satire. It is an angry, sarcastic comment on Florentine politicians. Members of the political group are put into worsening levels. An example of mockery in this style can be seen in circle five where Dante finally meets a political enemy of his, Filippo Argenti. Dante expresses his opinion clearly when he tells Virgil "O Master, great is my desire to see this arrogant bastard dunked in swill" (Dante, Canto VIII Lines 52-53). What little is known about Argenti comes from Dante, specifically this scene. An important takeaway is Dante's impression of Argenti as a wrathful man. This is in direct relation to the Juvenalian style of satire. Dante mocks Argenti for his anger and makes a point of the hot-headedness of many political leaders.

The language of *Inferno* itself is a rhetorical statement against Dante's society. Dante wrote *Inferno* in the vernacular language, better known as the Tuscan dialect. This dialect was the common language, which the lower-class citizens could read and write. In this act, Dante criticizes many of the texts that had been written in Latin, a language difficult for lower-class citizens who hadn't been taught. Dante explicitly wrote the Divine Comedy, and thus *Inferno*, in the common language to make it more accessible. "His fundamental intention was to break down barriers between the upper classes (who communicated in Latin) and the working classes, to allow even those who were not noble or educated to learn and get to know literary and philosophical works, with subsequent beneficial effects on morality and the civic sense of individuals" ("Why Dante Is the Greatest Genius of Italian Culture"). Simply, Dante wanted lower-class citizens who didn't know the scholarly language of Latin to educate themselves. This, again, was a mockery of the current intellectual society, especially considering the success of Dante's work. This text, and the way it was written, in the common vernacular, momentously influenced society. Dante's *Divine Comedy* led to the formation of a standard written and spoken language in Italy, purely by writing his trilogy of poems in that language.

The bias of Dante all comes to a head in the horrifying ending. In the last, and therefore worst, circle of Hell, Dante is introduced to the three-headed Lucifer. Not only that, Virgil and Dante find Lucifer eating Judas, Brutus, and Cassius; Judas being Jesus's betrayer and Brutus and Cassius being the assassinators of Julius Caesar. "With what a sense of awe I saw his head towering above me! for it had three faces: one was in front, and it was fiery red; the other two, as weirdly wonderful, merged with it from the middle of each shoulder to the point where all converged at the top of the skull" (Dante, Canto XXXIV Lines 37-43). This is an extremely important scene as it reveals Dante's opinions of Church and State. Although he believes in the separation of Church and State, he *does* believe in equal punishment for the betrayal of either side. He prosecutes each side equally. His opinion is brutal, and, in his mind, valid. This scene is also a look into Dante's satirical play at the balance of the two. Despite their separation from each other in his real-life society, they are both equally powerful, and are being treated as such. "Throughout the *Inferno* Dante believes in separation of Church and State, but should remain equal, and in the last circle Dante completes his vision of moral hierarchy and makes a last stand on his political views" ("Dante Alighieri And His Biased *Inferno*"). This is the reason *why* Dante believes in their separation, they are equally powerful and should thus be ruled separately. And while today betrayal is viewed as a lesser crime, the same was not true for Dante and his society. "The contemporary view of crimes of betrayal bears a curious resemblance to Dante's view of crimes of violence" (Chevigny 21). This is an important fact to remember when considering the layers of Hell and what they reveal about Dante and his world.

Dante's *Inferno*, and really the entire trilogy known as the *Divine Comedy*, is crucial to the education outlined in the works of the western canon. It enables readers to understand not only Dante's life, but his society as a whole. Specifically, Dante's use of satire is an angry, sarcastic joke on the politics and religion surrounding his life. He pulls on the pessimistic themes common to the Juvenalian style of satire to mock the current standing of his country, specifically in the balance of power between religion and politics. When analyzing *Inferno* with a biographical lens, these elements become extremely prevalent within the work. From the layers of Hell themselves, who is found within them, the conversations that are had, and the enlightening yet horrific end, Dante makes his opinions clear. He makes a mockery of the current social, political, and religious states with his grand comedy, especially considering the balance of power and knowledge. Thus, *Inferno* becomes a historical reflection which impacts modern literature and society. It is clear, then, that this work remains a crucial part of the canon as a reflection of Italian life, society, and literature both from the text itself and the author who wrote it.

Works Cited

Alighieri, Dante, et al. *The Divine Comedy: Inferno*. Thornwillow Press, 2018.

"Juvenalian Satire." *Encyclopædia Britannica*, Encyclopædia Britannica, Inc., 20 July 1998, www.
britannica.com/art/Juvenalian-satire.

Chevigny, Paul G. "From Betrayal to Violence: Dante's *Inferno* and the Social Construction of Crime."
Law & Social Inquiry, John Wiley & Sons, Ltd (10.1111), 28 July 2006, onlinelibrary.wiley.com/doi/
abs/10.1111/j.1747-4469.2001.tb00324.x.

"Dante Alighieri And His Biased *Inferno*." UKEssays.com. 11 2018. All Answers Ltd. 03 2019<https://www.
ukessays.com/essays/english-literature/dante-alighieri-and-his-biased- *Inferno*-english-literature-
essay.php?vref=1>

"Dante." *Biography.com*, A&E Networks Television, 12 Apr. 2019, www.biography.com/writer/dante

"Decameron Web." *Decameron Web | History*, www.brown.edu/Departments/Italian_Studies/dweb/
history/characters/filippo_argenti.ph

Edley, Luke, et al. "Understanding Different Types of Satire." *Thanet Writers*, 16 May 2017, https://
thanetwriters.com/essay/technicalities/understanding-different-types-of-satire/.

Ferrante, Joan M. *The Political Vision of the Divine Comedy*. Princeton University Press, 1984, http://www.
jstor.org/stable/j.ctt7zvgqq.

"Why Dante Is the Greatest Genius of Italian Culture." *La Piccola Fontana*, 31 May 2015, www.
lapiccolafontana.com/why-dante-is-the-greatest-genius-of-italian-culture/.

Tanya Lulla

Differentiated Instruction for Individuals with Developmental Disabilities

"Everyone is unique in their own way." This age-old phrase in its various forms has often been the topic of conversation when driving home the point that everyone is different. But this idea never truly sunk in for me until I became a teacher—specifically a volunteer art teacher for children with developmental disabilities. When holding my first class, my eyes were opened to a world of diversity among my students: different ages, different skill sets, different abilities, different interests, different personalities. Everyone was, indeed, different!

What did this mean for me as an art instructor? I knew that I had two main goals: to help my students grow as artists and to form meaningful relationships with them. This meant that I had to find the best method of instruction to achieve these goals. Working in a class of students with a wide range of ages and skill sets, I found that the best way to do this was to personalize my instruction to each student. In particular, I tailored my art teaching curriculum to take into consideration both the skill and age levels of my students, such as providing lessons on color theory for beginners, blending for advanced students and stippling for others. I was amazed by the results of this individualized instruction technique: not only did the students improve their art skills, but I began to connect with my students on a level deeper than just an instructional student-teacher relationship. That is when I realized that the most effective method of teaching students with developmental disabilities is differentiated instruction.

Individualized or personalized instruction, officially known as "differentiated instruction," (Lathan) is a style of teaching that deals with the creation of a curriculum specific to a particular student's learning needs ("Personalized Learning and Students with Disabilities"). This mode of teaching is one of many various teaching styles. In an article written by education specialist Joseph Lathan, Lathan distinguishes the multiple modes of classroom instruction into two primary categories: a teacher-centered approach and a student-centered approach.

As implied by their names, a teacher-centered approach is a teaching strategy that requires teachers to take the active teaching role, as they instruct students primarily through lectures (Lathan). Here, students' learning outcomes are usually evaluated through testing (Lathan). Some examples of this approach include direct instruction, which consists of learning content through the traditional lecture format, and a flipped classroom, which consists of learning content at home and practicing in the classroom (Lathan). On the other hand, student-centered approaches refer to when students take an active role to learn, while teachers simply serve as a guide (Lathan). Here, students' learning outcomes are usually evaluated through activities and participation in class. Some examples of this approach include inquiry-based learning, where students create and test research questions to learn content, expeditionary learning, where students take trips into the real world to learn content, and differentiated instruction (Lathan). Ideally, differentiated instruction—the style of teaching that I happened to implement within my art lessons—is utilized in classrooms consisting of individuals with disabilities "Personalized Learning and Students with Disabilities").

Weighing the pros and cons of these instructional methods in reference to individuals with developmental disabilities can be helpful in identifying the most efficacious teaching method for these students. Here, we will focus on the most common modes of teaching within the teacher-centered and student-centered approaches: direct instruction and differentiated instruction, respectively. According to the University of Manitoba, the biggest advantage of direct instruction is that it allows for a clear, consistent teaching structure through lectures. This is efficient for both the teacher and student in terms of both covering content and quickly using fewer external resources ("Using Lectures to Teach: Pros & Cons" 1). Furthermore, the teacher's role as the primary mode of delivering knowledge can promote independence among students. However, its greatest disadvantage is that it does not account for student preferences or skill, since the curriculum is created as a universal form of instruction ("Using Lectures to Teach: Pros & Cons" 1). As a student that has undergone direct instruction every year in high school, I have found all of these points to hold true—especially the drawback—which played a major part in choosing the way I conducted my own art classes. In particular, I realized that in high school, my preferences were not voiced with such a universal curriculum, and this ended up reducing my interactions with teachers. So when I became an art teacher with the goal of developing deep connections with my students, I felt that direct instruction was not the way to go, because I wanted to integrate the preferences and skills of my students into my lessons.

Differentiated (as opposed to direct) instruction presents a whole different set of pros and cons. Dr. Drew, an expert in the sociology of education, explains that the primary benefit of differentiated instruction is an attempt to ensure equal access to education. In addition, he explains that this mode of instruction allows for more student participation (Drew). In my art class, I too found that my students displayed an increased engagement when I implemented individualized instruction. Not only did they begin to ask me more questions, but they started to also share their own personal stories—both of which increased our one-on-one interactions, allowing me to form deeper connections with them. Another advantage of differentiated instruction was illustrated by a study that evaluated the literacy skills of a group of students receiving individual instruction compared to a group that did not receive this form of instruction: the growth of literacy skills was observed to be significantly higher in the group of students receiving personalized instruction (Conner et al. 77). As beneficial as the teaching method of differentiated instruction is ideally, it also has its limitations. Its major drawback is that it can be very resource-intensive and time-consuming, which makes it difficult to be utilized in large classrooms (Drew). Admittedly for my art classes, it did require more resources to plan my tailored curriculum, because I had to bring in extra volunteers to ensure that every student received the personalized attention that they deserved.

Another essential part to determine the best method for teaching students with developmental disabilities is to understand what a developmental disability is. In general, a developmental disability can be defined as a condition that causes "an impairment in physical, learning, language, or behavior areas" ("Developmental Disabilities"). One of the most prevalent examples is Autism Spectrum Disorder (ASD), which affects around 1.5 million people in the United States (Willis 81). ASD is a "spectrum," which means that individuals with it display a range of characteristics (Willis 81). For example, some may be nonverbal, some may respond strongly to sensory stimuli, and some may even display both these characteristics (Willis 82). Since individuals with ASD display such a wide range of behaviors, teaching them based on their individual strengths would be extremely beneficial to their academic growth. This was the primary reason behind my use of the differentiated learning approach within my art classes, since they consisted of many students specifically with ASD.

While individuals with ASD display many differences, their commonality resides in their struggle with communication (Willis 82). Willis explains that "because of communication and behavior issues, many children with ASD do not initiate interactions with others" (Willis 85). Since communication is an essential part of a student's success within a classroom, interactions should be encouraged to ensure that a student with ASD or any developmental disorder succeeds in a learning environment (Willis 86). From teaching students with ASD, I have found that one way to go about doing this is to identify the meaning behind a certain behavior a student displays in order to translate what they are conveying. Through this personalized, student-centered approach—in other words, this differentiated instruction approach—in my art classes, the student-teacher interactions between my students and I have immensely improved. Getting to know each student enough to understand the root cause of their behaviors has allowed me to communicate more with them, and these interactions have helped pave the path for their development as artists. Altogether, in a setting consisting of individuals with developmental disabilities, differentiated instruction is a great way to ensure a student's success.

For students with developmental disabilities, the pros of differentiated learning seem to heavily outweigh its cons: the time and effort it requires to create a curriculum tailored to each individual student is worth the positive growth it creates. Moreover, for a group of students who process information differently, being able to learn at a pace that makes them comfortable is crucial in adequately acquiring knowledge. In my experience, I found that this individualized instruction goes beyond just improved learning outcomes—it allows for deeper connections and increased engagement in class. From this, it can be concluded that differentiated instruction is the most effective mode of teaching students with developmental disabilities. Since this is currently not a prevalent teaching style for students with special needs, awareness should be raised to such a personalized instruction system—one that recognizes each student's differences. After all, everyone is truly unique in their own way, and the education system should acknowledge that.

Works Cited

"A Resource for Teaching in Engineering Teaching Matters." *Using Lectures to Teach: Pros & Cons*, https://umanitoba.ca/faculties/engineering/departments/ce2p2e/pdf/teaching_matters13.pdf.

"Developmental Disabilities." *Centers for Disease Control and Prevention*, https://www.cdc.gov/ncbddd/developmentaldisabilities/index.html.

Drew, Chris. "Differentiated Instruction - Strategies, Pros & Cons (2021)." *Helpful Professor*, 19 Mar. 2020, https://helpfulprofessor.com/differentiated-instruction/.

Lathan, Joseph. "The Complete List of Teaching Methods." *University of San Diego*, onlinedegrees.sandiego.edu/complete-list-teaching-methods/.

McDonald Connor, Carol, et al. "Individualizing Student Instruction Precisely: Effects of Child Instruction Interactions on First Graders Literacy Development." *Child Development*, vol. 80, no. 1, Blackwell Publishing, 2009, pp. 77–100, doi:10.1111/j.1467-8624.2008.01247.x.

"Personalized Learning and Students with Disabilities." *NLCD*, 11 June 2017, www.ncld.org/research/personalized-learning/.

Willis, Clarissa. "Young Children with Autism Spectrum Disorder: Strategies That Work." *YC Young Children*, vol. 64, no. 1, National Association for the Education of Young Children (NAEYC), 2009, pp. 81–89, http://www.jstor.org/stable/42731035.

Victoria Faith Miller

Building the Foundations for a Bright Future: Educated Girls Can Transform the World

In January of 2008, when she was just eleven years old, Malala Yousafzai said goodbye to her classmates, not knowing when or if she would ever see them again. The Taliban had taken control of her town in the Swat Valley of Pakistan, and they banned the ability for girls to go to school. A few years later, Malala began speaking out publicly on behalf of girls and their right to learn. This made her a target. In October 2012, on her way home from school, a masked gunman boarded her bus and demanded, "Who is Malala?" Once she was identified, he shot Malala on the left side of her head. She woke up ten days later in a hospital in Birmingham, England, with people around the world praying for her recovery ("Malala's Story").

According to UNESCO (United Nations Educational, Scientific, and Cultural Organization), more than 129 million girls are currently out of school around the world ("Girls' Education"). To put it into perspective, this represents approximately one-third of the population of the United States. As a proud 7-year graduate of an all-girls Catholic school and now a student at a highly regarded urban research university, these statistics are nothing short of core-shaking. For me, education has been a lifelong priority. From my parents encouraging me to achieve my full potential through my academics and extracurriculars, to my own self-driven desire to be a lifelong learner, I have been raised among the resources and support systems necessary to succeed. But this is not the case for millions of girls around the world. As girls in developing countries grow into young women, the prospects of completing a primary or secondary education, let alone a college education, become dimmer and dimmer. Barriers such as poverty, sexual violence, menstrual inequities, gender biases, and poor governance, prevent girls in developing countries from attending school. But by prioritizing girls' education we can combat these problems and many others. Education builds the foundation for a stable future for girls around the world and allows developing nations to thrive both socially and economically.

One of the most formidable barriers to getting girls to school is poverty. Many families in impoverished communities cannot afford the cost of supplies, uniforms, or tuition, to allow their children to attend school. Additionally, the value of a boy's education is placed at a much higher level than a girl's education. If a family must choose between sending their daughter or son to school, in almost all cases, the son will be chosen. Because of this, girls are often left to stay home and collect water and supplies for the family, assume domestic tasks, and care for younger children ("Menstruation and Education"). But even girls who do get the opportunity to attend school face a multitude of challenges to remain in school. Many children commute long distances (often on foot and alone) to get to school, which poses a serious danger to young girls. Approximately 60 million girls are sexually assaulted on their way to school, leading to detrimental consequences for their mental and physical health and overall well-being. This leads to lower attendance and higher dropout rates, even resulting in adolescent pregnancies ("Girls' Education"). In low-income countries, only 36 percent of girls complete secondary education, compared to 44 percent of their male counterparts. These percentages further plummet for girls' completion of upper secondary (high school level) and higher education ("Girls' Education"). I was raised in an environment where failing to complete primary and secondary education was not in question. My commute to school was about ten minutes each way and I was able to be driven by my parents or a friend. Although my parents were tasked with managing the whereabouts of four children at once, I did not have to worry about being unable to make it to or from school because of transportation challenges or violence. This feeling of security allowed me to focus my attention on my academics and well-being.

For girls in developing countries, the focus is placed on other, considerably more important factors, including status in the home and the responsibility to become a mother and a wife. Once girls in developing countries reach middle school, there is a notable change in school attendance. More than 50 percent of girls will drop out of school after they start menstruating. This marks the beginning of a lifelong struggle facing inequality due to their sex ("Menstruation and Education"). In developing countries, menstruation is a symbol that females will have to sacrifice schooling due to inaccessibility to feminine pads and tampons. Instead, girls use newspapers, dried leaves, and old cloths, leaving them vulnerable to infections, falling behind in schoolwork, and discouraging them to continue their education past middle school. Girls are then pushed to get married and have children while they are still teenagers. Not only does menstruation rob girls of educational opportunities, but it takes from them the powerful tool that an education can be to break the cycle of poverty, oppression, and the ability to see an adulthood beyond caring for children and husbands ("Menstruation and Education").

While there is taboo all around the world surrounding menstruation and menstrual education, menstruation is often celebrated as a mark of womanhood in a young girl's life in many countries like the United States ("Menstruation and Education"). I remember the day that I first got my period when I was 14 years old. One of my best friends also got it on the same day. We celebrated the fact that we were now "women" and we turned to classmates and teachers who always offered sanitary supplies when needed. Learning in a same-sex school greatly lessened menstrual taboo and created a supportive environment for all students to learn how to manage their periods and become educated about the menstrual cycle. Most girls don't have this luxury. Gender biases in classrooms and homes in developing countries often reinforce messages that affect girls' ambitions and their own perceptions of their roles in society ("Girls' Education"). Gender stereotypes can be communicated through details as specific as the design of the school and learning environments or through the behavior of faculty, staff, and peers in a child's school. When girls are constantly reminded of what they "can't do" because of their sex or are seen as inferior to males, this impacts academic performance and choice of field of study, especially negatively affecting young women pursuing STEM (science, technology, engineering, and math) or other male-dominated disciplines ("Girls' Education").

Beyond poverty, violence and menstrual inequalities are the fundamental measures or lack thereof within nations' governments for protecting the rights of girls. An article from the Oxford University Press' academic journal, *Social Journal*, provides extensive field research that identifies governance in girls' education as central to improving human and economic development (Sommer and Fallon). Proper governance on local and national levels has been proven to increase the effectiveness of education expenditures in improving girls' secondary education enrollment compared to males (Sommer and Fallon). In a panel discussion on girls' education that occurred at the White House among multiple women of diverse fields in 2015, former Prime Minister of Australia, Julia Gillard, stated that in many poor countries where she works, there has never been a concrete plan for schooling. Many developing countries don't see girls' education as a key problem to address, letting it fall behind overshadowing issues of poverty, violence, and civil unrest, for example. These government officials don't seem to realize that by giving girls equal educational opportunities they can directly address these issues.

Organizations like Gillard's Global Partnership for Education and many others have made major strides in increasing educational opportunities for girls in developing countries. The results of these efforts prove the investment is more than worth it. Equity in girls' education leads to delayed marriage and pregnancy, decreased infant and maternal mortality, reduced levels of HIV (human immunodeficiency virus), and ultimately, greater academic achievement among young girls (Sommer and Fallon). AIDS (acquired immunodeficiency syndrome), which is caused by HIV, is the number one killer of adolescents (specifically females) in Africa, and the number-two killer of adolescents globally. According to the Global Health Campaign, education is a social vaccine against HIV/AIDS. In Zimbabwe, for example, girls are five times less likely to become infected if they stay in school ("Panel Discussion").

Girls' education also has profound economic impacts. Keeping girls in school increases economic growth, democratic and community involvement, income equality, and poverty alleviation (Sommer and Fallon). According to a recent report's estimates (conducted by the World Bank), limited educational opportunities for girls, and barriers to completing 12 years of education, cost countries between 15 to 30 trillion dollars in lost lifetime productivity and earnings. Ending child marriage could generate more than 500 billion dollars in benefits annually ("Girls' Education"). When girls can earn money through higher-paying, skilled labor backed by at least 12 years of education, they become young women who can support themselves, their families, and their communities, with the ability to lift entire countries out of poverty.

There are many sub-topics to delve into under the umbrella of women's and girls' rights but they all seem to circle back to one: the right to a stable education. Education has the power to provide the foundations for lifelong prosperity. For me, education has surrounded me with incredible people and opportunities. My experience at an all-girls school has empowered me to believe in myself and in a world where all girls are afforded the same privileges. In truth, girls have never been the problem. The systems and stigmas surrounding them are the problems. I believe that the next step to solving this worldwide education crisis is accountability. Attitudes must be changed about the role of girls in society. We need male allies who are willing to see and support the value of girls' education and we need this to start in the home. Malala's father was instrumental in her journey to becoming a vocal activist for girls' education. As a man in Pakistan, Ziauddin Yousafzai went against the grain and decided that educating his daughter mattered. By running a girls' school in his village, he positively influenced the trajectory of his daughter's life and so many other girls' lives. We need more people like Malala and Mr. Yousafzai who are prepared to stand up and say, "let's educate our girls" ("Panel Discussion").

I firmly believe that as citizens in a country where education is made available to all, we have a responsibility to positively use technology and specifically, social media platforms to spread awareness of this issue and other important issues. My interest in girls' education started by simply watching a powerful documentary film in my high school theology class. But that newfound awareness was not squandered. It led me to take every project and every opportunity possible to learn, read and write about issues that oppress women and girls worldwide. I was inspired to become a leader in my community and participate in service projects for women in need in my community. Awareness leads to action. We must keep creating in the modes that reach people. We need entire communities, governments, and countries on board. We need the world on board. Let's close the gap and give every girl the tools to transform the world. Let's create a world where no girl has to face what Malala faced, ever again.

Works Cited

"Girls' Education." *World Bank*, 26 Oct.2021. https://www.worldbank.org/en/topic/girlseducation.

"Malala's Story." *Malala Fund*, 2021, https://malala.org/malalas-story.

"Menstruation and Education: An Obstacle for Young Girls." *University Wire, Uloop*, Inc, 2014.

"Panel Discussion with the First Lady, Julia Gillard, Former Prime Minister of Australia, Charlize Theron, Actress and Activist, and Nurfahada, Girl Project Ambassador on the Importance of Girls' Education." *White House Press Releases*, Fact Sheets and Briefings / FIND, Federal Information & News Dispatch, LLC, 2015.

Sommer, Jamie M., and Kathleen M. Fallon. "The Pathway to Improving Human and Economic Development: Girls' Secondary Education, Governance, and Education Expenditures." *Social Forces,* vol. 99, no. 1, Oxford University Press, 2020, pp. 205–29, doi:10.1093/sf/soz143.

Allison Lord

Lia Thomas and the Inclusion of Transgender Women in Intercollege Athletics

A few miles from Drexel's campus is the University of Pennsylvania's Sheerr pool. Here, the University of Pennsylvania's varsity men's and women's swimming and diving teams practice and compete, and one swimmer has become the center of the American news cycle. It is not her skill in the freestyle that has garnered this attention, but her identity as a transwoman. Lia Thomas, a senior swimmer and member of Penn's Varsity Women's swimming team began hormone treatment before the start of the pandemic. Before transitioning, she was a top college swimmer in the Ivy League and her times beat some of the best female swimmers and Olympians. As a transwoman, she went through puberty before beginning estrogen and testosterone suppression treatments. Thus, she maintains some of the stereotypical features of males, such as broad shoulders, being taller, and having larger hands and feet. Her success in the Women's division has sparked debate over including transwomen in female sports and under what regulations transgender athletes should be able to compete.

Many believe that due to transwomen's being biologically male, their biological makeup and physique yields better results, and thus must be prohibited from the female divisions to preserve fairness in their field. According to Elizabeth Ziegler and Tamar Isadora Huntley, for men, "Differences in testosterone and estrogen levels lead to men outperforming women in athletic events by approximately eleven to eighteen percent" (Ziegler, Huntley). Along with males typically being taller, having greater muscle, greater aerobic and anaerobic capacity, greater lung capacity, and greater strength, men often outperform women in athletic events like track and field. In 2008, there was a 17.2% difference between the world record for men and women in the high jump, a 22.6% difference in the pole vault, and a 37.4% difference in the javelin (Ziegler). Additionally, for years, men's sports have always been more popular, with the 5 major professional sports leagues in America all being men's sports. Women have been fighting for equality in sports for centuries, from the creation of Title IX to ensure equality in the sexes for American schools in sports, to fighting for equal funding and pay. It is thus expected that people fear disruption to the women's sports divisions, as they are often behind in men's teams in development, funding, and fan attention.

Opposition to including transwomen is not at all uncommon, in 2020 alone there were 20 states who introduced bills to regulate or ban transgender athletes from competing in the division that matches their gender identity (Goldberg). Shoshana Goldberg argues that transgender athlete bills rely on "scare tactics, stereotypes, and unwarranted claims that transgender women have a physiological advantage over cisgender women—despite a complete lack of evidence that transgender sports participation has had any measurable impact on the success of cisgender athletes." This is true, there are no examples of women's sports changing as a result of transwomen being included. Lia Thomas is not the first transwoman competing in sport, as rules permitting transgender athletes have existed since before 2004. And in that time, the landscape of women's sports has not changed in favor of transgender athletes. Firstly, there are few transgender women athletes in the first place, with a researcher at Loughborough University, Joanna Harper, saying that out of 200,000 women in college sports, only 50 are transgender or 0.025%. (Chen) Furthermore, transgender athletes are not dominating their leagues. At the Olympics, only one transgender athlete has medaled, as a member of Canada's Women's Soccer Team, and only one trans athlete has made it to a US National Team, a trans man (Goldberg).

A common argument is that including transwomen is not feminist, as it favors an individual over the good of a team. In the case of Lia Thomas, a group of parents and a group of female swimmers both sent letters arguing that Thomas being able to compete created an unfair and inequitable place to compete and argued in favor of preserving the "integrity of women's sports" (Rieder). This argument, however, fails to acknowledge that transwomen are women, and for an action to work in regard to feminist principles, it must support transwomen and their right to participate in athletic competition.

It is also a common argument that men will just identify as women to do better in athletics. Those opposed to Lia Thomas' swimming often point to the idea that she was ranked as 462nd in the country in the male division to the top of the country in the women's division (Lev). However, Thomas was not a bad swimmer as a male, considering she was a finalist in the 2019 Ivy League championship, and looking at the number of college swimmers, 462 is far from the bottom (Sutherland). Additionally, Thomas has lost races since transitioning; she has not beaten every one of her competitors in the women's division (Rushing).

Lia Thomas did not transition to win more races. For her, and many trans athletes, switching divisions is not an easy task and is not done on a whim. To compete, under NCAA regulation, transwomen must undergo testosterone suppression for at least one year (Witz). Besides the athletic requirements, transitioning is not a decision taken lightly by any trans person. Coming out as transgender can result in broken relationships with friends, families, and communities, and is a process that comes after years of self-exploration and gender dysphoria. Lia Thomas described how before her transition, she "was struggling, [her] mental health was not very good. It was a lot of unease, basically just feeling trapped in [her] body. It didn't align" (Sutherland). She didn't want to race in the men's category, not because it was more competitive, but because it added to the already destructive amount of gender dysphoria she had. After transitioning and being on testosterone for two and a half years, her times have gone down, and she has not broken any national records. Since transgender athletes have been allowed to compete in 2004, there have been no instances of fraud or switching genders (Gorton). Additionally, transitions, as seen with Thomas' case can result in intense scrutiny and hate speech. 16 of Thomas's own teammates at Penn wrote a letter to the NCAA against Thomas being able to compete. Winning races would not be worth putting herself through the criticism she receives for racing in the category that matches her gender identity.

Supporting women in sport should mean expanding opportunities to play, not restricting which women get to play. Women statistically play sports less than men, due to budget cuts to female sports, men's sports being more culturally valued, and the cost of women's sports being higher (Goldberg). In states where there are bans on transgender athletes competing in accordance with their identity, the percentage of women playing sports has decreased, while the number of women playing sports in states without these policies has remained the same (Goldberg). This insinuates that when transgender youth are allowed to play, more women and girls, not fewer, play sports.

Being a transgender youth or college student is not easy. Transgender young adults are more likely than their cisgender peers to report worse mental health, including a higher risk for depression, suicidal ideation, and suicide attempts. Additionally, transgender youth are far more likely to experience bullying and harassment (Goldberg). However, as Shoshana Goldberg argues in her report, "when transgender youth encounter accepting and affirming policies and peers, including transgender-affirming sports policies, their risk of poor mental health and suicidality decreases—and where these supports are lacking, risk is substantially higher." Besides the physical benefits of sport, student-athletes may be at lower risk for anxiety and depression, suicide attempts, and tobacco and drug use. Sports have also been linked to better academic performance, feelings of community and social connectedness, and could lead to friendships and positive relationships with coaches, and the building of feelings such as sportsmanship and comradery, as well as building work ethic (Goldberg.) From data gathered from the National College Health Assessment III during the 2019-2020 school year, 17.4 of transgender students were student-athletes who competed at the varsity, club, or intramural level. Compared to their peers who did not compete in sports, transgender athletes reported higher levels of psychological well-being and were less likely to report mental health issues. Additionally, they were more likely to report feeling "very safe" in their schools and report a feeling of belonging (Goldberg). Denying transgender women from participating in sports prevents them from reaping the positive benefits athletics give. For a minority so affected by mental health issues and bullying, sports offer an opportunity to feel a part of their school community. Restricting trans athletes to participate in the divisions that do not match their gender identity, or not at all, can only result in increased feelings of isolation and lack of acceptance from their school community.

In 2011, the NCAA released its policy on transgender athletes' inclusion in sports. In accompaniment, they released a handbook detailing the data behind the policy and giving guidelines on ensuring transgender athletes felt included and accepted. In a piece written by Dr. Nick Gorton, in the handbook, he argues against the misconception "that being born with a male body automatically gives a transgender woman an unfair advantage when competing against non-transgender women." He argues that transgender women vary like every human, that some may be small and slight, not unusually tall with large bones and muscles. He argues that "the assumption that male-bodied people are taller, stronger, and more highly skilled in a sport is not accurate." Additionally, many of these advantages are decreased after estrogen and testosterone suppression treatments. This is true in Lia Thomas' case, as compared with her times before starting hormone therapy, Thomas' top times in the 200-freestyle dropped by 3%, her 500-free time by 6%, and her 1,650-free time, dropped the most, at 7% (Rushing).

The NCAA policy is based upon the International Olympic Committee's framework, which argues that "no athlete should be precluded from competing or excluded from competition on the exclusive ground of an unverified, alleged, or perceived unfair competitive advantage due to their sex variations, physical appearance and/or transgender status." (IOC) This means that regardless of a transgender woman's biological sex, she should not be banned from competing on the unfound presumption of advantage. And statistically, this presumption is not supported by any studies. Dr. Gorton also argues that there is no evidence of transgender women having a competitive advantage "outside the range of performance and competitive advantage or disadvantage that already exists among female athletes" (Gorton). Due to the small sample size and complicated choice in what to study, there have been no studies done to determine that trans women have an athletic advantage; it's all based upon assumption.

Additionally, skill in sports is not just based upon physical quality. Just because someone has a lot of muscle mass or the endurance to run, does not mean that they are good at a sport like field hockey or soccer. Skill in sports is physical, but also intellectual. It is something that must be honed and practiced for years. Just because a trans woman may possess larger muscles or a bigger frame does not mean she will outperform her competitors due to the other aspects of sport needed for success. Additionally, due to this long time needed to build skill, it is unfair to deny transwomen the opportunity to compete and utilize their skills in fear of beating those who are female.

A common idea suggested is the idea of a third category specifically of transgender athletes. This is the complete opposite of inclusion, as it purposefully excludes transwomen from being considered women. It puts them in an "other" category. Additionally, in college sports, transgender women are far underrepresented. Joanna Harper, of Loughborough University in England, argues that transgender people make up about 1% of the population, and there are more than 200,000 women competing in NCAA sports, and to be equally represented, there should be about 2,000 trans women in college sport (Rushing). But there's not, there is far less. Putting transgender women in such a small category ruins one of the most fun aspects of sport: competition. Transgender women would have far fewer competitors and could be likely the only trans athlete at a meet, racing against no one but themselves.

The fourth principle of the Fundamental Principles of Olympism in the Olympic Charter states "the practice of sport is a human right. Every individual must have the possibility of practicing sport, without discrimination of any kind." This statement includes transgender women. A woman's choice to transition and present as her true gender identity should not prohibit her from competing in a sport that she is passionate and skilled at.

A lot of the argument surrounding transgender women's inclusion in sports surrounds the idea of opportunity. That by including transgender women, it will take away opportunities from those born female. Well, what about transgender women? Do they not deserve the opportunity to succeed and compete in the sport they have spent years training in? In a letter written by 16 members of Penn's Women's Swimming team and their parents, they claim that while they "fully support Lia Thomas in her decision to affirm her gender identity" and to "live her life authentically," they argue that "when it comes to sports competition, the biology of sex is a separate issue from someone's gender identity" and that by her "inclusion with unfair biological advantages means that [they] have lost competitive opportunities." They say that they "hope the sport will adapt; that swimming will find a place for Lia to compete," and invited Thomas to train with them. The idea that Thomas must "find a place" to compete because of her identity as a transwoman is a perfect example of the exclusion she faces by those who wish to preserve biological women's sports. The want to exclude transwomen from competing in women's categories perpetuates the idea those who support "Saving Women's Sports" don't have problems with trans women competing unless they're winning. It is not unfair or challenging the integrity of women's sports until biological females are not the only ones on the podium.

They argue that "Lia's wins, records, and honors should not come at [their] expense, the women who have worked their entire lives to earn a spot on the Penn's Women's Swimming Team." But they fail to realize that Thomas has too. She has worked just as hard and should not be excluded from competing because of her identity. Her wins, records, and honors are deserved regardless of what division she is in because she is an athlete who competes well. She, as a single individual, is not changing the shape of women's sports forever and preventing biological women from winning. Also, what makes her different at winning from a skilled biological female? No one argues a skilled biological female who wins doesn't deserve it or is taking opportunities away from other members of the team. They just support her as a teammate. Or if they want those opportunities? They train harder and beat their teammate. They don't call for her exclusion from the competition.

They finished the letter by referencing National Girls and Women in Sports Day and the "Title IX pioneers who have worked so hard for women to have opportunities and sports and for educational opportunities for all women," and asking the university to, in honor of these pioneers, "recognize the importance of providing fair competition and safe spaces for its biological female athletes." Do transgender women not deserve these safe spaces or fair competition? Why is it exclusive to biological women? Transgender women face sexism and transphobia too, they are not exempt from discrimination because they went through male puberty. And if these Title IX pioneers worked so hard to help "all women" it must include transwomen. Transwomen are women. Transwomen deserve the rights and protection from sexism that biological women get. By alienating them, suggesting they don't experience sexism, it not only minimizes the experiences of transgender people but excludes them from their fellow women. Feminism is not based upon fighting just for those born female, but for anyone experiencing sexism, whether that be trans women, trans men, women of color, or queer women. Saving women's sports means including these women instead of fearing their success.

This conversation also begs the question: why do college athletes participate in sport at all? The majority of college athletes don't win championships or races. The majority of college athletes don't go on to be professional athletes. So, this means many must do it for some other reason, likely the experience they get from competing and practicing a sport. If this is true, why should transgender women be denied the experience of college athletics just because they may win? College athletics are an experience to compete and be part of a community, in a less stressful environment than professional sport. The small chance of athletic success should not deny transgender women the experience and opportunity college athletics provide.

Works Cited

Brassil, Gillian R. "N.C.A.A. Responds, Tentatively, to Transgender Athlete Bans." *The New York Times*, 12 Apr. 2021, https://www.nytimes.com/2021/04/12/sports/ncaabasketball/ncaa-transgender-athletes.html?searchResultPosition=6.

Chen, David W. "Transgender Athletes Face Bans from Girls' Sports in 10 U.S. States." *The New York Times*, 27 Oct. 2021, https://www.nytimes.com/article/transgender-athlete-ban.html?searchResultPosition=3.

Devries, Michaela C. 2008, "Do Transitioned Athletes Compete at an Advantage or Disadvantage as Compared with Physically Born Men and Women: A Review of the Scientific Literature," https://athletescan.com/sites/default/files/images/do-transitioned-athletes-compete-at-an-advantage-or-disadvantage-as-compared-with-physically-born-men-and-women-a-review-of-the-scientific-literature2.pdf.

Goldberg, Shoshana K. 2021, "Fair Play The Importance of Sports Participation for Transgender Youth," https://www.americanprogress.org/article/fair-play/.

International Olympic Committee. "IOC Framework on Fairness, Inclusion, and Non-Discrimination on the Basis of Gender Identity and Sex Variations." *Olympics*, https://stillmed.olympics.com/media/Documents/News/2021/11/IOC-Framework-Fairness-Inclusion-Non-discrimination-2021.pdf?_ga=2.195521836.1048075235.1637092563-834742310.1637092563.

International Olympic Committee. "Olympic Charter." *Olympics*, 17 July 2020, https://stillmed.olympic.org/media/Document%20Library/OlympicOrg/General/EN-Olympic-Charter.pdf.

NCAA Office of Inclusion. "NCAA Inclusion of Transgender Student-Athletes." *NCAA.org*, Apr. 2010, https://ncaaorg.s3.amazonaws.com/inclusion/lgbtq/INC_TransgenderHandbook.pdf.

Rieder, David. "Penn Swimming Parents Write Letter to NCAA against Lia Thomas' Participation in Women's Events." *Swimming World News*, 17 Dec. 2021, https://www.swimmingworldmagazine.com/news/penn-swimming-parents-write-letter-to-ncaa-against-lia-thomas-participation-in-womens-events/.

Rushing, Ellie. "Penn Swimmer Lia Thomas' Success Has Prompted National Debate About Trans Athletes. Here's What to Know." *The Philadelphia Inquirer*, 21 Feb. 2022, https://www.inquirer.com/sports/lia-thomas-penn-swimmer-trans-athletes-rights-20220214.html.

Sutherland, James. "Penn's Lia Thomas Opens up on Journey, Transition to Women's Swimming." *SwimSwam*, 10 Dec. 2021, https://swimswam.com/penns-lia-thomas-opens-up-on-journey-transition-to-womens-swimming/.

Teetzel, Sarah. "Transgender Eligibility Policies in Sport: Science, Ethics, and Evidence." *Reflecting on Modern Sport in Ancient Olympia: Proceedings of the 2016 Meeting of the International Association for the Philosophy of Sport at the International Olympic Academy*, edited by Heather L. Reid and Eric Moore, Parnassos Press – Fonte Aretusa, 2017, pp. 161–70, https://doi.org/10.2307/j.ctvbj7gdq.17.

Webb, Karleigh. "Lia Thomas Competing at Ivy League Championships Is a Fair Deal." *Outsports*, Outsports, 16 Feb. 2022, https://www.outsports.com/2022/2/16/22926059/lia-thomas-ivy-league-penn-swimming-championships-transphobia-equity-fairness.

Webb, Karleigh. "Samantha Shelton, Lucas Draper and Brooke Forde Show Wisdom and Sportsmanship in Support of Lia Thomas." *Outsports*, Outsports, 28 Jan. 2022, https://www.outsports.com/2022/1/28/22905807/lia-thomas-shelton-draper-forde-harvard-oberlin-stanford-ncaa-transgender-swimming-inclusion.

Witz, Billy. "As Lia Thomas Swims, Debate about Transgender Athletes Swirls." *The New York Times*, 24 Jan. 2022, https://www.nytimes.com/2022/01/24/sports/lia-thomas-transgender-swimmer.html?searchResultPosition=10.

Ziegler, Elizabeth M., and Tamara Isadora Huntley. "It Got too Tough to Not Be Me: Accommodating Transgender Athletes in Sport." *Journal of College and University Law*, vol. 39, no. 2, 2013, p. 467-512. HeinOnline.

Victoria Faith Miller

The Implications of De-Extinction: Are We Living in Mary Shelley's Imagined Reality?

In Mary Shelley's famous gothic novel, *Frankenstein*, Dr. Frankenstein ventures to create a new being out of old human body parts. He believes that by giving life to a creature, he can discover the secrets of life and death. But his desire to achieve something great comes at a cost. Frankenstein soon realizes that his actions have major implications and he is forced to take responsibility for what he and his monster have done. In our current world, it can be argued that a similar philosophy is being applied to a scientific process called de-extinction. De-extinction can be simply defined as bringing extinct or no longer existent species back to life (Okuno 581). Through these efforts, scientists hope to re-introduce past biodiversity into modern ecosystems. But there is a lot of grey area in the policies and practices surrounding de-extinction, not to mention the extensive amount of ethical, political, and ecological concerns it raises. In reality, de-extinction is inhumane, unnatural, and often ineffective. While de-extinction seems on the surface promising, it is ultimately not a viable or sustainable method for wildlife conservation.

There are three primary methods that have been proposed for de-extinction, including cloning, genetic engineering, and selective back-breeding or strategic mating (Okuno 592). The first method, cloning, involves implanting nuclei from an extinct animal's cells and a host animal's unfertilized egg cell into a surrogate. The second method, genetic engineering, uses DNA fragments from a closely related living species, allowing scientists to fill gaps in incomplete genetic sequences of extinct species. The third method, back-breeding, involves identifying desired traits and selectively breeding living relatives of an extinct species until the living specimens begin to resemble extinct species (Okuno 592).

Upon analyzing these methods further, it is clear how much uncertainty and inconsistency are involved in all three methods. Without even acknowledging the ethical, political, and ecological concerns of de-extinction, one must question whether authentic de-extinction is even possible. Scientists have questioned whether or not animals created through these methods can count as members of the original species (Browning). In the case of genetic engineering, there are likely to be millions of differences between an extinct and living species' genomes, given the potentially hundreds to millions of years of evolution that may separate the species. Since it is impractical to edit every base pair in DNA to exactly replicate a target species' genome, scientists are tasked with figuring out which of the millions of differences are the most significant and require alteration (Barnosky 139). Therefore, any species created through one of these methods or a combination of all three could be genetically similar to the target species, but there will still be considerable differences in genotype, phenotype, and development between the species. It is uncertain whether a given species can even be said to have been brought back from extinction or whether a new, similar species has been created, designed to fill the same role (Browning).

Semantics aside, it is the process towards achieving this goal of "de-extinction" that presents the most implications. From an ecological and conservationist standpoint, de-extinction diverts crucial financial and other resources away from existing conservation and management programs (Okuno 590). De-extinction weakens conservation policies by providing a riskier alternative solution to preventing extinction (Valdez, Kuzma, et al.). Instead of resources being used to protect existing species habitats, populations, and public reputations, they are used to fund costly and time-intensive de-extinction projects that have proven to yield a high rate of failure.

Not only can de-extinction negatively affect a re-created species' own livelihood, but it can also affect that species' surrounding ecosystem. De-extinct animals are likely to be unable to adapt to contemporary ecosystems (Valdez, Kuzma, et al.). Additionally, de-extinct animals may exhibit characteristics similar to invasive species by creating ecological disruptions or out-competing native wildlife species. This can broadly impact ecosystems and increase wildlife disease risks and transmission. In order to release de-extinct animals into the wild, they would have to be closely monitored to prevent unforeseen species interactions (Browning). It is impossible to predict exactly how a de-extinct animal will interact with pre-existing species or the negative impact it could have on an ecosystem, leaving a large margin for error in the process. De-extinction has the potential to interfere with natural evolution processes and even uproot natural selection. It can be argued that restoring species will inspire awe in the public eye and lead to additional support for conservation while satisfying a moral obligation to revive extinct species due to our impact (Valdez, Kuzma, et al.). But de-extinction could also give the public an impression that extinction is reversible, therefore diminishing the gravity of humans' impact on a species (Browning). Considering this, we are much better off finding more time and cost-effective ways to protect the species still existing on our earth. The focus should instead be placed on preventing extinctions rather than reversing them.

De-extinction can have significant effects on a re-created species and its local ecosystem, but also on human populations and the planet as a whole. According to a study conducted for the *Journal of Responsible Innovation* that interviewed experts in multiple scientific disciplines, including both the social and natural sciences, experts perceived de-extinction to be more hazardous than beneficial to human health and the environment (Valdez, Kuzma, et al.). Almost half of the participants indicated that diseases emerging from de-extinct animals may impact human health. Concerns have been raised about de-extinction causing the rebooting of encoded viruses that are harmful to humans. Like many other factors in the process of de-extinction, it is difficult to assess the potential problems of a reintroduced species acting as a vector for human disease (Valdez, Kuzma, et al.).

In addition to the potential effects of disease on human populations, de-extinction poses questions concerning public acceptance of the process. In terms of the public's perception of de-extinction, the public could be more concerned about the uncontrollable nature of the technology as portrayed in science fiction interpretations of biotechnology in the popular media, rather than the principles of de-extinction itself. An imagined future where de-extinction is a common practice has been compared to the reality of the film, *Jurassic Park* (Barnosky 135). Many people perceive de-extinction to be a plot to bring back the dinosaurs or other long extinct species. While aspects of this ideology may be true, it is ultimately an exaggeration and can detract from the truths of the matter. The public may fear this technology that they don't fully understand, clouding de-extinction efforts. And even if a *Jurassic Park* reality entices people, this would further monetize the conservation world, rooting conservation in capitalism rather than balancing this perception with a genuine desire to conserve species.

When conservation is rooted in capitalism, it detracts the public from the innate value of the animals themselves beyond perceived monetary value. One of the most touchy subjects surrounding de-extinction is its ethical and moral impacts. Many people in the science community believe that de-extinction can be discredited solely by its harmfulness towards animals. In an effort to diversify populations and re-introduce extinct species, de-extinction encroaches upon the ability for re-created animals to live as free from human contact as possible.

In 1951, hundreds of embryonic cells of a northern leopard frog were implanted with the goal to produce new members of this extinct species. Of 197 attempts, the turnout was only 27 tiny tadpole clones. In the case of the Finn Dorset sheep, the experiment started out with an initial pool of 277 mammary gland cells, yielding twenty-nine embryos, only thirteen pregnancies, and one birth (Church and Regis). In the fall of 2002, scientists captured Celia, a Pyrenean Ibex mountain goat. They had tissue scraping done on her ear in an effort to preserve the cell line and had a radio-tracking collar put around her neck. To try to clone Celia, scientists placed thirty domestic goats into a state of superovulation, using hormones to stimulate the ovaries to produce egg cells. The cloning was unsuccessful (Church and Regis).

Displayed by these examples, cloning and the overall process of de-extinction is hard on the subjects and often results in stillbirths, as well as misshapen, abnormal, and impaired offspring. Animal welfare is one of the most critical considerations when it comes to de-extinction. Animals used as surrogates or for obtaining samples of their genetic makeup as well as wild animals in a de-extinct animal's reintroduction ecosystem and the cloned animals themselves are all involved in this taxing process (Browning). Cloning has proven to be problematic for animal welfare, causing rapid aging, ongoing health problems, and premature death. Dolly, the famous goat, who represented the first-ever successfully cloned individual was plagued with heart problems including arthritis and lung disease. She died at 6 years, only around half the normal lifespan of a regular sheep of her kind (Browning).

With de-extinction, it seems that in the attempt to create new life, we are causing more harm and often death to helpless creatures. These dim prospects create major legal and political hurdles when it comes to justifying de-extinction. By nature of the practice, de-extinction will eventually be introduced to new locations with the potential to cross national boundaries. Accordingly, there will be significant foreign and international, legal, and policy implications caused by the practice (Okuno 593). One of the major legal issues is how to define the status of de-extinct animals. In question is whether they'd be considered native or introduced, endangered or not and how this would affect conservation and protection legislation (Browning). Currently, a legal framework, including policies, regulations, and laws, does not exist for jurisdiction over de-extinct species. Immense measures would have to be taken to protect humans and the environment from these species and vice versa. The creation of adequate regulations would take many years and could create disagreement and disruption in political settings (Okuno 593).

Immense measures must also be taken to protect humans from themselves. Attempts to reconstitute genomes and re-create species can be viewed as hubristic or similar to "playing God." This connotes a human desire to transgress fixed limits on human capabilities, a label that has been affiliated with biotechnology since its inception (Valdez, Kuzma, et al). The desire to develop cloning techniques to copy the genetics of an extinct mammal or currently living being raises questions about whether humans are next. If this were to ever occur, the ethical issues involved in animal de-extinction would be magnified ten-fold.

Many people know how the *Frankenstein* story plays out. Dr. Frankenstein's unquenchable desire to "renew life" results in a monster, a bloodthirsty creature who is miserable and ghastly in appearance. Because Dr. Frankenstein attempts to transcend the rules of nature, he lives the rest of his life in regret. If we do the same, who is to say that we won't live regretting our decisions? Who is to say that we won't create a worldwide catastrophe? Will we too allow our ambitions to be our downfall?

Works Cited

Barnosky, Anthony D. *Dodging Extinction: Power, Food, Money, and the Future of Life on Earth*, University of California Press, 2014. ProQuest Ebook Central, http://ebookcentral.proquest.com/lib/drexel-ebooks/detail.action?docID=1710996.

Browning, H. Won't Somebody Please Think of the Mammoths? De-extinction and Animal Welfare, 2018. *J Agric Environ Ethics* 31, 785–803. https://doi.org/10.1007/s10806-018-9755-2.

Church, George M., and Ed Regis. "Regenesis: How Synthetic Biology Will Reinvent Nature and Ourselves," *Basic Books*, 2014. ProQuest Ebook Central, http://ebookcentral.proquest.com/lib/drexel-ebooks/detail.action?docID=1595856.

Okuno, Erin. Frankenstein's Mammoth: Anticipating the Global Legal Framework for De-Extinction, 2016. *Ecology Law Quarterly*, Vol. 43, No. 3, 2016, https://ssrn.com/abstract=2962391.

Valdez, Rene X., Kuzma, Jennifer, Cummings, Christopher L.& Peterson, M. Nils, 2019. Anticipating risks, governance needs, and public perceptions of de-extinction, *Journal of Responsible Innovation*, https://doi.org/10.1080/23299460.2019.1591145.

Noah Entz

The Unbreakable Bond Between Hands-On Experience, Confidence, and Information

It's no secret that confidence plays a huge role in a person's choice of job. It's also not a secret that many people lack that self-confidence when it comes to seeking out their dream jobs, if the job is in the STEM field. Many people can have trouble remembering terms and procedures that they have never been able to perform which only furthers this problem. I know that I see these qualities in myself, and have heard my friends speak on similar issues. There was one experience, however, that helped me gain this confidence and information like nothing else. Hands-on experience can not only boost information retention, but it can also boost self-confidence and lead more people to find themselves in STEM fields.

It is well known that hands-on experiences improve the ability for a person to recall the learned information. Many people know this from either personal experience, studies, or both! In one such study conducted by the American Association of Neurological Surgeons, a group of students participated in a neurological surgery bootcamp. These students were surveyed before and after about the effect the course had on them. The surveys came back with an almost unanimous agreement that the hands-on exposure during the boot camp was beneficial to the students. Even six months after the course had ended, the information learned during the bootcamp was retained and 99% of students thought the courses helped them gain skills and knowledge that would continue to help them in the future (Selden et al.).

While it wasn't exactly a "bootcamp" I joined a year-long veterinary assistant program, which ended in a month-long internship at the age of 18. In the year before the internship, all of the work that I did was online and through textbooks. This meant that I never had the opportunity to test my skills and had a hard time recalling things since I had to memorize lists rather than experience things. In the one month of internship, I learned far more information that I am still able to recall well to this day because I was given the opportunity to perform and demonstrate my skills. This, in turn, had a direct impact on my overall confidence in the field. Walking into the internship, I was incredibly nervous that I would misremember things and consistently mess up. By the end of the month, however, I was performing difficult tasks like they were second nature, because I was granted the opportunity to try. Many of these tasks still feel like muscle memory even though it has been a year since I have been able to do them.

This confidence boost is not something unique either, in an article published in the 68th volume of *Academic Medicine* students were asked to rate their confidence levels after encounters with patients where they had to attempt a diagnosis. Several encounter variables were assessed and were noticeably positively correlated with the confidence rating given by the students. The most significant of these were seen when students had already gained experience with the presenting problem, or had done lab work during their studies. The study concluded: "Our data suggests that hands-on clinical experience may be more important for building confidence than any other encounter variable" (Harrell et al.).

Despite the clear evidence that hands-on experience is beneficial to learning, many high and middle schools seem to shy away from this, which can have a huge impact on the grades of the students attending the schools. I know that many of my friends in high school were never given the opportunity to do any hands-on work at all, which led them to struggle in subjects they had previously excelled at. A study in the 33rd volume of the *Journal of Research in Science Teaching* supports this as well. A randomly selected group of eighth graders were picked from around the country and given an achievement test. This test was a cognitive battery test developed by the Educational Testing Service. To quote the study directly, "Eighth-grade students who experience hands-on activities either every day or once a week score significantly higher than eighth-grade students who experience hands-on activities once a month, less than once a month, or never" (Stohr-Hunt). This, paired with the previous examples, begs the question, does this hands-on experience lead to more people looking for jobs in fields that they otherwise would have shied away from?

The answer is, maybe unsurprisingly, yes! Even just speaking from my own experience, I know that if I didn't seek out my veterinary internship, I would be far less likely to pursue a veterinary career, even though it is something I have wanted to do for as long as I can remember. An article published in the *RIT Scholar Works, Journal of Science Education* surveyed several students twice. The surveys themselves asked the same question posed above and while this study calls attention specifically to those students who are disabled, the main conclusion can still be applied broadly. They found that a majority of the students they asked had an interest in STEM work; they said they found it fun and engaging. Yet, when asked whether they would pursue a STEM major, only 8% reported they would do so. After given access to a hands-on lab, however, the same students were more likely to agree with the question from survey A: "I plan on enrolling as a science major in college and my educational experiences, so far, have given me the confidence that I need to decide on majoring in an Examination of Hands-on Science Learning Experiences area of science in college and then a career in science" (Michaels, Roth). On top of that, answers from survey B indicate that hands-on experience can lead to an increase in confidence regarding one's own abilities (Michaels, Roth).

The links between hands-on experience, confidence, and retention are clear and strong. I know this, not only from the multiple studies documenting the phenomena, but also my own personal experience with hands-on learning. When one is given the opportunity to test their skill and demonstrate what they learn, it strengthens the connections between information. When they are able to have this information at the ready, they feel more confident in themselves and their abilities. When they feel more confident in their abilities, they are far more likely to enter fields they would have previously been scared of. These are three concepts that build on each other and lead to more people pursuing their dreams.

Works Cited

Harrell, P., et al. "Medical students' confidence and the characteristics of their clinical experiences in a primary care clerkship." *Academic Medicine,* vol. 68, no. 7, July 1993, pp. 577-9. https://oce-ovid-com.ezproxy2.library.drexel.edu/article/00001888-199307000-00020/HTML.

Michaels, Michelle, and Alan Roth. "An Examination of Accessible Hands-on Science Learning Experiences, Self-Confidence in One's Capacity to Function in the Sciences, and Motivation and Interest in Scientific Studies and Careers." *RIT Scholar Works, Journal of Science Education,* 15 Nov. 2016, https://scholarworks.rit.edu/jsesd/vol19/iss1/7/.

Selden, Nathan R., et al. "Society of Neurological Surgeons Boot Camp Courses: Knowledge Retention and Relevance of Hands-on Learning after 6 Months of Postgraduate Year 1 Training." *Jns, American Association of Neurological Surgeons,* 1 Sept. 2013, https://drexel.primo.exlibrisgroup.com/discovery/fulldisplay.

Stohr-Hunt, Patricia M. "An Analysis of Frequency of Hands-on Experience and Science Achievement." *Journal of Research in Science Teaching,* vol. 33, no. 1, Wiley Subscription Services, Inc., A Wiley Company, 1996, pp. 101–09, https://onlinelibrary.wiley.com/doi/abs.

Drexel Publishing Group

Creative Writing

Introduction

The following creative works were selected by faculty judges from student submissions (of creative nonfiction, fiction, humor, and poetry) to the Drexel Publishing Group Creative Writing Contest. There were many strong entries in all categories. These pieces engage with issues of culture, gender, education, and the challenges of living though a global pandemic. They are as diverse as the students who wrote them. These writers demonstrate insight, humor, and a profound understanding of our current times.

—*The Editors*

Anh Quach
Home and Away

Newark, April 2, 2020

Spring is here. Cherry blossoms are here. Baby-pink, soft, fluttery sun-kissed petals. Cherry trees line the walkway around her dorm. Picturesque. Inviting. Instagrammable. The Northeastern American spring lies mere inches away from her window, delicate, sweet, full of life, and cheerful beyond imagination.

What's the weather like today?

Are there cherry blossoms yet?

Mở cửa ra cho nắng sớm vào phòng,[1] she tells herself. *Open the blinds. Let the sun in. Please.*

Her blinds are drawn. Darkness blankets the room. *Day or night?* she wonders. Her chest throbs. Coughing fits torture her, haunt her dreams. The air feels hot and cold and bland and thick and sticky and pestilential. She's exhausted. Slowly drowning.

She's too ill to open the blinds.

She reaches for her phone next to her. Her chest tightens. Two missed calls from her parents, which she has no plan to answer lest they find out how ill she sounds. Fingers trembling, she opens Instagram, acutely aware of how much her eyes hurt. Her head is pounding. She coughs, gasping for air. But she keeps scrolling. Instagram is her only way of communicating with the world ever since this all began.

Where did this all begin?

No idea, she snaps. Her brain is too foggy to recall anything right now.

Sourdough starter. Cookies. Someone picked up their cat from an animal shelter. Another person is at a virtual concert. Someone else partied despite lockdown orders. Her friend back home went to brunch—in pandemic-free Vietnam. She wants to scream, cry, turn off her phone, throw it at the wall. How she wishes she were home safe and healthy! But she is not well. Her exhaustion is eating her alive—too suffocating to ignore.

How's everyone doing, reads an Instagram story from a fellow international student.

Rising panic. *It's all coming back now,* she shudders, horrified, *the chaos and terror of what went down.* Tears blind her. She had fallen ill with some COVID-19-like thing as the first COVID-19 tsunami crashed into Newark; she wasn't allowed a test because there weren't enough tests, and she was "too young

---

1   The first line in a popular Vietnamese children's song, *Nắng Sớm* ("Morning Sun").

to die anyway." She watches the repatriation flights trickling into the country and leaving her behind. She watches her university close; she sees hordes of people running for safety. She watches her plans vanish into thin air. Coughing, trembling, she hastily types her response to the story. *Ill. Probably COVID. Denied test. Quarantined in an empty room with four white walls. No one's here. People leave food at the door. No more summer plans.*

What am I doing? she wonders. She barely knows the person. And she hasn't even told her loved ones her ordeal.

You alright? comes the reply.

She's sobbing, gasping for air. Her despairing cries sink into the blanketing silence. The walls are caving in. Her chest throbs: she feels another coughing fit rising. *I'm scared,* she's dying to text back. *Talk to me, please. Talk to me about anything: school, spring, cherry blossoms, your family, anything to make me forget how sick I am. Say something. Please.*

I don't want to die here alone, she types.

Sent.

Rotterdam, June 21, 2020

"Did you get the box of masks we sent you?" Mom texts.

He glances at the heavy box sitting at the corner of his tiny room and imagines the piles of blue surgical masks stacked inside. Rotterdam is once again running out of masks. "I did," he replies, "yesterday evening."

"Can you PLEASE count how many bags of masks are in that box NOW, so we know if we need to send you more?" screams Mom's next text.

Woah, chill, he thinks. He can't be bothered to count masks right now. He pictures Mom yelling into the phone and reads her text again in her voice. Is she mad? Where did his parents get all these masks from? Why aren't they keeping them? Don't they need masks, too?

"Later," he answers. "I'll send some of these to my friends, too. You guys can keep the rest. That's plenty." *They'll just mail another giant box over here anyway,* he chuckles. *Funny.* He knows his parents all too well.

"How's Rotterdam?" Mom asks.

Bad, very bad, he wants to tell her. He, exhausted, frightened, has seen it all: the numerous lockdowns, the case surges, the people who have fallen ill or died, the mobs of panicked grocery shoppers at the beginning of lockdowns, the anti-lockdown protests, the gloomy news reports, the empty streets, and his deserted campus. The very thought of leaving his dorm—his safe haven—horrifies him: what if he catches *it*? What if he gives *it* to someone else? How many times have they announced another case surge? Will there be more? When can he go back to school? Will they all be okay? *It never freaking ends,* he thinks. An ambulance passes by his room every five minutes or so, its unmistakable sirens burning its way into his eardrums before fading into the distance. Someone's sick. Unwell. Dying. He shudders. He wants to scream. Ah, Rotterdam, ailing Rotterdam! COVID-19 has brought the city to its knees.

"Not great," he types. Mom need not be troubled with the details.

"Will you please come home if you can?" Mom texts. Again, he reads it in her voice. *Is she exasperated? Worried? Scared?* he wonders aloud. He can never seem to tell.

"I'm good," he tells her. "I don't want to take up a spot on one of those repatriation flights. Someone else might need it more than I do. And I'll probably catch COVID-19 on my way back because everyone's sick. Then I might bring it home. That's no good."

"Come home to us," beckons Mom. "We'll take care of you if you're sick. *Về nhà với bố mẹ đi con. Về đi, bệnh bố mẹ chăm.*"

Về nhà với bố mẹ đi con.

He's hugging himself. He's crying. Wailing. He hasn't in years. Tears are welling up in his eyes faster than he can blink them away. How he misses his parents! How he longs for the warm and safe embrace of home, away from all of this! How he craves certainty in this world! But there's no way out. He shudders at the suffocating omnipresence of COVID-19. Flights are few and far between, even for those who are lucky. Home is only two flights away, yet home has never felt farther, almost like a distant memory he's desperately trying to hold onto before COVID-19 wipes it off the face of the Earth.

He can't bring himself to reply to Mom's text.

"Stay safe, okay?" says Mom. She *knows*.

"Promise," he texts back.

Hanoi, April 8, 2021

The iPhone ringtone pierces the silence. He jumps. He fumbles for his phone. *Who the hell is calling at midnight?* he groans, annoyed and tired.

"Dad, I got the vaccine," exclaims his daughter.

He sits up, no longer sleepy. *Wait.* He clutches his phone to his ear. His eyes widen. "What?" he asks.

"I got the COVID-19 shot," says his daughter. "Pfizer."

His hands are trembling. He cannot believe his ears. His thoughts are racing in his head. His daughter, stranded in a pandemic-stricken country for months. The kid who cried herself to sleep on the phone every night. The kid who phoned the Vietnam Embassy in tears, desperate to go home. The poor child who never set foot anywhere close to an airplane ever since she arrived home on a repatriation flight. *Yet she won't stay,* he marvels. His memories of her are bittersweet. He recalls begging her to stay home until things got better, to no avail. He recalls helping her pack her suitcases. *I wouldn't leave if I didn't have to,* she said the night before her flight. He recalls dropping her off at the airport just weeks ago so she could fly back to college. Back to chaos. Back to where she fled. His wife sobbed as their little girl disappeared down the empty airport aisle. He remembers how he and his wife stayed up all night praying to their ancestors for their daughter's safe arrival and good health, praying that her life would return to normal, that she would be given the strength to survive whatever lies ahead. The world was hell when she returned home, hell when she left. But Pfizer? The vaccine? *Dare I hope?* he wonders.

"How are you?" he asks her.

"My left arm's sore," she sighs. "One more and I'll be fully vaccinated."

"I'm assuming school's gonna be back in person soon," he remarks. He knows how much she hates online school. His wife is up now, staring at him, listening in.

"I'm excited," his daughter gushes. "I get to go to classes and see my friends again. After a year. Isn't it fun, Dad? Imagine."

And he does. He pictures his daughter conversing with friends he has never met on their way to class, laughter filling the air. He imagines her confidently boarding the subway without having to dodge large crowds and fear for her life. He envisions her living her life—a year of which she lost to COVID-19. Yes, he dares hope! Is this the beginning of the end? Will she be safe and healthy? Will the world be kinder to these kids? He suddenly finds himself giddy, excited, hopeful. *This is it. The new normal.*

"Are you asleep?" his daughter laughs. "Did I wake you up?"

His wife snatches his phone; he doesn't notice. A smile is plastered on his face. Happiness and pride fill his soul.

My daughter was gifted a huge scientific achievement, he's dying to scream to the world.

Maybe tomorrow.

Maybe now.

Ho Chi Minh City, July 9, 2021

On the hard floor of the dimly lit, humid, cramped room she sits, poking at her measly dinner. Mosquitoes swarm. The TV is on. The evening news plays.

It feels weird being back early, she thinks. How oddly liberating, even, to no longer have to work overtime. The factory closed yesterday, and for the first time in forever, she's home early. In fact, she's been here all day. She's no longer busy. *What do I do now with all this time?* she wonders.

Who's paying rent? whines the small voice in her head.

Not now, she snaps at it.

She turns up the volume. She stares at the reporter's mouth as he rambles about Directive 16. *Ho Chi Minh City commenced strict lockdown as Directive 16 came into effect on July 9,* the man babbles. His camera shows a deserted street with a checkpoint in a distance. *People are strictly following public health guidelines there.*

Old news, she chuckles. She and her co-workers lost their jobs yesterday as their factory began shutting down; hugs, phone numbers, and well-wishes were exchanged. She stood in line for two hours at the market for some stringy vegetables and a fish. She came home to the awe-inspiring sight of a makeshift barricade surrounding her poverty-stricken neighborhood. Someone stuck a giant green sign atop the growing pile of chairs and tables: COVID-FREE ZONE. RESIDENTS ONLY. NO UNAUTHORIZED ACCESS.

Like a warzone, she thinks. She shivers. It's summer, but she feels cold.

A graph appears on her TV screen. The number of cases keeps climbing and climbing. The reporter's voice suddenly becomes irritatingly cheerful. *The number of COVID-19 cases and deaths in Ho Chi Minh City is rising,* he says. *This lockdown may be extended.* The screen blurs. She's seen her co-workers get sick one by one; she recalls their hushed conversations as they held back tears, of family members, friends, relatives that passed away. *Mom died. Grandma died. Dad didn't make it. Alone in a hospital room. Couldn't even have a funeral.* She sighs. Death is everywhere. Everyone seems to know someone who died.

She takes another bite of her measly dinner.

The little voice returns, but she can no longer shut it up. *Who's paying rent?* it begs her, implores her. *Who's getting food? Who's earning money? Who's sending money home to your mom? Who's paying your kid's tuition?*

Bitter. Bitterness everywhere: bitterness lodged in her throat, bitterness running down her spine. She lays down her food. She can no longer eat another bite. Her son—poor little baby! When did she last hug him, make him dinner? *Sweetest kid ever,* she smiles forlornly. Her heart aches. She left him in her mom's care in one of those villages full of children and old people to find work; for the first few months of her being here, she'd cry herself to sleep, missing him. How she would dream—of visiting her son during the holidays, of saving up enough money to one day bring him and his grandmother to the city to live with her! Like a real family! Ah, his laughter. His tantrums. His singsong voice. His nonsensical stories. His warm little hugs. She grimaces. No *crying,* she snaps at herself. But what can she do? Her neighborhood is sealed off. Barricades and checkpoints surround the city. COVID-19 is here. People die. People are ill. There's no way out. She's trapped. Can't leave. Jobless, fearing for her life, running out of money. What will happen to her poor baby? What now? What even is there to do?

What even is there to do?

So much for dreams, she snickers, bitterly, hopelessly.

Her food is cold. She turns off the TV and stares ahead.

Ho Chi Minh City, September 20, 2021

He clutches two water bottles in his hands. Squirming, he feels his damp t-shirt underneath the blue hazmat suit. His forehead is peppered with sweat.

His shoulder aches. His girlfriend is resting her head on it, sleeping peacefully; he dares not wake her up.

Awful shift today, he thinks, watching the row of fellow hazmat-suit-clad volunteers quietly napping. He's too exhausted to fall asleep.

Aspiring dermatologists, their whole lot, less than halfway through their medical degree. *Very experienced,* he snickers. They came to the quarantine centers a few weeks ago, wide-eyed and hopeful, as COVID-19 ravaged Ho Chi Minh City. Busload after busload of them dispersed into the city's pandemic hotspots. Someone scribbled on the back of their hazmat suit in giant block letters, SINGLE AND READY TO MINGLE. He remembers singing with them on the bus, screaming, laughing, tears in their eyes. He watched them bicker about world affairs and share their hopes, dreams, and deepest secrets. *Online school sucks,* they cheered. He smiles at the memory. So many of them later got COVID. That online school is terrible is the only thing they agreed on before more than half of them got shipped off either to work or to be treated, not yet seen again.

He quietly removes his mask and draws a long breath. The hot, humid air fills his lungs. Readjusting his mask, he chuckles. What do they even look like? He knows too much about his fellow volunteers, and he hasn't seen their faces.

Did we know what we signed up for? he sighs. His parents never knew he left; they would *not* have let him go.

It's 4:30am. Thirty more minutes. *Sleep,* he tells himself. He closes his eyes.

He sees them again. The patients. They arrived in droves, carrying SARS-CoV-2 with them as they slumped down the flimsy plastic chairs. They were all masked and tired and long-suffering. Some looked well, others coughing and shivering; some got worse overnight and left quarantine the next morning in ambulances. How different yet similar they were—tired and worried eyes, unkempt, asking the volunteers when they'd be let out! He'd try to remember their names as he checked them in. He'd recite them to his friends. That *chú,* two rows down, the uncle in the untucked blue button-down shirt, was Sáng. The *cô,* that auntie waddling toward a chair with a *nón lá* in her hand—her name was Nga. But he and his fellow volunteers would always forget. He shudders at the patients' long-suffering eyes. *Someone's worried sick about them,* he thinks. They remind him of his parents and sister. How he wants to see their faces, to know who they are, to know what's happening in their lives! But he can't. Nobody can. No one spoke; no one ever speaks. COVID-19 keeps them apart. He never finds out what happens to the people who arrived well or sick or left in ambulances. He never sees *chú* Sáng or *cô* Nga or anyone again. He feels cold. More of them will arrive again. So many of them. Sick. Coughing. Dying. Waiting for help, waiting to die. *Rinse and repeat,* he reminds himself.

Rinse and repeat.

A rustle. Another volunteer stands up and stretches. He opens his eyes. It's 5am.

Ho Chi Minh City, November 19, 2021

One by one, lights go out. Darkness envelops the houses and alleyways.

By the snaking canals, motorcycles quietly stop.

Inside, a candle is lit, its warm flame flickering, illuminating the blanketing darkness. Yet another lights up. Then another. From the canal banks, flowers flutter, dance in the evening breeze, and land atop swirling waves.

Church and pagoda bells toll from afar. Ship horns echo. The wind carries the symphony of bells and ship horns to the candlelit alleys and the flower-covered canals, where the aroma of incense lingers and people stand together in silence, grieving, reminiscing, praying, hoping.

Today, Ho Chi Minh City slows.

Today, its residents mourn more than 23,000 Vietnamese citizens who have lost their lives to COVID-19—family members, friends, neighbors, acquaintances.[2]

Today, Ho Chi Minh City residents celebrate the lives and memories of people they never got to say goodbye to.

Tomorrow, life goes on in the city that never sleeps. Life is slowly returning to Ho Chi Minh City in its own new normal—louder, busier than ever. Vaccines are arriving at the city's every corner. Vaccination rates are climbing nationwide.[3]

Hope is in the air.

References

VnExpress. (2021, November 20). *Hình ảnh xúc động đêm tưởng niệm nạn nhân* COVID-19 [Highlights from Vietnam National Day of Observance for Victims of COVID-19]. vnexpress.net. Retrieved February 16, 2022, from https://vnexpress.net/hinh-anh-xuc-dong-dem-tuong-niem-nan-nhan-covid-19-4390679.html

VnExpress International. (2021, August 5). *Covid-19 vaccination in Vietnam: Statistics*. COVID-19 in Vietnam. Retrieved February 17, 2022, from https://e.vnexpress.net/covid-19/vaccine

---

2 As of November 19, 2021, Vietnam recorded more than 23,000 deaths due to COVID-19. See VnExpress (2021).

3 As of February 15, 2022, over 77% of Vietnam's population has been fully vaccinated (VnExpress, 2022).

Upoma Chakraborty

Eat

A Bengali man in his late 20s has killed himself. My family vaguely knows his family, enough to go to the funeral, but not enough to cry at said funeral. But I will tell you that story later. Let me start from the beginning.

There is not much that is sweet in Bengali culture. This is ironic given the fact that this culture has produced what has constantly been voted "the sweetest language in the world." Not to mention, Bengalis have consistently produced an array of desserts that are now popular throughout South Asia. *Roshogulla. Payesh. Roshmolai. Mishti doi.* You get it. Most of what is cultural never started out as culture but was based on the art of survival. Over time, Bengalis have taken out survival and have been left with only art. But this shift only happened after Bengalis learned how to live and not just survive.

Bengali ghost stories are rich and vivid, not because we want children to have a real childhood, but because we are afraid what will happen if they go out in the dark, and so ghost stories serve as a cautionary warning.

Before a woman gets married and goes off to live with her in-laws, we host what is called *Aiburobhat.* This is where you cook and feed the bride-to-be all of her favorite foods, not because you love her but because her in-laws may be cruel and purposefully starve her. It is the one last time you can make sure she is properly nourished.

Bengalis gift gold jewelry at every occasion they can. Not because they love each other, but because gold is easy to transport and will always be valuable. Gold is gifted as an asset, a safety net, not because it's pretty.

A Bengali parent will pay for their child's school tuition and books, even if it means selling their soul, life and limb. Not because they love their child, but as a way to set them up for success in their careers. The rich and educated always survive.

You get the point. The love comes later in these cultural gestures. Survival was always the main focus.

Yet, I can only think of one thing that is done out of love and love only: feeding children by hand.

This makes sense for small children. They don't have the ability to feed themselves, but Bengali parents will feed you by hand until it becomes embarrassing. I've seen 11, 12, and even 13-yearolds being hand fed by their parents. I have sat and tried to understand why they do this, but I can only come to one conclusion: parents do it out of love.

"You're not understanding why parents feed their children out of love? You monster."

No, I understand it, but I don't understand why that love is so open and out there.

Bengali love has always been historically quiet. Soft and shy glances at your lover during your wedding, giving your children the last piece of chicken without hesitation or resistance, and always asking about every single family member when seeing a friend after a long time. Bengali love is quiet and simple, never loud and extravagant.

So, when my mother fed me for the first time in over a decade, I was taken aback. Her love was always quiet. She buys the kind of grapes I like at the supermarket. She does not allow me to buy her expensive gifts because "she doesn't need it," despite wanting it. She puts potatoes in every single curry because I love potatoes. She hates them (a fact she didn't tell me, but that I learned after overhearing a conversation). She has kept every single birthday candle of mine for the past 22 years. She keeps her childhood trauma of war and poverty to herself and makes sure her children never experience the same.

That is Bengali love, quiet. It's not telling your child "I love you" at the end of phone calls or showering them with extravagant, meaningless gestures. Ma is a quiet lover.

She had just come home from a funeral. The son of a family friend had passed. He was in his late 20s, dating a woman he seemingly loved, had a good family, and a great paying job. He killed himself anyway. Depression is a silent killer.

She came into my room and sat down. She was quiet for a very long time then finally spoke. "Buri, you are my life, Buri. Always be strong. Never give up. Your parents are behind you..." She trails off. She sighs. "You can't leave me. I need you. Your Ma needs you. If you ever have any problems, you tell me. You tell me. I'm your Ma. I am behind of you. I am your well wisher. But you cannot leave me. I'm your Ma. You can do anything, but you cannot do *that*."

She is red, on the verge of crying. I can see tears well up in her eyes, begging for their sweet release. But my mother does not allow the tears to escape. Ma is a Bangladeshi woman of a certain generation. She does not cry.

And so, there she is, moments later with her wet slicked back hair, freshly applied sindoor, and unblended Nivia cream on her chin, making me a plate of pure Bengali comfort food. I'm talking freshly cooked *phena bhat* with added layers of homemade *ghee* drizzled on top, crispy fried *bora* on one side, and savory *shorshe ilish* on the other.

She sat on the sofa with me, then aged 21, and began to feed me just like she did when I was younger. Feeding someone, with your bare hands, is the most intimate experience there is. The skin-to-mouth contact. *I'm your Ma.* The feeder separates the bone from the fish and you, as the one being fed, trust they will do a sufficient job so you don't choke on a bone. *I am behind of you. I am your well wisher.* You are at the mercy of the hand feeding you—they dictate what you eat and when. *But you cannot leave me. Your Ma needs you.* The hand feeding you could be feeding themselves, but they choose to feed you instead. *Buri, you are my life, Buri.*

And yet despite having one of the most emotionally intense moments, Ma never spoke more than a word. A heavy silence was all there was in the room. She said one word and one word only that encapsulated all her love, grief, and pain for me and the man who killed himself: "*Eat.*"

Maya Micci Morrison
The World Moves On

In 2020, the world shut down. Millions remained stuck at home, unsure of what lay ahead. Isolation impacted us all physically, mentally, and emotionally. For me, isolation was a familiar feeling. After years spent in and out of doctors' appointments and hospital visits due to post-concussive syndrome, I had learned to live in my own form of self-quarantine long before the global pandemic.

I opened my eyes and all I could see was the room spinning around me. Time had slowed down as I heard muffled yelling off in the distance. The screaming sounded more frantic as it moved closer to me. A loud mechanical beeping followed. I could make out figures moving around me. All I could feel in that moment was a pounding sensation in my head that clouded my senses.

With a gasp of air, I became conscious of my surroundings. As my vision cleared, I was able to make out a dozen or so adults wearing white jackets. The yelling was so loud that it was all I could hear. The only words that I could understand were, "Don't move!" I realized that I couldn't move even if I wanted to. Panic set in and my eyes darted around the room, trying to make out any clues that could help me piece together the scene I found myself in.

The bright white LED lights that shone down on me seemed to bounce off of everything that I looked at. I winced and my hand flew over my eyes, a tingling sensation running through that arm. As the adrenaline began to wear off, the pounding in my head turned into a deafening ringing in my ears. I felt pain rush through my whole body. I cried out and began to move but was quickly held down by those surrounding me.

My eyes began to adjust slowly to the light, and I could see that I was in a hospital room, splayed out on the cold tile floor, surrounded by doctors. In the corner of the room, I saw a woman yelling hysterically. She was attempting to swim through the wave of lab coats to get over to me. Through the yelling, I heard her calling my name. Seeing this woman so upset made me feel sick.

That was when I became aware of the sharp pain in my stomach. I remembered that was the reason I had come to the hospital in the first place, but I still did not remember why I had a splitting pain emanating from my skull. As I assessed my surroundings, I looked back up at the woman in the corner who was now holding her head in her hands, weeping. I realized that that woman was my mom.

I looked at the doctor closest to me who was putting a stiff brace around my neck and managed to form a couple words.

"Wha...what happened?" My words slurred as if this was my first time speaking.

"We're not sure yet. Just stay still and try to relax." She tried to smile at me reassuringly, but she could not hide the panic in her eyes.

As a handful of doctors firmly lifted me back onto my hospital bed, they began to run my vitals. I laid there staring at the drop tile ceiling as they hurriedly yelled across the room to each other. After hours of tests, doctors slowly trickled out and the yelling turned into hushed whispers. The roaring sound in my ears had quieted itself to a dull ringing. The pounding in my head now focused itself to one lump on the base of my skull.

The doctor that was originally assigned to me when I first arrived at the hospital stepped over and placed a hand on my shoulder. I believed he was trying to reassure me that I would be alright, but it felt like he was actually trying to reassure himself. His name tag sat crooked on his perfectly ironed coat. It read *"Dr. Ferguson."* He walked over to the corner of the hospital room and sat at his computer, reading over some notes on a nearly blank screen before speaking.

With his back facing me, he said, "I'm sorry you had to go through all of this, Maya." He paused for a moment, looking over at me with a glance that almost showed remorse before quickly looking back at his screen. "The good news is it looks like all that happened was you had a bad reaction to the medication we gave you to relieve your pain. You passed out from a vagal response while trying to stand up to get something. Do you remember that?"

I shook my head, waiting for him to continue.

"That's what I figured. You hit your head on the wall and on the floor as you fell. You're lucky you didn't get more injured than you did. Now...the bad news is we believe you have a severe concussion from the fall." Dr. Ferguson looked towards the ground as he muttered the last few words.

I was speechless. I laid there with my neck resting in a brace and my stomach still in excruciating pain, now with a severe concussion to top it all off.

"What about the reason she came to the hospital in the first place?" My mom blurted out; her eyes wide from hearing this news.

Dr. Ferguson shifted his swivel chair towards us. The metal creaked as he turned. "Well, we are still not sure. I know this must be immensely frustrating for both of you, but we are trying our best to figure out exactly what is going on." I watched the doctor lower his head as he continued, "I'll be back soon to get more of your tests done." As Dr. Ferguson left the room, he shut the door firmly behind him.

That night I was moved out of the emergency unit and into the children's hospital, still unsure of what other news was to come. During my stay, I was woken up hourly by nurses checking my vitals. It did not matter much to me because the constant ringing in my ears left me unable to sleep for more than fifteen minutes at a time. Whenever a nurse would come around to my room, I would ask if everything was normal, and they would simply nod their heads and continue on their way.

For three more days, time stood still as I spent every waking moment staring at the ceiling waiting for some sort of answer. I was now able to pick out the constellations of stains and indents on the tiles above me. I lost track of the number of tests that the doctors ran. The drone of the machines I was hooked up to started to sound like instruments that harmonized with the drum-like beating in my ears. Finally, on the afternoon of my fourth day at the hospital, Dr. Ferguson came into my room with a pile of papers thick enough to be a short novel.

"Alright, Maya. It looks like we've done all that we can for you. As we've discussed, all of the tests that we've run on you look fairly normal. We believe all of your stomach pains are from a stomach virus that has been going around. That should get better with time." He paused and shifted his footing. "Thankfully, we haven't found anything more serious than that. Unfortunately, that is all we can do for you at this time. You'll be going home in a few hours."

I sat up slowly in my cot, careful not to make myself dizzy with sudden movements. "What about my concussion?" I asked, baffled by the doctor's news.

Dr. Ferguson hesitated before speaking. "That will also only get better with time. We can set you up with some of our best neurologists who will work with you further." Before leaving the room, the doctor muttered, "Once again, I really am sorry all of this happened to you." As he left this time, the door closed a little harder behind him.

My mom and I left that day feeling defeated. The concussion would get better with time, but how much time was unknown. Little did I know that the decision to go to the hospital for a stomach virus would follow me for years.

After a week of recovering at home, my symptoms seemed to only get worse. I was living with severe migraines day and night, unable to eat or even walk at times. The migraines became so debilitating that I would pass out if my body was under any amount of physical stress. My doctors recommended sleep and rest. But when I slept, all I was met with were nightmares. I dreamt of my worst anxieties coming to fruition, my waking life haunting me even then. The state of my condition had not gotten better with time, and my symptoms only became more frightening.

For the time being, my school was understanding and accommodating. They assigned me a high school tutor who worked with me as a homebound student for the remainder of the school year. Thankfully, the last few months of freshman year went by quickly with support from my school and friends. But when sophomore year started, and my symptoms hadn't changed, my school began to fight my mom on my need to be a homebound student. Teachers threatened to fail me and hold me back a year for not being physically present in their class, even though I was completing my work with all As. At first, I reassured her that I could go back out of fear of what might happen if I didn't.

I returned to classes a couple times a week and my teachers would report back to the school that while I looked tired, I seemed well enough to be in class. These comments would lead to my school actively working against my doctors' recommendations even though they were based solely on my appearance. What my teachers could not see was my sensitivity to light and sound, constant nausea, and extreme dizziness. They could not see me barely holding my head up as their classroom spun around me or the countless times I nearly passed out in front of my classmates. Because I was able to hide my pain to make those around me comfortable, my teachers ended up thinking that I was lying.

As I continued pushing myself to go to school, I only ended up making my symptoms worse. My memory was failing me as I struggled to recall conversations and simple things I had done throughout each day. As I began to realize that my memory was severely impacted by this fall, I thought of my future in high school and how this could impact the rest of my life in college. I remained unable to sleep as these anxieties consumed me. My fears came to fruition as it felt like my life was falling apart before it had even begun. But, as far as anyone else could tell, I just got headaches.

By the third month of sophomore year and after several more doctors' visits and letters sent to my school, my administrator grew tired of fighting with doctors and allowed me to be a homebound student once again. But by this point, I had lost most of the support I once had. My academic advisor set up biweekly meetings with all of my teachers, herself, and my mom, in which my mom would have to show physical proof of doctors' notes and extensive tests that proved that I was, in fact, suffering from post-concussive syndrome.

"Lisa, if I can be frank with you, you can't show proof of a headache. Do you really expect us to believe that she's *that* unwell to the point that she can't just show up?" a teacher questioned my mom as I sat across from him at a round table in an empty conference room. In the center of the table sat CAT-scans of my brain and cognitive tests that showed the exact proof he was looking for. Yet all these adults did was judge my health based on my composure and grades, both of which were all I spent my time maintaining to keep what little pride I felt I had left. Unable to say or do anything to convince them otherwise, I watched as adults who barely knew me decided my fate.

Not only did my school not understand my situation, my friends could not understand why I was unable to go to class after being at school for several months. As far as they could tell, I looked fine. When I stopped showing up to class, they stopped reaching out. The isolation I felt at that point was beyond any loneliness I'd ever felt before. The few times I was able to make it to class, I was bombarded with questions like, "Where have you been?" or even worse, "Why are you here?" My friends saw me receiving academic accommodations for what they only knew as headaches as they struggled to juggle classes, work and college applications. While I could still go out if I felt well enough, I was met with scrutiny from my peers when I did.

So, I stayed home for months on end as the rest of the world moved on without me, in a sort of self-quarantine. I was unable to live my daily life and socialize without the fear of judgement and speculation on how sick I really was. As the months passed, I saw everyone's lives change and grow while I felt like I was still stuck at home, unable to live my own. Sophomore year passed and junior year began, but not much changed for me. My friends began to visit colleges, have relationships and make new friends, all the while I was living in solitude at 16.

It wasn't until my senior year that I was able to return to classes part time. Slowly, my symptoms began to subside just as Dr. Ferguson had said. As the migraines became less severe, I was able to return to normal life. I had already missed out on two and a half years of high school and by that point I felt like no one my age could understand what I had gone through. They couldn't relate to me, and I couldn't relate to them. I watched my friends live out their last year of high school through social media posts as I lay in bed only to go out for my afternoon classes and the special occasion of a doctor's visit. As everyone else celebrated their last year of childhood before college, I mourned the memories I was never able to make.

I graduated high school on time with a nearly perfect GPA and proved each of my teachers wrong. After taking a gap year, I moved to Philadelphia to attend Drexel University and made a new life for myself. When I moved four hours from home, I acted as if my past didn't matter anymore. In an attempt to move on with my life, I pretended like this life-altering experience never happened.

When COVID-19 shut down the world during my sophomore year of college, lockdown and self-quarantining took me right back to my teenage years. Isolation was a familiar feeling, an old friend that I had wished to never see again. As everyone else was complaining, rightfully so, about not being able to go out and see their friends and family, I felt a bizarre sense of closure. I felt like my peers could finally relate to the experience I had, stuck at home and unable to leave my house. This isolation was under a much different, scarier circumstance, but that feeling of separation from the world was there. In this shared experience of quarantining away from those we loved, I learned to find solace and opened up to those who knew me in high school about my experience. That peace I felt was validation for the loneliness I went through. As strange as it may sound, when the world stopped, I was finally able to move on.

Lucy Song

My First Heartbreak

It was a typical rainy day in Seattle, yet it was a day that I will never forget. Outside, I could hear the splash of water hitting the cement as cars drove by and I could see pedestrians ducking under their umbrellas. Inside, I could hear the machines beeping and blinking, along with the numerous dangling tubes. There were hushed whispers, with an occasional voice over the speakers and a sour smell of bed sheets and socks.

It was around 1 or 2 am when a nurse came in to check on my mom, probably to give her more medication to ease her pain. My mother's eyes were closed, her mouth open, lips dry. She looked almost peaceful as if being in the hospital for the hundredth time was normal. I shifted my weight on the small futon to let the nurse through the small crack of space between me and my mom. As I laid there in a light sleep, the memories came flooding back.

I was in fifth grade when I first heard about it. Cancer. Just starting middle school, I didn't know much about it. I didn't understand how much pain and suffering it would truly cause my mom. Yet, every day when she picked me up from school, she had a smile on her face, asking me how my day was.

"Hellllooooooo, mooommm!! I'm hooommee," I announced as I barged through the garage door. On good days, she could walk up slowly to me and give me a warm hug, but on the bad days, I met her in the living room where she sat on her worn recliner sofa chair. The routine was to make her hot tea as we talked about our days. Mine usually consisted of, "Today this person said this, this, and this, and I learned about this, this, and this." While her day usually consisted of, "Today I was able to walk around the house and I took a nap in the afternoon." I tried to make her laugh and smile as much as possible; I wanted to help get her mind off the pain and discomfort. One time, I remember she laughed so hard when I did those Snapchat filters on her. You know, the ones that make your mouth and eyes enormous. Her genuine laughter filled up the room and it made my heart happy. I could tell my grandparents and dad were so glad to see that she was having a good time.

When I was younger, we loved to cook together. She was the amazing chef, and I was her little apprentice. Once, while my mom was ill, I found a recipe on Pinterest that I couldn't wait to make for her. I spent hours chopping up veggies and prepping the meat. When the shrimp sizzled in the pan and turned into that perfect golden-orange color, boy I knew it was going to be delicious. The aroma filled the room as the various meats and colorful vegetables steamed over the rice. I remember how proud she looked when I presented it to her as she lay on the couch. She grabbed her phone and took several pictures, wanting to show off my cooking to her friends. Later when her health worsened she was barely able to walk, let alone cook, so I stepped in to prepare dinner for the family.

I did anything and everything I could to make my mom smile. I realized that I could never repay her for her unconditional love and support. My mom raised a beautiful and loving family while battling a nasty illness. And if that doesn't say superwoman, I don't know what does.

"It's time." I felt a nudge on my shoulder as I blinked my eyes open, back in the hospital room. *What time was it? 8? 9?* I got off the futon and walked over to my mom's bedside. My dad said so many times, *be prepared.* What the hell did that mean? It didn't even feel real. I cupped her soft face in my hand and leaned in real close. "You did so good, mom." I whispered as tears slid down my face. She looked at peace, with a slight smirk on her face like she was going to laugh any second. That's when it hit me. I hate crying in front of people, yet I turned to hug my aunt as tears streamed down my face. I cried and cried till I couldn't breathe.

Not going to lie, the next couple of months were tough. I felt so lost and detached, like I didn't know what to do with myself. How was I supposed to move past this? How would an almost sixteen-year-old girl survive without her mother? I wouldn't get to tell her about my college experience, my relationships, my struggles, my goals, and so much more. I wouldn't get to hear her calm and collected voice, to smell her distinct smell of roses and vanilla, and most of all, I wouldn't get to see her bright, genuine smile.

I was angry. Not at a particular person or thing but just at the world. The person you see every day, you talk to every day, you laugh with every day, is just gone. I was heartbroken for many days, regularly wondering why this had to happen. Why did my mom have to get sick? Why did she have to suffer? Why did I have to lose her? Yet, over time, I was able to rely and depend on my friends and family to get through this difficult time. People would constantly check in on my family and provide any support they could, whether it was cooking numerous meals or taking us out on adventures.

I am not going to pretend that I have healed, because I haven't, but I am working on it. I realized I had two choices; I could sit in my own puddle of sadness and do nothing, or I could pick myself up, work hard, and continue to move through life. I chose the latter because I saw that life was still worth living. I wasn't going to let my mom or myself down. She showed me the stars in the darkness, she has taught me to Never. Stop. Fighting. And that's going to stick with me forever. I look at life from a different perspective now. Instead of thinking, *why did this happen to me?* I now think, *what has this taught me?* Day by day, I began to find myself again by focusing on what I love to do, what the future holds, and what I can control.

My first heartbreak? This is it. My mom's goal was to see me off to college, and now here I am. My mom's strength was so powerful that I somehow channeled it to help me continue through life. As weird as it sounds, I can hear her cheering me on and telling me to keep going. My family's journey shaped me into who I am, and I know she'll be proud if I work hard and love hard, so that's what I strive to do.

Qwuacii Cousins
To My Brother

To my brother

Dear Boise,

You have been gone for a long time, but I need some advice. Those Friday nights we used to venture to the country; do you still remember them?

The middle of the night, early morning rather, before dawn had yet to wipe its backside. The taximen used to recount the stories of duppies[1] they had inadvertently picked up. We used to think that they were smoking something a little stronger than sinsemilla.[2]

Remember when Shady said that he picked up a nurse on the side of the road, in the gorge, just after midnight? He brought her to the address that she gave him and waited for her to leave the car. When she didn't get out, he and the other passenger glanced back to discover no one else was there.

As Uncle Tuku would have said, he sounded like he was smoking rum.

When you left, you left me with instructions to take over the business, you know which one. So that I could protect Mummy, Shirley, and the rest of the family.

But Boise,

Lord, I don't know where to start.

We had a little war with some youths from Corner, but we dealt with them. When I first took over, I thought that the crew only entertained me because I was your brother. However, after I handled the business with the thieving boy Potbottom, they have come to respect me. Six-foot-six, under six inches of grass, as it were. When I talk everyone is on standby. When I say do, they do and if I say dirt,[3] they dirt, like a real executioner.

Remember my one tired black jeans pants and knockoff Clarks boot, with the bottom peeling off as if it were begging for bread? Now bricks[4] and pieces[5] are lined out; so, you know everyone is iced out[6]. We have the city on lockdown. We don't instigate; we don't bother anyone that doesn't bother us. And if somebody gets dropped in our area, they never understood the road code.

Teachers still command a lot of respect. We ensure that they get out and get in safely; children too, to get a better education than we did. The ballers are

---

1   duppies: ghosts or spirits
2   sinsemilla: highly potent marijuana
3   dirt: kill
4   bricks: stacks of money
5   pieces: guns
6   iced out: well dressed

still balling, the field has never been greener, the skills are top notch, and we are reigning champions as always.

Boise, I have been addressing all these other things because I don't know if I should tell you. I don't think you will believe me but Boise, I need to get if off my chest.

Likkle

Chatty Mouth Boy

Likkle,

Do you think this is Dear Pastor, that you can write to me like I'm your agony aunt?

Continuing to talk about the scheme as if you don't know that Mummy tells me everything.

Do you think this is a confessional and I the Father; that you need to lay yourself bare as though you don't know that the gossip ring is in full effect?

Need?

Did I not tell you to stop using words such as "need" and "want" — you sound weak and fearful. We don't fear men we fear God, anybody that looks at us too hard gets dropped like a bad habit.[7]

Get to the point.

Boise

To my brother

Dear Boise,

You know where my luck with women lies but I met the nicest catty[8] the other day.

Do you know what people mean when they say Benz Character?[9]

Jr. Gong[10] can stop searching[11] because I found his jubee[12] right here.

I found her in the country, while walking through Sip Hall.

I was coming back from a dance[13] one of Valentine's sons started a Round Robin.[14]

---

7 Jr. Gong. "Welcome to Jamrock." *Welcome to Jamrock*. Lion's Den, 2005.
8 catty: female usually gorgeous
9 Benz character: describes a woman whose appearance mirrors that of a luxury car
10 Jr. Gong: Damian Robert Nesta "Jr. Gong" Marley, son of Bob Marley, is a Jamaican musician and Grammy Award-winning artiste
11 Jr. Gong. "Still Searchin'." *Halfway Tree*. Motown, 2001.
12 jubee: virtuous woman
13 dance: all night party, featuring disc jockeys and a sound system
14 Round Robin: a partnership among bar owners to save money

You would never guess who I saw.

That boy Murdera.

Boise, time has not done him justice. I wonder if we will look as old as he does one day. I didn't know that people without a passport and visa could still travel. Maybe he could give you the link.

Likkle

Loggerhead Boy

Likkle,

If this were a phone call, I would hang up.

If I were near you, I would clobber you so hard Mummy would feel it.

The girl Likkle, what about the girl?!

How many times do you want me to tell you to believe half of what you see and none of what you hear?

Murdera was deported three years ago and has been living in Boscobel, he only pretends to fly in from America, his baby mother sends him clothes and money.

Next time you write to me it had better be about the girl.

Boise

To my brother

Dear Boise,

Cold sweat a wash mi.[15]

I feel like a sinner in church.

Boise,

As I walked through Sip Hall, me one and God.[16]

When I say "*mi corna dem dark*"[17] this is what I mean.

I couldn't even make out the colour of the shirt I had on. I was taking my time because as you know, the road is narrow and steep, bordered by a gully on one side and hillside on the other.

I got to the bottom of the hill, where the last lamppost is until you get to the hilltop over the other side, where Darling and Hog live.

---

15 cold sweat a wash mi: I feel like I am bathing in cold sweat
16 me one and God: I and God alone
17 mi corna dem dark: colloquial expression meaning you can't see your way out of a situation - verbatim translates to "my corners are dark" in reference to the corners on a roadway being too dark making navigation difficult

As I left the light of the lamppost, I was trying to make sure I didn't go too far to the right and fall over the edge or too close to the left and risk dirtying my shirt on the retaining wall.

It was a good thing that I had sobered up already because if I fell into the gully, I don't think anyone would find my body.

As I continued to walk, the little fireflies ceased their incessant flickering, not that they were providing light anyway, so I didn't pay them much attention.

Then I heard click, click, click behind me.

Through the valley of the shadow of death.[18]

I stopped.

My first thought was which idiot was so brave and so stupid to try an' aim for me. He should have taken his chance when I walked under the light.

Right then, I couldn't even see my hand in front of my face, I was relying on memory alone. How was he going to find me in the dark?

As I continued walking, I heard the same click, click, click.

On second thought, it sounded like shoes.

Then a sultry scent serenaded me.

Now Boise,

No decent girl would be walking in high heel shoes in the dead of night, when the moon and the stars had long since turned their backs and there were no witnesses to provide a description.

I was trying to imagine what she looked like, she didn't walk as if she was afraid of anything. Her footsteps never faltered. She just went click, click, click, like she owned the road, and I was paying toll. I swore she was going to step on me the way she was walking strong.

I decided that she must be a good girl and I started to imagine what she was wearing, maybe a skin-tight skirt, soft silk blouse and jacket. She could work at a bank, or better yet the tax office. Maybe she was a teacher and had just left her class in town[19] to come and visit her family for the weekend.

Boise,

The girl smelled like she looked good. I couldn't wait to see her when we passed under the next light. I was planning on doing the chivalrous thing and offer to follow her home. Make sure she got in safely and that pervert Bangy didn't assault her.

Rhatid,[20] I was planning to carry her home to meet Mummy an' wondering what we were going to name our children. If she wanted to continue teaching—

---

18 Psalm 23:4
19 town: Kingston, Jamaica
20 Rhatid: used to express surprise, bewilderment or frustration.

by then I swore she was a teacher—it wouldn't be a problem but I would support her if she wanted to stop.

Maybe she would want to live in America or the U.K. I could find a house somewhere near you and fly out Mummy too and leave DinDin to look after the business.

Start a different life with her.

10 yards from the lamppost I was gearing up to meet her,

Impress her with my lyrics, can't sound too desperate.

5 yards...

Maybe try a little Kartel,[21]

...*Loving and sincerity is all that my agenda is...* [22]

1 yard...

Boise,

I was ready to meet your future sister-in-law.

I felt like I was at church approaching the altar with my beautiful bride sauntering down the aisle behind me, waiting to greet her, maybe cry a little when I lifted the veil.

I stopped right under the light, my heart racing, palms sweating, ready to meet the new missis.

Boise...

The only thing I heard was the footsteps in front of me.

I swear to you on Pappa's grave,

She did not pass under the light.

the footsteps left from behind me to in front of me with no transition.

Boise, I was so frightened I felt sick.

Only taximen have these stories.

I just stood under the light staring after the sound of her footsteps.

I couldn't even move; my own legs were too weak.

Maybe it was a trick of the night.

Brought about by a fanciful imagination,

Motivated by a lack of sleep

And talent for the dramatic.

---

21 Kartel: Adidja Palmer aka Vybz Kartel is a Jamaican dancehall artiste, record producer and entrepreneur.
22 Vybz Kartel. "Teacher (Lyricist Pt. 2)." *Kingston Story*. Mixpak, 2012.

Boise,

I should have dismissed it.

Guess what I decided to do?

I could beat myself, I should have just gone home to Spanish Town

But no.

Boise,

I sat on it for two days,

Until frustration and curiosity won out.

I told the boys I was staying in the country and put DinDin in charge.

Clearly all those years of indulging in vices had addled my mind and dulled my senses.

I stopped smoking.

I was seeing in 20/20 plus tax.

Every night for the next five days I walked to the first lamppost at Sip Hall and back.

Aunty Lola said she was going to call the madhouse.

Boise, I finally saw her.

Pretty like money.

Clad in white.

A dress.

Floor length.

Gathered on one side and tied at her hip fashioning a thigh length split.

The top draped lazily about her shoulders and cinched at the waist, accentuating her hourglass frame.

Floating in the air, her feet barely touching the ground beneath her.

A vision of beauty.

Her presence hushed all the chirping crickets and even the fireflies seemed to stop and stare. The dress was unfit for the masterpiece in front of me. I doubt one sewn from the stars in the sky would be worthy. In that moment, the sole purpose of the moon, if there were ever one, was to shine on her.

Besotted,

Beguiled,

Bewitched,

So Enticed, Enchanted, Ensnared, Entrapped was I by her beauty, it was only after she had passed, I realised that the click, click, click...

Was a clank, clank, clank,

From shackles around her ankles, wrists, and neck.

...she was a duppy.[23]

Her neck snapped back at me then,

As if taking in my presence for the first time.

It wasn't as though I had said it out loud.

My fight or flight response kicked in.

Boise, I was halfway down the hill, past Darling and Hog's gate before my brain caught up with my legs. It was the quickest I ever reached the yard.

Likkle

Likkle,

Look under the mango tree and you'll see a bottle of seawater.

Shake it up and sprinkle some around the house.

Go to the kitchen, remember to walk through the door backway.[24]

Find the salt and pour some at each doorway, windowsill and around your bed.

Look in Granny's old dulcimena,[25]

Find the Florida water and use some of it to wash your face.

Wet up[26] your head with some john crow batty rum.[27]

You are the only person I know that walks and looks for duppies.[28]

Tomorrow you better find a pastor or a good obeahman[29] to pray over you.

Boise

---

23 duppy: ghost or spirt
24 backway: backwards
25 dulcimena: valise
26 wet up: soak
27 john crow batty rum: highly potent white overproof rum
28 duppies: ghosts or spirits
29 obeahman: A leader in the practice of obeah

Second Place—Fiction

Sanjana Ramanathan

Sweet as a Siren's Song

A twist on the Greek myth "Orpheus and Eurydice," in which the musician Orpheus attempts to lead the shade of his dead wife, Eurydice, back to life.

Eurydice can't remember how she first met Orpheus, just that she doesn't care much for his manner. He's dull, even for a man. His legs are like thin white reeds as they slip into the pond, where she likes to float on her back and sunbathe away from the other nymphs.

But his music—*oh*, his beautiful music. If a single thought of leaving enters her mind, one strum of that lyre chases it away. His song makes grass sway in rhythm, makes the willows weep, makes the birds fall silent to listen.

So Eurydice swims to the pond's edge, pushes the cattails aside to rest her head on the bank... and stays.

A few months pass that way, though Eurydice can't say they've become closer; their conversations are often one-sided. Everyone and everything is in love with Orpheus' voice, and that includes himself.

He spins hymns of his own life stories. He's descended from Apollo, he says. Just look at his godly skill with a lyre! He had travelled with Jason and the Argonauts on their mighty ship. Though he is but a humble bard, he has witnessed bloody battles and beasts!

One day, he addresses a song to Eurydice—more specifically, a proposal. She looks up from the lake into Orpheus' eyes, a soft denial caught in her throat. His company is kind enough, of course. But marriage?

The sweetness of his song still rings in her ears, drowning out her thoughts with a sudden, unnatural lethargy. She feels herself nod.

Their marriage passes the same way, only that Eurydice now listens to Orpheus at a kitchen table, instead of the lovely grove she left behind. He smiles at her each day, tells her that he's the luckiest man in the world, and she the most beautiful wife. The words only fill her with a sense of wrongness.

Then, he picks up his lyre.

Though other heroes populate his songs, his favorite stories still involve himself, his ancestor Apollo, or his time with the Argonauts.

The day he tells her about the sirens, Eurydice sits at the table—splitting open dates and filling them with honey, the way Orpheus likes to eat them. Her motions still as soon as he begins his tale, painting a picture with his voice. Himself with the Argonauts on the great Jason's ship. The siren song luring them towards the rocks. Orpheus strumming his lyre and singing in response, drowning the sirens out and breaking the sailors' trance.

"But how?" Eurydice asks. A date is crushed in her palm, stickying her fingers. "The sirens are such powerful creatures. Surely not even Olympian blood in your veins could defeat them?"

Orpheus frowns at her, bemused as he always is when she questions him. "Perhaps it's not only Apollo's blood in my veins. Some say my mother was a muse. Maybe she was something stronger." He grins. His teeth glint like sharp rocks in the sea.

Then his song starts again, and Eurydice finds herself lulled like a child in a crib—or a boat on calm waters. Her thoughts drown once more in his melody.

When Orpheus is gone, Eurydice spends her time in the meadow by their home. She walks barefoot, letting her feet soak up the morning dew and wishing for the marshy sand of a riverbank.

It's on one such day that the viper sinks its teeth into her ankle. She feels the sharp pain, feels the venom course through her leg, feels her body fall to the ground, then—darkness.

In that darkness, before Charon comes for her, she hears Orpheus' voice. Praying, begging, singing. *"Eurydice, my sweet, come back to me."*

In her last moments, all she feels is utter relief—for once, his song fails and her soul refuses to listen.

Being a shade suits her well. Eurydice spends most of her time floating on her back in the river Cocytus. The strange ghostly flowers of Asphodel bow their heads over the bank to meet their reflections. Sometimes she sings, her voice floating up to join the other joyous wails of the dead. It's peace as she's never known it.

Time ceases to exist, so Eurydice doesn't know how long she spends submerged in that peace before a familiar melody shatters it. She feels herself being pulled from the river, walking towards the palace of Hades as if in a trance. Her feet float towards Orpheus' turned back, his tune a tether.

"Orpheus, please," Eurydice begs. "Leave me be! I don't want to go back."

"Do not worry, my wife," Orpheus calls back. His eyes stay fixed ahead. "All you need to do is follow me. So long as I don't look back, Hades has allowed you to return to life."

"No! I'm no longer your wife. I belong here now. Are you listening to me? Orpheus!"

His hands thread his lyre, and he takes up his song again. The shades part way for him. Eurydice reaches out to clutch at them, but her hands pass through their pallid forms. She begs and begs to be left alone, raising her voice to be heard, but Orpheus' siren song carries on.

Too soon, sunlight shines upon them. Orpheus' laughter is a bewitching melody. "Do you see that, my love? We're nearly there."

Eurydice falls silent in despair, feeling herself start to solidify.

"Do you hear me? Call out to me, my love! I cannot turn back."

An idea sparks in her at his words. She stubbornly clenches her jaw shut.

"Eurydice? Speak to me! Did the Lord of the Underworld keep his word?"

Her silence keeps. Orpheus' fingers tremble against his lyre strings. He bounds forward towards the sunlight, clawing through the crack in stone that leads back to the surface world. Still worried over Eurydice's quiet, for once wishing for her words—he turns back in haste.

Through the gap, he catches a glimpse of Eurydice's closed mouth curving into a defiant smile before she disappears.

Max Gallagher
Confetti Kids

My first concert since seeing *The Wiggles: Live*. Florence and The Machine—a highly revered artist in my friend group. Sadly, our seats were far enough away that she'd be reduced to little more than a figurine. But hey, the tickets were cheap! I'm a slut for a bargain, any time, any day. And my friends and I didn't end up sitting in those seats for long. I'll get to that later, though.

I was carrying a rather large, forty-ounce water bottle with me. Being my first concert in some time, I neglected to consider the inevitable bag and bottle checks that would follow our arrival; I even opted to fill up the bottle extra high right before leaving my dorm. Hydration and all that. The kids love it. It's all they talk about, really. Water *this*, water *that*.

"Water that," the teen exclaims, pointing at a dried and abandoned cicada shell.

Silly teens!

Upon arriving, I was greeted—not kindly, mind you, but with wariness and suspicion—by a beefy, grass-fed man. This security guard asked to look into my bag, which was a high fashion, eco-friendly hemp pouch, obtained from my local *vegan* festival. Yes, that's right: I'm one of *those* people. I'm a *vegan*! When I whine in the night, Mother Earth shoves her swollen and leaky tits deep into my gaping maw, nourishing me with all that she can sustainably provide.

Anyway, my bag was absolutely stunning. I could tell the security guard agreed by the way they handed it back to me without smiling or making eye contact. I was then asked to pass through a full body... metal detector? Scanner? Whatever they're called. The plastic archways in airports. Part of me believes that they're part of a massive conspiracy, truly just plastic archways with no metal-detection abilities, no special powers or properties of any kind. But that's more than a little far-fetched... right?

Just before passing under the archway, I was stopped in my tracks by a booming voice: "Leave the bottle."

Right! Sure. I get it; you don't want me to expose the whole plastic-archway-charade by walking through the "detectors" with my metal bottle and having no alarms go off. I get it! It's fun. It's performance art! Maintaining the illusion. That's cool with me.

I set my bottle down on the conveyor belt adjacent to the 'metal detectors' and tried again to walk through the archway, only to be stopped *again*.

"No liquid in the arena!"

Oh.

Oh.

I see.

Right.

I can't? Are you sure?

Right. Sure. Well...

You've tested my hand.

My friends had already passed through their own respective plastic archways with zero problems and zero cares, ready to see the ethereal being we all paid as little money as possible to see. I saw them looking around in the lobby.

"Where did Max go?" I could hear them all asking themselves.

One of them pulled out a conch shell and trumpeted for my return. Another put up 'Missing Child' posters with my unedited headshots on them. *Unedited.* That bitch. Now everyone in the town is going to know I have acne. The third and final friend was the only one to spot me. "OMG," she screamed into the open air. "What're you doing back there? Why didn't you just pass through the plastic archways like we did?"

They all watched me. Everyone did: the guards, the people in line behind me, the people hiding behind the walls on the lookout for suspicious activity (peeping through the eye holes carved out of those grand Victorian portraits). They had all come to see me and my show—one night only! Tickets are already sold out!

I opened the top of the bottle and looked deeply into the waters. Someone who looked almost exactly like me stared back, with the backgrounded ceilings suddenly so close to my reflected head. I did what I had to do.

"Bottles to the sky," I cried aloud. "Raise them high! In solidarity, in defiance. Raise it!"

A cool, conditioned breeze graced the hairs on my knuckles and the rim of the bottle, now several feet above my head. How did it get that high? How could one bottle be so far away from me and still inexorably linked, so inescapably *mine*?

It happened so quickly.

The bottle tipped. The first few drops fell into my hair, flooding my scalp. I don't think I have *dandruff*, per say, but I definitely do struggle sometimes with a dryer scalp. I felt *relief*. Wetting my shoulders, spilling down my shirt, the endless waters soaked into the fibers of my being. And my clothes! Ha ha, do you get it? Fiber?

It's hard to say really how much water I dumped on that day, but it felt like gallons and it rained for hours, like the sky had opened above me and dropped all of the tension it could no longer ignore. I now carried that weight in my socks. In my briefs. In my ears and in my heart.

The guard looked at me in disbelief. The whole world looked at me in disbelief. I looked at myself in disbelief. Who did I think I was? Who the hell *did* I really think I was? Pulling a stunt like this in a public place? What happened to that sweet child I used to be? Who was this person I saw before me? Are they even me anymore, or have I just gone stumbling past the point of no return? I stepped closer to the security guard, who shuffled back in submission. Their arm passed through the archway—an arm adorned by a *metal* watch.

No buzzers went off.

A silence befell the arena.

I lifted an eyebrow and a finger, and I wiggled them both. I was right! These arches have no real power.

"Shit," they spat from a dry mouth.

I grabbed the guard by the face and looked deeply into their eyes. Winked. Kissed them, gently. And they fainted. All of the guards fainted. Simultaneously. Looks like they couldn't secure me. Not knowing for how long the guards would be unconscious (or how angry they may be when they awoke), I snatched my bottle, kicked down the plastic archway, and leapt over the wreckage of this broken thing we call "public safety."

All of my friends stood, stunned to the point of paralysis. The lights flicked off, and when they turned back on moments later, my clothes were dry. In fact, I was wearing a new outfit entirely: denim on denim. Nice.

"Are y'all ready to go in?"

And they were. We put on our wristbands - and once we put on the wrist bands, we were different people. We had been *banded*. Promoted. It felt great just to be nominated.

We entered the arena.

Several minutes after getting to our seats and snacking on crabby fries— or should I say *crappy* fries? Am I right, ladies (specifically you, ladies in the back struggling with digestive issues)? They tasted very good but also gave me a stomach ache.

It only took a moment's survey of the arena to realize that the standing area, the mosh pit, was ungated, unguarded, and only about half full. Without much thought at all, my friends and I snuck our way down to the pits and injected ourselves deep into the growing crowd, fractionating the distance between us and the incoming Florence (and her machines, of course). One of my friends in attendance, Elyse, said that she appreciated how densely packed everybody was. She could fart as much as she wanted and never be suspected.

Edging our crew were several groups of drunk teens, drunk adults, and one Sober Boy. As the drunkards encroached upon the boundaries we'd established, my crew adopted this lonely Sober Boy. We kind of had to. He was too physically close to us for us not to adopt him. It would be like chewing and spitting out food. Like... you're so close. And you need the sustenance. It's good for you. Just swallow it. You'll like it! And besides, everyone's a stranger until they're somebody. Until they're no longer just *some* boy but *the* boy. *My* boy. One of the crew!

I don't remember what songs Florence sang, and I don't remember how they sounded. I don't remember much of the night, aside from how it tasted. Some song had just begun. We were probably dancing, or maybe just swaying. Me and my crew. *My crew.*

Confetti began to rain down from the ceilings. The pieces started so high up that they were unrecognizable as anything but shards of light and fluttered down at us. A fleet of butterflies inspired by sounds of belonging, even if only for a night. Sober Boy wrapped an arm around me as I looked up in awe. I was everywhere. I was crying. Everything around me was shimmering, the ceilings, the walls, even my crew. The crew. We were all so alive at that moment.

Sober Boy picked a translucent pink piece out of the air and dangled it above me.

I opened my mouth.

He placed it on my tongue, and it immediately dissolved.

"Salty."

He winked.

My mouth opened again involuntarily, hungry for another load.

I snagged another out of the air and held it over his head as his mouth fell open.

I pressed the confetti into his tongue, dragging my finger down his tongue and across his bottom lip. I held his chin and closed his mouth.

Our gaze never broke as he swallowed.

At some point, the songs ended. The concert ended. Everything ends. Sober Boy tried to get my phone number, but somewhere deep inside me, I felt the collision of love and fear. I picked some final pieces of confetti from his hair, and with my crew, we all shared the last tastes of that night: just a moment of salt, flashing across your senses, before fading away.

I hope you're well, Sober Boy. And I hope you escaped before the security guards finally woke up and tore the arena to shreds. Maybe I'll see you again someday.

Katelynn Rudolph

A Dedication to a Bear

When I was eleven years old, I snuck a grizzly bear on a plane. I came across the brown mammal in Houston, Texas, while on a trail walk with my mother. As she strolled down the brown and green pathway, I had gone ahead to get a closer look at the oddly shaped leaves peeking out of the woods and onto the path. I bent down and soon enough, I was face to face with a small cub. However, it did not scare me. I had seen large horses walk through the trails of the park, so a small bear did not seem unusual. There was something about its frail body and silky ash brown fur that gave it a kind disposition. It could not have been taller than three feet, so I could see the reflection of my curious face in its black glossy eyes. Perhaps it was all of these features combined that compelled me to reach out to the small mammal and hold it in my arms. After all, who could be afraid of a smiling bear with a red necktie?

At least, that was the origin story I created for my new stuffed friend. In truth, the bear was a gift from my aunt who lived in Houston when my mother and I visited her home. During my fifth grade of middle school, my mother and I had moved from Philadelphia, Pennsylvania to Houston, Texas. Initially, I was extremely excited to move. I had family in Houston that I had not met before, and I looked forward to spending time with them. Yet that excitement gradually turned into something else. For the first time in my young academic career, I started to fall behind in school. My teachers covered material that was ahead of what I had originally learned in Philly. I struggled with geography, hated mathematics, and deeply missed my childhood friends. Despite falling behind, I refused to ask classmates or teachers for help. The thought felt equivalent to admitting defeat, and my Virgo heart couldn't handle it—plus, I was too shy. Thus, I spent free periods like recess and lunch alone and often kept to myself.

So, when I was face-to-face with the brown bear with the wide smile and necktie, I was a bit skeptical. I had a full-time job as a struggling lonesome student, and I didn't have time to parent a cub too. Would it require walks? Would I have to teach it how to hunt and survive like a reversed *Jungle Book*? About a week after adopting Big Bear (at the time the name seemed appropriate), I learned that he was actually quite easy to raise. As predicted, he was terrible at hunting. However, he was surprisingly good at cuddling, listening, and playing—all the things I unknowingly longed for. After a tiring day of school filled with frustration and isolation, I was always welcomed home by a smiling bear sitting at the edge of my bed. He would listen to my worries and childish complaints, and sometimes had insightful advice despite his young age. In return, I shared with Big Bear the story of his lineage—the creation of the first stuffed bear (although he corrected me to say "teddy" bear, as "stuffed" is considered a derogatory term).

Similar to how Big Bear was raised in the South, I told him how the first teddy bear in America was also born there. One of the few things I remembered from history class was reviewing presidents like Theodore Roosevelt. A fun story I later learned was about the hunting trip he attended in Mississippi on November 14, 1902. When he couldn't find any bears, his assistants tied a black bear to a willow tree for him to shoot. Roosevelt declined the gesture as he saw it as unsportsmanlike. The event was illustrated as a political cartoon that appeared in the *Washington Post* and was viewed by a Brooklyn candy shop owner named Morris Michtom. Inspired, Morris, along with his wife, created a stuffed bear in Roosevelt's honor and named it "Teddy's Bear" ("The Story of the Teddy Bear"). Big Bear contemplated his origin story on the plane ride back to Philadelphia, since etiology interested him.

After about six months in Houston, my mother and I moved to Montgomery County, PA, and eventually back to Philadelphia. I was back at school with friends whom I missed dearly. I was also excited to give Big Bear a tour of the neighborhood I spent so many years in. Before coming to Philly for first grade, I lived in Modesto, California, where I was born. Since then, I moved about four more times. Yet what made the latter time special was that no matter how many times I moved, how many times I had to start over, relearn the geography, and make new friends, I always had my special confidant with me. Big Bear has always been compassionate, and the older he gets, the wiser he becomes. Although he prefers hibernating, he was kind enough to teach me tips and tricks on how to deal with migration that he learned from his cousin the black bear. As for those days when I didn't feel like learning about my "new" homes, Big Bear never hesitated to offer me a shoulder to cry on.

Even during a time of worldwide unrest and fear of Covid-19, my teddy bear was a foundational part of my day. In a *HuffPost* article by Aileen Weintraub titled "I'm a Grown Woman and I Still Sleep with a Stuffed Animal," she explained how her bear, George, became a highly valued object to her. She also wrote about her sickness with Coronavirus and how George stayed with her. Weintraub explained, "When everything seems hopeless, when it looks like we will never get out of the hellfire that is 2020, perhaps it's OK to admit to finding softness and comfort from something as simple and familiar as an old threadbare stuffy."

Following Weintraub's advice, I wanted to dedicate something to my favorite teddy bear for the first time. A special thank you to the bear who was by my side when I was alone in Houston, who accompanied me to my first sleepover, who traveled with me to many states, and who always made my rooms feel like home. Thank you to Big Bear for keeping me company during a global pandemic, and for following me on-campus to be my secret freshman roommate (don't tell Drexel Housing). Despite his brown fur that is now dull and matted from multiple washes, his disproportionate stuffing, his neck that's too weak to hold his head, and his potbelly stomach, he is still the most precious stuffed animal I've ever owned. His eyes still hold that childlike wonder from when we first met in the park trail, and his smile has never wavered a day in his life. He may now be small in size, but Big Bear, you will always hold a large place in my heart.

Thank you.

References

"The Story of the Teddy Bear." *National Parks Service*, U.S. Department of the Interior, 15 July 2021, www.nps.gov/thrb/learn/historyculture/storyofteddybear.htm?platform=hootsuite.

Weintraub, Aileen. "I'm a Grown Woman and I Still Sleep with a Stuffed Animal." *HuffPost*, HuffPost, 29 Aug. 2020, www.huffpost.com/entry/adult-sleep-stuffed-animal_n_5f469ac3c5b6cf66b2b1eece.

Grace Fisher
In Defense of Whom

This essay is about one word, and the word matters. Although the conflict over the word may be emblematic of the cultural battles of our time, full of well-intentioned destruction as they are, I did not write this essay with any political aim. I wrote it, setting aside all broader philosophical disputes, because I fear the loss of something beautiful. That is enough to warrant a thorough response.

In *A World Without "Whom": The Essential Guide to Language in the Buzzfeed Age*, Emmy Favilla, at the time Buzzfeed's copy chief, writes:

> Face it: You hate *whom*. If you don't, you're likely a liar or someone with an English degree who actually still really hates *whom* but can't bear to come to terms with your traitorous hatred for fear of your overpriced degree being snatched from your cold, dead hands, never to be seen again.

This sentiment is reiterated throughout her book, which is a combination dictionary of Internet slang and descriptivist (that is, linguistically majoritarian) manifesto. I found her position to be this profoundly ignorant in terms of harmful consequences. And, sorry, I love *whom*. Thus, my appeal:

To whom it may concern (that is, Ms. Favilla and all her supporters):

Is life not dull enough already? Must we leech every last drop of life and spirit out of our language in the name of ease and a perverted image of democracy? I am sure that I am going to lose this fight; sooner or later *whom* will be obsolete and another bastion of honest eccentricity and quiet refinement will fall, crashing, beautiful in its death, into the rising tide of plebeian utilitarianism, never to rise again from those terrible, efficient depths. (Is that a mixed metaphor? I think not; I can imagine a bastion falling into a tide.) Nevertheless, there is no good reason to get rid of *whom* and there are plenty of good reasons to keep it.

Grammar is a matter of taste. It has to be. It was not discovered, hidden in the laws of the universe; it was not written by a single author; it was not handed to us on a tablet by the prophet of God. Unlike French, English has no official governing body to create rules; to speak of any English grammar being truly, *objectively* correct or otherwise is nonsense. The only criterion left for us to judge by, therefore, is taste. (I suppose one could also argue for a firm majority-rules stance, but even if it were possible to gauge accurately, it would be ever-shifting and hence impractical.) Favilla pushes for a casual approach to grammar, but even she recognizes the authority of some kind of structure and admits that some usages are wrong—after all, she calls the incorrect use of *whom* "the worst offense." Since this structure must also be based on taste, neither Favilla nor I own an inherent advantage; what matters is the potential of *whom* for (linguistic) good or evil.

The case against *whom* is based on several fallacious points: It is not necessary for meaning, it is offensive when used incorrectly while being difficult to get correct, and it is elitist.

Of course, *whom* is not necessary for meaning, but what a misconception of the value of a word! No word with synonyms is "necessary" in a strict sense, but the wonderful value of English is its immense vocabulary, vaster than that of any other language, with millions of words each containing different shades of meaning. "Slender" means the same thing as "skinny" means the same thing as "svelte" means the same thing as "thin" means the same thing as "slim," but each has different connotations and calls up a slightly different concept in the mind of the reader. *Who* used as an object pronoun is not the same as *whom*. It has different connotations—and yes, connotations that are generally not what the writer is looking for, but connotations that are sometimes, as in the case of formal writing, desired! Note that I am not arguing for universal use of whom. At one point in time that was appropriate, but yes, Favilla, language has changed, and I embrace it! I do not use *whom* in casual conversation. My point is merely that whom is not solely a pretentious version of who. Every word that dies is a tragedy in that it diminishes the expressive power of English. Why would we ever purposefully reduce our ability to communicate? Again, I am not suggesting the use of *whom* in all possible instances—but at least leave the door open! Ironically, grammatical conservatives in this case are the more descriptivist of the sides, since Favilla's support for losing the word is essentially prescriptivist. It is Favilla that is creating rigid rules.

So that argument is, hopefully, knocked aside. (See my embrace of linguistic change? I can be reasonable.) As to the argument that it's simply too hard to use *whom* properly, at the risk of being labeled draconian, do better. Of course we should have grace for those who fall into error here, or indeed at any grammatical pitfall, and in fact *whom* is not a particularly easy word to use correctly. But to urge abolishing the word because some people have trouble with it is like banning books because illiteracy exists. By all means, if you are unsure which is correct, use *who*—although it is hard to imagine a formal context (typically the only kind in which *whom* would be appropriate) where, in this age of instant information, the writer could not swiftly and easily check their work.

It is conceivable that the use of *whom* might jolt readers out of a text by its unexpectedness, but I think unlikely—after all, those of us who are proud defenders of the word are hardly shocked and shaken at a technically misplaced *whom*. Our law should be to live and let live—if an author dislikes *whom*, there is no need to use it!

But oh, for that small, eccentric, and passionate fraction of readers who care! To them, how lovely a well-placed *whom* is! Perhaps it is my ego searching for proof of my own intelligence (I do feel a strange reluctance to analyze the source of the feeling) but to me each *whom* generates a small jolt of delight. Each is a cheerful, stylish little wave directly from the author to me, across time and space; a cordial intellectual reminder of the complexity and richness of the language we both speak; even a bit of a puzzle, a genial wake-up call to my brain cells. What a tragedy if *whom* should die.

A more serious criticism of the word is that its use is a sign and tool of elitism. This I wholeheartedly and passionately reject. The solution to a significant section of our population not knowing some piece of knowledge is *never* to suppress it, (how Orwellian that would be!) but to teach it more effectively! Grammar's primary purpose is to facilitate communication. Its *secondary* purpose, which grammarians tend to avoid all acknowledgement of in their over-compensation to a skeptical public, is a self-contained beauty of its own. That beauty, as well as that facilitation, should be shared with the entire population, not destroyed because at one point it was the sole property of the elites! Else why shouldn't we burn all literature written before mass literacy, all art that was created for private collections? Our language and its grammar are a shared heritage of all those who speak it. It would be a crime to pretend it is owned by the privileged few.

Empowerment does not result from the discovery of the right model to impose on society, but from the facilitation of individual choices. If *whom* disappears from our vocabulary, we all lose the expressive power of that choice, as well as the unique beauty of the word itself. If the bell tolls for *whom*, it tolls for thee.

Upoma Chakraborty
97%

You don't understand.

My mother was the protector of protectors.

If the gates of heaven were to be embodied in a person,

it would be her.

Always watching, always keeping the bad away,

always guarding the innocent.

So radical in her ways, I thought of her as wicked growing up.

But I understand her now.

So I didn't understand,

when it happened to me, because it happened to me.

The first time was quiet and shy,

like my small footsteps walking downstairs afterwards;

perhaps even forgettable.

The second time bold and brutal,

there is no analogy that would ever suffice.

And in the same way it happened to me,

it happened to almost all other women.

I sometimes wonder if it happened to her,

in a life before my own.

I don't understand,

if someone like my mother had failed,

perhaps it was never her fault at all.

Most of life's worries, after all, traces back to uneducated sons.

Yet it is always women picking up the pieces,

and hiding the trauma away deep in her womb,

wanting to protect the next life

from the life she has known.

So, then you must understand,

why I am awake at night during these ungodly hours

and thinking.

Thinking one day I will be a protector,

and if the math is correct,

I too,

will fail.

Geneva R. Gigliati
Birthmarks

I was born with Orion's Belt across my back,
Destined for a few arrows.

Fell in love with a boy at eighteen—
His fists made of fire,
Car full of bottles,
Closet full of skeletons,
Words of what I called love,
I became a mirror;

'Drunk' just another word for 'Clueless—'
'Clueless' another word for 'Innocent—'
How I dreamed of being innocent.

I walk with keys between my knuckles,
Knives in my fists,
A chip on my shoulder—
Orion: A hunter,
His belt on my body,
I will not be hunted.

Honorable Mention—Poetry

Sanjana Ramanathan
Sita's Trial by Fire

This is what it means to wed a hero:
the heat of flames before your feet,
the crackling laugh of smoldering wood.
Praying before a pyre
of your brother's making.

For years, your prison has been
green gardens and fresh air;
you almost welcome the fumes.
(Your love's silence chokes
more than the smoke.)
Your purity will protect you; you know.
The flames will spit you out
like a fishbone,
you'll make lotus petals of the lit coals
with your toes,

> but in the moment before you leap
> you feel not fear, but grief
> You mourn for the faith
> you did nothing to lose.
>
> Your own blind belief
> will burn with you.

Writers Room

Introduction

Writers Room, now in its 9th year, is a university-community literary arts program engaged in creative place-making and art for social justice. We are a diverse intergenerational collective of students/alumni, faculty/staff, and neighborhood residents whose work demonstrates a desire for collaborative opportunities in our joint communities.

This year Writers Room enjoyed its first full year in our space in Ross Commons. We offered workshops, classes, and student-run open mics. We organized special events for notable authors and produced numerous publications, including *The Story So Far*, which brings together our creative work along with research produced by the Second Story Collective. The offerings in this year's *The 33rd* were written by a student, a faculty member, and a community writer and were first published in *Anthology 8*.

Learn more about us at writersroomdrexel.org.

—Valerie Fox, Faculty Writing Fellow with Writers Room

Kirsten Kaschock
More than a Sonnet

It came to be I met a man some few years beyond
my years. His kindness stirs in every move, his mind
a searching one. He likes to get things right, to put
things down, to understand the how and why and what
of life. There was a fire once, a girl lost to time
on Olive Street, where his younger self could be found
on occasion, when he wasn't in school or on a train
South to spend summer with his kin. He became a man,
branched out, got his degree, he lived in Panama, he taught.
Still does. Each place, each word I've lived through him has
taken root and grows in me. The way a thing was
is the reason it is—the meaning it takes on, it got
from how he tells it. How I'd love in all men to plant
a seed of the fierce, dancing soul of the poet Norman Cain
who transforms pain to truth by how he learns to know it.

Cosmo Randazzo
C# Reprise

That night, I heard

Nothing from you.

Nothing, nothing, nothing.

I keep part of it,

As in rusting

There is no better cradle

Than a scrapheap for

Frames with sturdy bones.

Every now and then, I

Peel off an electric blue,

Berry red, daisy yellow wrapper,

"Low-fat, low-cal, low-sodium,"

Studded to a pavement

By rainfall and animals.

I keep all of them,

As paintings do paint.

There could be a day

For us, and real,

Real color—

Soft as wind chimes.

Lakes of pores for us to

Touch, dip, find

It is egg-shell canvas I miss

On the steeled arm.

Carol Richardson McCullough
The Anatomy of My Hilltop

The handprint design represents a genealogy of my childhood neighborhood. I grew up in the Black section of a white neighborhood called South Hills in Charleston, West Virginia. It is my understanding that it has since been gentrified, like much of America, but back in the day, from the late 50s up through the beginnings of the New Millennium, that vanilla sundae had a concentrated dash of chocolate sprinkles augmenting its flavor with sweetness.

So as not to mix metaphors, let's get back to The Hand. The palm print is made up of my immediate family, the center-most part of my being: my mother, my father, and my sister. Both of my parents were teachers, my mother, sixth grade elementary school, and my father, high school phys. ed and health, along with coaching. My dad was a great athlete in his time, a football star on the West Virginia State College (now University) HBCU team. Sports were in his blood, and throughout his career as an educator he also coached football, basketball, and track during the school year, and Little League-Farm League baseball during the summers. My mom sponsored the school safety patrol group, and each year took three classes of gangly sixth graders on a bus trip to our nation's capital in May, usually on the weekend of Mother's Day.

That's true dedication, being off mothering other peoples' children on a holiday designed to celebrate you. My mom and I were close from the moment I was conceived til the moment she passed away, and then beyond. She died a young 59, but she filled the years we had together with enough love to last my whole lifetime. My father lived a longer life, passing away a month after he turned 80. This gave us time to get to know each other, and me, to understand and appreciate him with a fullness that would never have been had he been the one to leave this earth first. Some aspects of his nature I did not understand until I got older. Others, not until I had children myself. If he were still alive, I would first apologize to him for all I must have put him through during my brief time of mild rebellion. Then I'd ask him about his experiences as a Black man in America for the first three quarters of the last century. I'd have a book of Wisdom, for sure...Mama and Daddy were a team, she the Ying to his Yang; he the strong provider to her sweet and nurturing spirit. They held and supported me during my childhood growth and encouraged me to reach for the skies beyond the mountains.

I also had a sister nine years my senior, Elizabeth Ann, or Tibby as many called her. That age difference made for some interesting (challenging) times between us growing up. At first, I am sure she must have looked upon me like a living doll who actually cried and pooped, to cuddle and gently brush my hair and pat me to sleep while singing soothing lullabies. As that wore off when I began to grow and command language and develop my own curiosity, she most likely resented my getting into things while unknowingly stealing some of her thunder and grabbing attention that had previously all been on her. We moved through our childhoods like an ocean wave, cresting in admiration and love, then crashing with irritation and resentment. We were in different stages of development. Sometimes we got along. Others, we conflicted. I like to say, in the early years, I was into dolls while she was into boys. At times I was a little snitch who thought it my duty to report on things I peeped that seemed like reportable offenses. She often warned me, "Don't tell Daddy." Other times, she looked out for me, and taught me things, and played the big sister role with grace. We shared a bedroom in our small two bedroom house, so nobody had any real privacy. But then, when she actually married the guy she was sneaking around with, and moved out of the house, we became the best of friends, for a good long time. But later, the wave crashed on some differing opinions-turned-squabble, and we each kept to ourselves. Time passed and we were on good terms again. However, there was one major fall-out of our adult years that left us permanently estranged. Ebb/flow/crash/burn-to-ashes in an urn. Read between the lines....

Continuing a downward gaze, that's me at the base of the palm right on top of the arm. I guess you could call me The Wrist, a moveable joint. I lived in my father's house at that neighborhood location for half of my life, but I have also moved around—off to college, into the deep south, back to reality, working in the DMV, then settling in Philadelphia, the northernmost point of my re-location. I became a teacher just like my parents. Had they become lawyers, or doctors, or even criminals, I loved them so much I would probably have grown up to be just like them. Who knows what I would be had I had more time with them? Now, I toy with being a writer-poet, staying flexible, flexing as needed.

But looking back to the Hand, bordering the palm are digits representing extended family members who lived close by—across the street, up the hill, beyond the field, down the way. They were born in a house across the street from the one where I grew up...so that mid-50s date I gave earlier actually goes back to the turn of the two centuries, late 1800s or the early 1900s. I know my mom was born in 1913 in that house. She was the third oldest child of eleven, I believe. Several uncles eventually moved off of The Hill once they married and started their families. One aunt moved to the midwest. But two of my uncles remained in the neighborhood, building their houses within two blocks of The Homestead. They show up as fingers at the end of the palm. The two other fingers represent Gran, my step-grandmother who lived across the street from me and next door to the birth home I'll call The Homestead, and Aunt Sally, my grandfather's sister who lived up the street and around the corner from me in a little pink house. (Sample John Cougar Mellencamp here, briefly, then cut the music because we mostly listened to Motown Soul music back then.) Sidenote: Aunt Sally was instrumental in shaping my childhood development. She babysat me from the ages of three to five, from the time my mom went back to teaching until the year I started first grade at the elementary school where she taught. Sally was a former schoolteacher herself, and she was a strict disciplinarian. She gave me the advantages of daycare, pre-school, and one-on-one homeschool kindergarten all rolled up into one. She taught me to mind my manners, toe the line, and act like a little lady. Looking back, I think she is the reason that my sister and I were so different, after you account for the nine year age difference. She did not have the same strong influence upon my big sister. But that is another story for another project....

This leads me to the last digit, The Thumb, which signifies my Aunt Isabelle, known as Sis to her siblings and Aunt Sis by her respectful nieces and nephews. Come to think of it, there was that one cousin who thought she could stop using the Aunt title once she reached her teens. Ha!

That child almost did not make it into her fourteenth year, but she did learn to show her Elder some respect. Aunt Sis lived across the street from me, in The Homestead, next door to Gran. I used to love to walk across the street to visit her, first with my mom, then as I grew older, by myself. Her house was small to have contained thirteen or so people growing up, but it held a lot of stories and a lot of love. A few items of her furniture were antiques from when she was a child herself. I remember a Victrola she let me crank to play a vintage 78 rpm record we listened to, and a big brass double bed in the back room where her mother had given birth to all ten of her siblings assisted by a midwife who lived a block and a half away. When my grandmother died a year or so after my youngest aunt was born, Aunt Sis laid her dreams of a college education to rest and stepped up to help her father, my grandfather, look after her younger siblings until he later met and married Maime, the step-grandmother I affectionately called Gran.

Gran was cool. She had smooth, nut-brown skin that stood in sharp contrast to all her light-skinned step children and even her new husband. She was short and bow-legged, and she had a goiter on her neck that concerned me as a child because the growth seemed so big I thought it must have hurt her. She assured me it did not. I found a picture of her not too long ago. Seeing her image now, as an adult, the goiter is not nearly as large as I had remembered. I guess I am bigger now, and that is what makes the difference. One other thing to note about Gran is that she rubbed snuff. Yes, that's right. I guess she was what kids today would call a badass. She had a little Mason jar (or was it a soup can) she would sit at her feet as she sat on the sofa, or in her favorite chair, or on the front porch, and every now and then she would pick it up and spit the juice in it, discreetly. This was years before the Surgeon General warned us all about the dangers of carcinogenic tobacco products. Plus it was in the hills of Appalachia, so yeah, my Gran rubbed snuff. On occasion she would send me to the corner store three blocks down the hill to buy her a tiny can of it, and she would give me a nickel for my effort. I would purchase penny candy or a single-scoop ice cream cone and feel like a little big shot.

But Aunt Sis was the Real One. She never had any children of her own, but she had a house full of siblings who grew up to give her many nieces and nephews, all of which to love. She lived in that family Homestead house all her life, buying out her siblings' portions to place her name solely upon its deed after Papa passed away. That house is where she was born, lived, and actually died—in the bathroom, steps away from the antique brass birthing bed in the adjoining room—slumped over an antique original claw-foot tub, while drawing water for her morning bath. Since a hand does not have a backbone, a spine, I placed my Aunt Sis in the thumb position.

Thumbs play a key role in the grasping mechanics of the hand. They are vital to its dexterity, its ability to smoothly function effectively. Aunt Sis was a vital extended member of our family. She became revered like a matriarch on my mom's side. She was the one who took my mother to the hospital the night I was born, and was one of the first people to meet me as I came into this world. The day before she passed away, we spoke about her upcoming eye surgery that next morning. I could hear a hesitation I took as fear in her voice, so I assured her I would stop by to check on her after my other aunt brought her back from the out-patient procedure. But her heart gave away that morning while she was preparing to leave, drawing water for her morning bath. She did not even have time to place the stopper in the tub. As I entered the house when Aunt Frances called me before the ambulance arrived, the water was still running. We went solemnly into the bathroom, and there she was, on her knees, slumped over the tub, reaching, hand gracefully poised on the faucet. Before she could even complete placing the stopper, Death had taken her home to Glory. So I was one of the last to see her on this earth. We had a closeness, from beginning to the end. I carry her sweet memory with me, even today.

Continuing this anatomical reflection, if you look down underneath the hand and wrist, there are rows of names positioned to represent other Black families, the arm of the neighborhood, the couples and their children who were all friends of my family. They were teachers, an artist, a lawyer, a doctor, postal workers, a department store mailroom clerk, coaches, a seamstress, a hotel bell captain, retirees, a truck driver, the "first Black fashion buyer for a major department store in our city," a principal, and the Director of the West Virginia Department of Mental Health/Division on Alcoholism and Drug Abuse, who gave me my first summer job right after my high school graduation. We children looked up to them as models of Black Excellence as they pushed forward in a society that constantly tried to hold them back. These grown folk nurtured, provided, loved, and protected our spirits as best they could with however little or much they had, to set us on a path to a more perfect future, in spite of the times' imperfections. They...WE barbequed, danced, played cards, studied, rode bicycles, played all kinds of ball games, held luaus in the summertime, dreamed, partied, worked hard, laughed, cried, lifted each other up, cared for our sick, sat by the bedside of the dying, inspired, hoped, rose, raised families, respected elders, built friendships, loved, made love, looked out for one another, worshipped—All in the shadow of Jim Crow and his Uncle White Supremacy, a cancer on the body of the America we fought, bled, and sometimes died for, too.

This hand holds many memories, some bitter but mostly sweet, stories yet untold.

Faculty Writing

Introduction

Faculty writing reflects current, published work by Drexel University faculty. These texts have previously appeared in academic journals, books, conferences, magazines, newspapers, and websites. These examples of fiction, poetry, satire, essays, memoirs, and personal narratives serve to demonstrate all the wonderful forms that writing can take. Each piece is a product of their lived experiences and expertise, and come together to form this poignant and thought-provoking collection.

—The Editors

Jennifer Britton and Gwen Ottinger
Let's Start Crafting Environmental Policy
Through an Anti-Racist Lens

The effects of climate change will hit communities of color first and worst, due to long-standing patterns of segregation and redlining.

Creating an equitable, sustainable Philadelphia requires integrated solutions, but these cannot be limited to strategies that aim for a vaguely defined greater good. Initiatives that improve the environment "for all" are likely to perpetuate structural environmental racism. Conversely, initiatives that foreground the needs of the most vulnerable tend to work to everyone's benefit. Explicitly anti-racist approaches are necessary.

Environmental racism is a well-recognized phenomenon. By design, pollution concentrates near communities of color, who are also the most vulnerable to the effects of climate change. In Philadelphia, that includes intensifying summer heat and the kind of persistent flooding that the Eastwick neighborhood contends with. Government programs to address environmental injustice focus on one community at a time, as issues flare up. Their solutions don't address underlying capitalist and racist logics that allow environmental hazards to pile up in already-vulnerable communities.

Policies to address other environmental problems, including climate change and pollution, are seldom designed with consideration for how they may differentially impact people of color—and thus often end up reinforcing structural racism. The federal Clean Air Act makes cities and regions accountable for average pollution levels, but not for levels in the specific communities where pollution is most concentrated. Pollution trading schemes, meant to reduce greenhouse gas emissions overall, have been shown to increase the exposure of communities of color to pollution.

Pursuing equity and sustainability together requires a paradigm shift. Environmental policy cannot continue to treat environmental racism as a problem that exists as a discrete challenge, or that can be solved independently of other environmental issues. Rather, all environmental policy needs to take an explicitly anti-racist approach.

Anti-racist environmental policy would prioritize protecting the health and well-being of people of color and other groups most vulnerable to pollution and the effects of climate change. Organizations like the Climate Justice Alliance and Philly Thrive envision replacing extractive, polluting industry with a new economy that offers sustainable livelihoods for people of color. Policy makers should work with organizations like these to translate their vision into policy. It should reject polluters' demands to be treated as "stakeholders," and instead recognize them as entities invested in activities known to endanger human life, especially the lives of people of color.

An anti-racist paradigm for environmental policy would also honor the knowledge, insight, and creativity of people heavily burdened by pollution and climate change. Communities of color are experts on their own conditions.

They can see the subtle and not-so-subtle ways that environmental problems intersect with health disparities, food insecurity, economic injustice, and police brutality.

Anti-racist environmental policy would establish community knowledge as on par with that of credentialed scientists, engineers, and health professionals. While undeniably important, the knowledge of credentialed experts is neither infallible nor all-encompassing, and it is inflected by cultural biases associated with class privilege. Integrated approaches to sustainability and equity require a diversity of insights, from the earliest phases of problem definition.

The defining challenges of the 21st century—equity and sustainability—cannot be solved separately. The City of Philadelphia will need to invent anti-racist environmental policies to secure the city's future. Adopting two guiding principles—prioritizing the health and livelihoods of people of color, and valuing the expertise of communities impacted by pollution equally with those of scientists—will make the city a trend-setter in environmental protection.

Paula Marantz Cohen
The Seminar Course Can Save Civility

When well run, it combines free speech with a safe space.

The only college courses I remember taking happened around a seminar table. I became an intellectual at those tables by talking about ideas in an intimate, authentic way. Now, I teach seminar courses, and when I walk into the classroom for the first time in the term, I am always moved by the faces around the table, by their distinctiveness and willingness to open their minds to me—and each other.

The seminar format is sometimes called the "Harkness table," derived from a gift by Edward Harkness to Phillips Exeter Academy in 1930. It is associated with liberal arts schools that pride themselves on small classes and seasoned teachers. And yet the seminar is not a luxury. It is fundamental to the education of resilient, thinking citizens. This is especially true in the era of isolating social media.

To put this in the terms of the present moment: The seminar course combines free speech with a safe space. It reconciles two ideas that have recently come into conflict within academia.

Free speech used to be a sacrosanct, nonpartisan value but has lately been subject to qualification in some left-leaning quarters. The assumption is that certain kinds of speech and even singular words can inflict psychic pain. Establishing a safe space is a physical response to this apparent threat. The theory goes that college students can't learn if they feel vulnerable or experience mental discomfort.

If free speech is now seen by the left as an excuse for hateful and hurtful speech, safe spaces are decried by the right as excuses to shut down disagreement and encourage liberal coddling.

The seminar reconciles these warring values. When well-run, it is both free and safe. In this setting, students feel empowered to speak their minds. A good teacher can discern from the faces around the table the tremor of disagreement or the blossoming of an idea, and can tease out a thought that, no matter how initially incoherent or divergent from a mainstream view, can be clarified and discussed with civility. Once encouraged to say what they think, students tend to remain engaged. They grow more comfortable and more fearless, as well as more willing to change their minds.

My canvassing of former students shows that the courses they remember most are those that happened around a table. They say that these courses taught them to see themselves as people with ideas, as well as interested in and open to the ideas of others.

We respond to people around a seminar table as we would to those around a dinner table. Experiencing this intellectual intimacy improves our judgment and makes us more humane. A seminar is a safe enough space to allow for free speech and civil disagreement. It models encounters that can spill from the classroom into life.

Tim Fitts
Gigi

I recently visited my buddy in Santa Clarita for his fiftieth birthday. It's a treat, in a way, knowing all the things that might have killed you haven't killed you—you can ease up on yourself a bit. It's nice, too, seeing a good friend emerge from middle age. He likes his kids. He likes his wife. I like them, too. The dog, though. Gigi, a poodle. Gigi is so old, she's gone bald on her back, and what's left of her fur has turned a strange type of purple, as if the purple had been applied by a generic brand of cosmetic powder. *Gigi*. Even the name is purple. On top of it all, Gigi is deaf and blind. She roams the house like Roomba, but joyless, seeking neither heat nor affection, bouncing from kitchen cabinet to garbage can, to the fridge, then back to the living room sofa and coffee table. Outside, Gigi roams from one side of the yard to the other. Fence to fence. Lately, however, a pack of coyotes have caught wind of Gigi. The coyotes live in the patch of wilderness that separates my buddy's neighborhood from the next. Keen to Gigi's disabilities, the coyotes have altered their game, abandoning the tactic of feigning gimp or playful, hoping to lure the dog into their grips. Instead, the coyotes have begun baiting the back of their yard with strips of jackrabbit.

During the birthday weekend, I found myself standing in their backyard staring at the patch of desert, sipping a cup of coffee or a Knob Creek, depending on the time of day. I started wondering why a dog like Gigi would even be worth their trouble. By the time the coyotes ripped her apart, how much meat would any of the coyotes even get—just enough to make it to the next meal? Hardly worth the caloric effort or even a fair return on their investments. On the last evening of the trip, though, just before the drive back to LAX, my eyes somehow penetrated the tangle of sagebrush, I spotted one of the coyotes hanging about. The thing had been looking at me the whole time. Probably tracking movements, counting my drinks. He was thinking way past that rabbit.

Tim Fitts
YMCA

The topic in Danny's Trans Am was the movie star we had seen at the YMCA pool, Warren County, Ohio. Had I not watched the movie star act on television throughout my childhood and been disappointed in his movies once his television career ran its course, I still would have noticed him in the same way dogs recognized wolves as wolves and we recognized chimps as apes. Similar, but different. First of all, the reflection of sunlight on suntan oil caused him to shine brighter than the rest of us, the glare just visible through the tangle of young girls, basting him with application after application.

The conversation changed, however, as we drove back to Danny's house, and we spotted a dead gopher in the middle of the road. We heard the thump against the floorboard, like a baseball bat, but when we turned around, the gopher had disappeared. Somehow, the TransAm had scooped up the carcass had stuffed it somewhere in the undercarriage. We knew it had been scooped the gopher, because we backed up and looked on the side of the road. We looked underneath the car, under the hood, behind the wheels. We knew the gopher remained with the car because the TransAm stank for weeks. The science of it was simple. Enzymes and microbes broke down that gopher bit by bit, wafting up dank and moist, so wretched you could taste it. We drove the car through puddles, through the car wash, jumped it over the railroad tracks, trying to jar it loose, but nothing worked.

A few weeks later, when school had started up again, Danny walked out of class after school to find that somebody had rolled his car in the parking lot, demolished it completely. Windows smashed, tires set on fire with black char up all four sides, upside down with the roof caved in.

Long gone were the thoughts of the movie star, why he had been in town, how his family was actually connected to organized crime and he had come to lay low, or the group of teenage girls splitting apart like vultures when he stood up to walk over to the high dive and climbed the ladder. I'll never forget it. He bounced thrice on the diving board, spread his arms wide, suddenly curled his body into a spin, then straightened his form, slicing into the water.

Valerie Fox
Belongings (in Six Boxes)

You could still carry your belongings in six boxes, in the small, maroon car. Records, books, paints. You make a detour, 2 a.m., to say goodbye to C., your childhood friend. You help her tidy up. She sings, tries to get you to stay. But you doggedly fly west.

The smells of the milky foods that C. had placed in the backseat make you queasy and hungry. Nevertheless, you're back on Street Road, where you first started. Unkempt warehouses stare, peripherally. People with strained looks mingle in lots. You pass them by and immediately forget their faces.

After twenty miles you miss the sign for the way you've been told. Another entryway is closed. A shadowy person waves you aside. Without map or GPS, you're being pulled in the wrong direction. You're looking for the river you know, scanning the sooty gray view.

On Red Lion Road you still have plenty of gas. If you spot the celebrated statue of Don Quixote, you'll know which way points west. Alas and oh boy. This was last night's dream. You're in a baking competition and keep getting partnered up with oddball Mr. Maloney, your middle-school math teacher. You hear a breathing sound coming from the front area, inside your car.

Soon you pass into a gated community, then back out. A sign looms: New Hope. You're going that way. They have a nightlife. You can ask, *where should I settle down?*

When you were a child, you spoke as a child, you thought and acted like a child, and Jesus was everywhere (a code for everything). Now you're 18. Eventually, after several more hours, you spot an alert coyote, red-eyed. One long look. Your heart flutters. The expansive road narrows. A fireman reaches into your window and shows you a number, saying, *here, turn here.*

Valerie Fox
Your Intemperate Life

Before you stopped believing in the God your parents feared, before you searched for your birth mother, before the heavy stick struck, before I was crouched by the snowy window and you said "let's get married" over the phone, before you realized your mother (the one you had) could not make out the patterns of words and learned everything by rote, before you forgot to go to the promising job interview with the pharmaceutical-maker, before our last night of silence in your childhood home on the steep hill, before you understood that you had to turn your head like a bird so that your good eye could see straight, before the metal company, before the world got too small and possessed only you, before the mine your father worked closed down forever, before the path winding through stacks of newspapers in the attic, before twenty years-worth of furry dust coated the framed picture of your last dog and, it's a good thing your mother did not live to find you there in her threadbare goose-neck chair and we didn't have kids of our own.

Henry Israeli
Survival Song

They were tough motherfuckers
with their tattoos, their stories
of hiding beneath floorboards,
under bales of hay, trading cigarettes
for crusts of bread, climbing out of pits
of bodies still warm, turning left
instead of right or right instead of left,
losing parents, brothers, sisters, husband, wife,
losing sons, daughters, then starting new families
before the ashes in the air settled to the ground,
before the last breath of the last SS officer
swung from a rope at Nuremberg.

My father's uncle was one—
he pulled his parents' killer out
of a bar at gunpoint and shot him
in the head. He jumped off a moving
train headed to Siberia. In his eightieth year
he buried his horse with his own hands
in his own yard on his chicken farm
in New Jersey. So tough were these
men that when they cried
the room quaked around them,

and when they died the air collapsed
into the lonely nowhere they'd held open.

Miriam N. Kotzin
116 Plan B

Love may change

leaf meal to leaf,

leaf to blossom,

blossom to bud.

Now I may be

blossom, blossom,

blossom, but what

will love do when

I am no more

than a bare branch?

Miriam N. Kotzin

A Scholar Flunks Romance

Nessa called Pete insensitive. Jack, she said, had watched the moon rise and recited poetry. To please her Pete studied haiku.

He took her hand the next full moon, "What cold light shines there, lantern hanging from bare branch, the full moon rising."

She pulled away, disgusted. "Risen," she said.

Miriam N. Kotzin
Daylight

Resetting the antique clock was an occasion—my mother stood behind me, coaching. Because the hands couldn't be moved counterclockwise without damaging the mechanism, the "fall back" reset required a progression through eleven hours. I opened the glass door covering its face and, using my index finger only on the minute hand, began the journey. As I approached every half-hour, she'd tell me to slow for the bell. For the hour, with its numbered chimes, she had more instruction. "Pay attention," she said. "Give each chime a chance to ring." Stopped now, that clock's silence offers more warning than advice.

Miriam N. Kotzin

Lessons

I rolled the paper
with your name
to a tight scroll,
my scrawl hugged
to itself like
a profession of faith.

You told me
yesterday is rain
in a desert   rain
in an arroyo
waiting with sentinel
cottonwoods   rain
water over rims
water cascading
water falling
into red rock
torrents
slot canyons
Red Rock
Antelope
Zebra
Echo Bell
Little Death Hollow.

You told me
today is a parrot
pale as her cuttlebone
you taught
pretty girl pretty girl pretty
girl to whistle the first
bars of "Casta Diva"
taught her to love
to cling to swing
on her pretty girl perch
to cling to the bars
of her pretty girl cage
a cage
I tell you is not
tomorrow.

Miriam N. Kotzin
Penmanship

Pete left his poetry on Nessa's pillow. *Moon light rain rose ribbon moon snow bone stone moon moon hair eyes lips moon light moon.* When "seas' curling fingers caressed the moon dying on the sand," Nessa scrawled a loopy "swill" in red marker. He read "swell" and wrote longer poems.

Lynn Levin
Student Rebellion

9:15 a.m.

The revolt against the humanities faculty begins as student rebels halt professors in the middle of class and usher them to the quad. Some of the professors assume that they are being led to an assembly honoring them for their service.

Rebel leader Gillian Jones passes around a box and orders the professors to hand over their pens and paper.

"From now on, no writing on dead trees," orders Gillian.

"And no reading from them either," chimes in cell-phone poet Billy "Bullz" Rohrer.

"How are we to jot down a thought?" Dr. Leon Babbage wonders aloud.

"Or write in our planners?" asks Dr. Nia Stone.

9:40 a.m.

The captive faculty mingle nervously as rebels march another group of professors into the quad.

"The more the merrier," says Dr. Kelly Donaldson.

"I love a good mass roundup," says Dr. Gloria Jiménez.

"Detain them in the library," commands Gillian.

"Not the library," counters co-leader Franklin Li. "They love the library."

"Yeah, no," replies Bullz. "Lock 'em in the computer center. They hate computers."

"No, yeah," says Karim Mohammed.

"Yeah, no," says Yael Cohen.

Gillian, Franklin, Bullz, Karim, and Yael herd the teachers into the computer center.

Stone says that she needs to use the ladies' room.

Gillian hastily tapes a "Gender Neutral Bathroom" sign on the nearest men's room. Glowering, Stone stomps into the facilities and strides past the urinals, some of them in use. Grateful to find a stall with a door, Stone attends to business. Why the term "gender"? What's wrong with the word "sex"? Does sex sound too sexy to them? When she was in college, she was all about sex. Had a lot of it, was a big fan. Yes, those were the days.

11:00 a.m.

The rebels torture the professors by forcing them to learn a new online teaching platform. Once the professors have mastered some of the basics, the young radicals send through an update that completely changes the system.

"We still have the power of grades," whispers Jiménez to Dr. Louis Greenbaum.

"Whom do you think you're kidding?" says Greenbaum. "They'll grind us down with their wheedling emails like they always do until we put through a grade change."

"I'm starving," moans Babbage.

"Hang in there, Leon. Maybe they'll bring in some non-allergenic, non-GMO, nut-free, gluten-free, organic, soy food," encourages Dr. Rita Chang. Images from the movie *Soylent Green* float into the consciousness of several of the faculty.

12:30 p.m.

Gillian arraigns the detainees. "We hereby charge you with criminal use of the sexist pronouns 'he, him, his' and 'she, her, hers' and your anti-progressive refusal to accept 'they, them, their' as universal gender-free singulars. We condemn your refusal to use the terms 'Latinx' and 'alumnx,' and we condemn, in advance, your refusal to use any x-suffix inclusive terms yet to be invented."

She takes a breath, "We call for an end to the time-wasting teaching of long works, such as novels and epic poems."

"From now on, it's flash fiction, haiku, and tweets," interjects Bullz.

"Furthermore, any so-called textbooks are to be provided free online."

"There go the royalties," sighs Babbage.

"You get royalties?" asks Donaldson, shooting Babbage a jealous glance.

"Our PDF Liberation Organization will upload all books to free open-access websites," says Franklin.

"That's theft of intellectual property!"

"Piracy!"

"Copyright violation!"

The professors shout out their protests, knowing that they are helpless before the tech-savvy rebels.

"And no more essay writing. Multiple choice tests and PowerPoint decks only," adds social media chief Elsie "L-Z" Lockhart, scrolling through their cell phone.

"How are you going to learn anything?" challenges Greenbaum.

"EduSnack Packs," Karim replies. "All prepackaged and free online. Gives students the highlights. Easy as popping Skittles."

"At least I won't get a backache from toting twelve pounds of books in my knapsack," says Chang. "My arthritis is killing me."

"And my bursitis. Don't get me started about my bursitis," adds Dr. Pete Milano.

"Does anyone know a good cataract surgeon?" inquires Stone. "Getting to be that time for me."

The young rebels shake their heads in pity. Karim fiddles with their nose ring. Yael adjusts their "Cancel Gender!" button.

"We furthermore accuse you," says Gillian, "of white privilege, Black privilege, Asian privilege, Latinx privilege, and Boomer privilege. We accuse you of homophobia, heterophobia, transphobia, and all the other phobias now known or yet to be developed. You stand accused of Islamophobia and antisemitism, the teaching of dead white male writers and live white male writers. We call for an end to syllabx and lecturx." The manifesto covers a dozen more biases and insensitivities.

"No lecturx?" says a perplexed Babbage. "How will I share my knowledge?"

"You give lecturx?" says Chang. "Leon, no wonder you're exhausted. You should just show videos in class like me."

2:00 p.m.

The rebels mercifully allow the professors to order their own lunches by old-fashioned phone calls. After lunch, the captives must face the horror of the gender-neutral necessary.

Yael, Karim, and Bullz break the professors into groups for intense self-criticism sessions. The professors apologize for their sexist and non-progressive use of outdated forms of grammar, obsolete pedagogy, flagrant use of paper, failure to offer trigger warnings before discussing disturbing material, unconscionable tolerance of opposing opinions, rejection of cancel culture, and every other social offense and insensitivity, real, imagined, or future.

"We trust that you will take this re-education session with the utmost seriousness," declares Gillian.

"Remember," warns social media chief L-Z, brandishing their cell phone, "we have command of Twitter, TikTok, Snapchat, Instagram, Facebook, and all the other platforms, plus we're on every professor-rating website."

A shudder runs through the captives. How often had they been pilloried on the professor-rating sites, always surprised by what mild remarks ignited fierce offense?

"We can hack anything," says L-Z.

Gillian makes a hand motion as if to tell the powerful social media chief to tamp it down.

"Remember when we used to say don't trust anyone over thirty?" Stone whispers to Babbage.

"Now, it's people under thirty," he laments. "It's either that or depend on them."

"Remember when we protested the war in Vietnam? Remember Black lib, gay lib, women's lib, and farmworkers rights?" says Jiménez.

"Now I feel so nostalgic," says Chang with a faraway smile. "My husband and I met at a sit-in."

"Maybe we brought this on ourselves," muses Milano.

"You think?" says Stone.

4:50 p.m.

The student rebels order the teachers to pose for a group mugshot. Milano extends his middle finger and covers it with the fist of his other hand. He nudges his colleagues to do the same. Soon all the professors, wearing sly smiles, display the secret gesture.

L-Z snaps photos and posts them on social media.

A torrent of responses pours in about the hand signal.

"Are you making some kind of elitist, Boomer privilege, retro hippie, white power, racist hand signal?" accuses Gillian.

"Not at all," 'splains Milano. "This is a sign of solidarity among the people of the remote Brazilian Amazon. Quite well known in progressive academia. Trending, really."

"We should try that," says L-Z. "We need to be more woke."

All the rebels form the gesture and salute each other with it, their faces glowing with new conviction.

5:00 p.m.

"I have to get to my job," says Yael.

"I have a midterm tomorrow," says Karim.

"My parents are expecting me for dinner," Bullz pipes up.

"I could use a martini," says Babbage.

Gillian gathers the rebels. They all give each other the secret gesture. Gillian dismisses the professors.

"We'd like our pens and paper back," says Chang feeling bold.

"Fine," concedes Gillian. "Just don't use them to write anything."

"We hope this will not affect our grades," says Franklin.

"No, yeah," says Greenbaum, attempting the senseless affirmative-negative collation popular with the youth.

Franklin stares darkly at Greenbaum as if double-crossed.

"I mean, yeah, no," Greenbaum corrects himself.

"No, yeah," says Karim.

"Yeah, no," says Yael.

"No, yeah," Babbage jumps in, thinking that logically the interjections should negate each other. Then he wonders if the "no" is a serious "no" or if the "yeah" could be a "yeah" of goodwill followed by the "no" of gentle disagreement. Gentle disagreement. That would be nice, but was the world ready for it?

Leah Mele-Bazaz
Second Sight

On our honeymoon, my husband and I had the same dream. We found ourselves lost in the red rocks. On our last morning in Sedona black ravens lined the fence, with Cathedral Rock in the distance. I waved my phone around for cell service, to check in on my family, worried the birds signified death. When I got a connection, no one had died, but I couldn't shake the feeling of those dark eyes and lush black feathers watching over us. I rubbed my belly with a sense of foreboding.

*

My great-grandmother was born with a veil over her head. Also called an "en caul birth," this is when a baby emerges out of the birth canal tucked inside its translucent amniotic sac. In Norway, many people believed that this rare occurrence meant she was gifted with second sight, something that I believe was passed down to me on my maternal side. I've always had moments of intuition that I've never been able to explain.

At twenty-six weeks gestation, I tended to the cornstalk dracaena in our apartment, clipping off the stale yellow leaves. The plant was the only other living thing in my husband's condo before we met, and it was a prized possession. We tended to it dearly. Suddenly, I heard a voice in my ear. *Your baby has died.* There was no one around me. Had the plant spoken? I decided it had to be anxiety, a manifestation of my innermost fear.

*

My back began to spasm as the epidural wore off. A nurse unhooked my arm from the fluids and antibiotics. My husband groaned as he got up from the plastic chair and guided me to the bathroom. He helped me undress. He turned on the water and tested it until it ran warm, the steam from the shower fogging up the mirror. A baby screeched from somewhere down the hallway, which caused the hair on my neck to rise.

The shower rid me of the coated blood between my thighs. I did a slow dance around the low water pressure, cupping my hands to catch the water like it was something sacred. I scrubbed the hospital soap against my skin. I looked at my body: the gooey tape marks from the I.V in my arm, my flat belly looking sad and lifeless, caked in hardened blood. I scrubbed harder, avoiding the water spreading to the bandage on my back.

I stepped out of the shower slowly, careful not to slip. My husband dried me off with a coarse towel and opened the overnight bag. He had been in a rush when he packed the overnight bag, packing the wrong size pants, no underwear, and a sweatshirt. I returned his innocent smile. We made do. He tried to help me with my winter coat, but it zipped easily, no more baby bump for the zipper to get stuck on.

*

When we arrived home, the cornstalk dracaena needed water. My husband froze when he went in to water it. One of the three stumps was completely uprooted and had fallen onto the floor. We'd often said the plant's three branches symbolized the three of us: husband, wife, and baby. Now one of us was gone.

*

My great-grandmother also had a daughter who died young, at the age of sixteen. The girl was deemed unfit, institutionalized, eventually dying of pneumonia at the state facility. *That's how things were back then*, my mother said, trying to help me understand.

I raided the fridge for a drink. I could only find the champagne we had planned to pop when we came home with our baby. When my husband entered the kitchen, I held the bottle up. His expression looked pained.

"Let's go," he said. "We need a proper breakfast."

At the restaurant, my blood orange mimosa was the first thing to arrive on our table besides the water. I washed my Lorazepam down with the first sip. Before I left the hospital, one of the doctors had given me a prescription, although he technically wasn't allowed. Extenuating circumstances, he said.

The champagne tasted bitter on my tongue, acidic with the fresh-squeezed orange juice. My steel-cut oatmeal arrived moments later. The last thing I'd tried to eat was the fruit from the hospital's sympathy basket, which had been sent to my room. I took a small bite, but dropped my spoon with a clatter when I saw a woman with a stroller passing by the window.

Jealousy coursed through me and I felt the tears start to come. I wondered if we would ever try again to have a baby, but somehow that felt like a dishonor to the baby we'd had to leave behind. It dawned on me that I didn't know where the hospital stored the babies who had died. I felt like a terrible mother since I forgot to ask.

*

A few years ago, the ghost of my great-grandmother materialized in the corner of my bedroom, just days after her death. Against the dim glow from my laptop, she appeared youthful, with her blonde hair curled under her chin. She looked happy. I wondered if she had been reunited with her daughter.

*

Back home, I was still bleeding. On the bathroom counter, my toiletries looked like a still life of my former existence. My cocoa butter for stretch marks was left out on the counter next to my prenatal vitamins. I swept the items into the drawer.

As I stripped down, I looked at my naked body again. It seemed even worse under the bright lighting. My breasts were red and agitated. A swollen rash on my back from the epidural was beneath a bandage on my spine. I ripped the bandage off.

I ran a bath, dipping my feet in first, even though the water was so hot they turned bright red. I squatted down and slowly sunk myself in. My engorged breasts floated like ocean buoys, close to three times their previous size. I traced the faint brown line extending down from my navel to my pubic hair, something I hadn't noticed before. As I followed the path down with my finger, a thick, white drop of breast milk escaped from my nipple and trickled into the water like a teardrop.

*

My first funeral was for a young girl. A middle school classmate had a sudden brain aneurysm that took her life overnight. We had history class together and a few days before her death, we were assigned to work on a in class activity together about Otzi the Iceman.

Side by side, we read through a chapter about the accidental discovery in the Alps of Europe's oldest naturally preserved mummy, found encased in a block of ice. We brainstormed ideas about what this discovery could mean. I cringed to look at the page with Otzi's shiny leathery skin, while she traced her hands around the image.

At her viewing, I bravely walked towards the casket, unlike many of my classmates. I peered over the casket; she was buried in her pajamas with a teddy bear in her arm. I blushed at the intimate scene, as if someone gently pulled her from her bed and placed her into the casket. She didn't look dead, only frozen in time.

*

I don't remember much about those three weeks I had off from work. I moved like molasses. I continued to drink. I refused to wear my maternity clothes, so I wore the same pair of green sweatpants. I could feel the eyes of the doormen in my apartment building looking at me with pity.

Sleep was pointless. My breasts throbbed without ice. I woke up from dreams about holding my baby again, and my nipples leaked through my pajama blouse. In my dreams, I didn't believe my daughter was dead. She was *my* baby. My sleeping baby. She was so beautiful, so peaceful, but certainly not dead. The doctors had it all wrong.

Do all parents go through this denial when they lose a child?

*

In the end, we chose to cremate her. I collapsed onto the kitchen floor when I sensed the moment she burned. My skin was on fire. I regretted not having a proper burial. She could have rested next to my great-grandmother's daughter.

*

On my first day back at work, I was still bleeding. My large maxi-pads felt like a sponge at overcapacity and gave me rashes. My body didn't fit into my pre-pregnancy clothes; my cotton midi-dresses were the only things that fit.

My thighs were pale from lack of sunlight and twice their normal size, full of fatty white cellulite. I went from being a glowing pregnant girl to a barren one. My dresses were too short because of my weight. My face lost its glow. My large breasts sagged. My hips were too wide. I walked around the office embarrassed and exposed. I took the back door to bypass the bullpen of men whenever I had to use the restroom.

*

The lady on the suicide hotline was very kind. I explained to her that my transition back to work had been terrible, and that I felt like a failure. I told her about the blame I imagined others felt towards me and, even worse, my own self-blame. My doctors tried to tell me that I had done nothing wrong, that gestational death can occur with no reason. People told me I should work through my grief, and since I couldn't, I thought, *how would I be able to survive this*? My own body was incapable of sustaining life. So why should I be able to live?

"Oh dear, that's understandable. It's good you gave us a call," the woman said. She gave me resources for local support groups, and asked if I had a therapist.

*

I told my therapist I dream about death because I think I will see my baby again. That's a normal response to grief, she said. I didn't want to push my luck and tell her about the woman in white who seems to live a parallel life with me. I see the woman behind my eyes when I'm about to fall asleep. She's not a dream, more like a premonition. I see her in a long white dress, rocking my baby on the same rocking chair I was rocked in when I was a baby. *Just wait*, the ghost tells me. *This will be you soon.* I think of the Iceman and self-preservation. I think of all of the little girls who died, and I think of my great-grandmother, who lived until she was one hundred and one, all those years without her daughter. I plead to her ghost to keep my baby safe without me, until we meet again.

Don Riggs
Occasional Communities: Academic Conferences and Arthurian Romance

One type of partially self-selected community is the annual academic conference, in which people who are within a particular range of interests and educational backgrounds commune for several days to a week once a year, or some similar arrangement. David Lodge's novel *Small World* explores one such type of gathering, which is of literary scholars in the humanities. He follows a set of characters from conference to conference for nine months following the interlacing plot structure of the medieval Arthurian Romance tradition. In so doing, he implicitly compares characters in Northrop Frye's Romance mode with parallel characters in Frye's Lower Mimetic mode. The element of the Fantastic is present in the element of Coincidence, which plays a major role in untying a very tangled knot of human interaction. Although the "realistic" Lower Mimetic fictional mode discourages belief in the existence of miracles and other quasi-magical forces, as when certain scholars dismiss Jesse L. Weston's identification of the Grail with a pre-Christian Celtic fertility ritual, Lodge directs his characters to coalesce and disperse following the *entrelacements* of the Arthurian quest cycles, which are shaped by what Jung would call "meaningful coincidence" and result in the discovery of the Question, the asking of which has a transformative and rejuvenating effect on the "world" of the international academic community.

The *Oxford English Dictionary* defines "community" as "[a] body of people who live in the same place, usually sharing a common cultural or ethnic identity." Hence: a place where a particular body of people lives. In another entry, a "community" is said to be a "body of people practising communal living (esp. with shared ownership of property) on ideological or political grounds; More generally: a commune." The stipulation that the members of a community live together is lifted in a "group of people who share the same interests, pursuits, or occupation, esp. when distinct from those of the society in which they live." An ecological definition turns the focus onto a "group of animals or plants in the same place; (*Ecology*) a group of organisms growing or living together in natural conditions or occupying a specified area."

A related term is "fellowship," as in: "The people collectively with whom a person habitually socializes or associates, esp. with reference to their (usually unsuitable or dubious) character." This of course, is in a deprecatory sense. A broader definition would be: "The fact or condition of being in partnership or alliance with another specified person or entity; (as a count noun) a partnership or alliance. Also: membership in a group, society, confederation, etc.; (as a count noun) an instance of this." The group of knights of the Round Table is referred to by Quene Gwenyver as a "felyshyp" (524), which is a community of a special sort. On Pentecost, when the Holy Grail floats around the Round Table, giving each knight a taste of the dish he finds the most delicious, and then leaves, all of the knights leap to their feet, swearing that they will pursue the Holy Grail—in Malory, "the Sankgreal"—in a quest that will not end until they find it. I refer to Malory's version of the Queste of the Sankgreal, as it is the most familiar one to English-speaking people—except, of course, for the much more recent *Monty Python and the Holy Grail*, which shares many motifs with Malory's text, although not, perhaps, the same purpose.

The sense in which a "community" is defined in part by physical proximity is alluded to by King Arthur when he laments, "I am sure at this quest of the Sankegreall shall all ye of the Rownde Table departe, and nevyr shall I se you agayne holé togydirs" (520). However, the knights shall continue to feel a sense of belonging to this "felyshyp" through all of their individual adventures, in which they will frequently encounter each other as if by chance, in a structural device known as *entrelacement*, or the interlace, in which knights who have parted on separate journeys occasionally run into each other and share an adventure before they part again. This is the device that allows David Lodge to bring his various fictional academics together at various conferences around the world and then send them on their separate ways, to return to their home educational institutions.

Not every event in Malory's text corresponds to an event in Lodge's *Small World*, but the 20th-century author avails himself of many of the motifs and structural gambits from the earlier text. One of these motifs from the Malory is the frequent appearance of a small chapel, or hermitage, or other similar hut inhabited by an isolated religious devotee such as a monk or hermit where the wandering knight can ask for advice or directions to their current destination. In Lodge's text the information booth in an airport frequently serves that function. Cheryl Summerbee is at the information desk for British Airways for Persse McGarrigle—possibly an embodiment of Percival—to ask where he can obtain a copy of Spenser's *The Fairie Queene*. No airport bookstore has such a title, although one helpful person points to a section on Gay Literature. However, miraculously, or perhaps coincidentally, Cheryl has a copy of that thick text with her. Persse is astonished, and admits that he thinks her reading is more on the lines of the Bills and Moon type of romance, when Cheryl responds, "I used to…But I've grown out of that sort of book. They're all rubbish really, aren't they? Read one and you've read them all." She continues to note that "[r]eal romance is a pre-novelistic kind of narrative. It's full of adventure and coincidence and surprises and marvels, and has lots of characters who are lost or enchanted or wandering about looking for each other, or the Grail, or something like that" (258). Lodge has given one of his characters the line that describes both Arthurian Romance writing strategies and his own, at least in that novel.

Coincidence, one of the features of "real romance" that Cheryl Summerbee lists, is defined by the OED as, among other meanings, "[a] notable concurrence of events or circumstances having no apparent causal connection." Such coincidences are frequent in Malory and other Arthurian texts, with a possible subtext that Divine Providence has determined that a certain knight will encounter a certain maiden under specific circumstances to test, or perhaps to display, whether said knight has the qualities allowing him to rise to the challenge. Modern readerships substitute Divine with authorial providence, as the author is the creator of the imaginal world, the characters, and can move them about as their creative spirit dictates. Even if authorial providence was assumed in the age of Malory, that author can always take refuge in the pose that he is translating from "the Frensshe Booke," indicated by such statements as, "HERE LEVITH THE TALE OF SIR GALAHAD AND SPEKITH OF SIR GAWAYNE" (534) and "HERE LEVITH THE TALE OF SIR GAWAYNE AND HIS FELOWYS AND SPEKITH OF SIR GALAHAD" (535). Malory seems to be implying that the story he narrates is structured on the events as recounted in the source text.

Lodge seems to be following a similar conceit, although he nowhere mentions a source text beyond the statement of Cheryl Summerbee above. However, his novel is a very intertextual narrative, as it starts with a translation of the Prologue of Chaucer's *Canterbury Tales* and continues with one of the characters quoting the beginning of T.S. Eliot's *The Waste Land* (3). The character Miss Sybil Maiden, a student of Jesse L. Weston, constantly remarks upon the origins of various practices in pre-literate rituals, reminding the reader that much of what passes for modern "realistic fiction" is in fact much more primitive but disguised in modern clothing. An unnamed "Oxford medievalist" states that this 'business of phallic symbolism is a lot of rot.' He stabbed the air with his knife to emphasize the point" (12). With this clever bit of business Lodge manages to highlight one group of academic curmudgeons— though, admittedly, more of another generation than our current 21st century group.

Small World sets up a world-wide network of connections among literary scholars as well as authors of novels and writers of poetry, translators, essayists, and editors, with one poet and scholar in particular, Persse McGarrigle, connecting many of them by coincidental encounters in his quest for love. Miss Sybil Maiden appears at many of the same conferences, Morris Zapp of Euphoric State and Philip Swallow of Rummidge, a red-brick university in the U.K., are merely the kernel of the nut that represents academia as the fellowship of wandering knights. It is this network that I am suggesting as the "occasional community" of my title, ignoring the geographical element of many of the definitions from the OED. The discontinuous nature of this network is like *Neuromancer's* character Ashpool, who opts for cryogenic life extension, described in the novel like a series of brief blips of light along a multiple years'-long line of continuity, the frozen parts of the line corresponding to time teaching at institutions of higher education, the brief blips of light corresponding to the once-annual conferences.

One other type of occasional community generated by scholars that encounter each other at unexpected times over the years is that of the publication, access to which has increased many-fold due to online databases. In researching for this paper, I came across a paper by Siegfried Mews, who had taught German at UNC-Chapel Hill when I was a grad student there. I never took a course with him—my languages were Romance—but I knew him by sight, and heard him speak at the Philology Club. "The Professor's Novel: David Lodge's *Small World*" was published in 1989, seven years after grad school for me. It gives one an overview of a literary scholar's take on the novel about literary scholarship, introduced me to Garrett Weyr's 1988 novel set in Chapel Hill, and sets the academic farce in the context of what Mews calls

"Lodge's metafictional stance" (714). Mews objects to "an expression of Anglo-American prejudice" in the reduction of two Continental literary points of view, the feminist-Marxist theory of Fulvia Morgana and the Reception-aesthetic of Siegfried von Turpitz (725).

All of which is to say that there is a range of moral and other personal qualities both in the occasional community of literary academics in the turn of the twentieth to twenty-first centuries and the knights of Arthur's Round Table in Malory's work. Certain Arthurian motifs have parallels, whether intentional or not, in Lodge's small world. For example, in Malory's *The Quest of the Holy Grail* there are ships that a knight will board, finding it to be without crew or passengers, and that sails as if of its own volition to a destination evidently in the destiny of that knight. This is not original in Malory; in Marie de France's 12th-century *lai* "Guigemar," the titular knight boards an unmanned vessel, complete with a bed covered by sumptuous blankets or *duvets;* the knight lies down on the bed and wakes up having been transported elsewhere, to a tower imprisoning a maiden claimed by an older knight. In Lodge's novel, there is an awards ceremony being held at a ship, the *Annabel Lee*, tied up on a piling on the Thames. A contemporary novelist, Ronald Frobisher, one the of Angry Young Men, has an altercation with an Oxonian literary critic, and leaves the ship. He unties one of the ropes holding the ship to the dock, and the other rope snaps, letting the ship to drift downstream (175). Where the passengers end up is withheld from the reader. Oddly enough, that seems to correspond somewhat with a steamboat ride taken by member of the ICFA at Beaumont, Texas.

In some ways, the occasional community of literary scholarship and creation is ideal for the participants: blending escape from the quotidian travails of first-year composition, visits to exotic locales, and interaction with peers of similar interest, with collegial interaction on theoretical and plot-driven levels. At the same time, people are still people, and incompatibilities can be lived with only so long until they drive people apart. So it is in the realm of Arthur where knights slay each other and of literary criticism where critics and authors slay each other with words.

Works Cited

Lodge, David. *Small World*. Penguin, 1984.

Malory, Thomas. *Works*. Clarendon Press, 1971.

Mews, Siegfried. "The Professor's Novel: David Lodge's *Small World*." *MLN*: 1989, 713-726.

Gail Davida Rosen
Curtain Up: Teaching the Broadway Musical

Broadway was closed, and a global pandemic meant my Introduction to Honors/Broadway Musical Disasters course in the Fall of 2020 and my Broadway Musical in American Culture course in the Winter of 2021 would be taught remotely. Would these students, many trapped in their childhood bedrooms, want to watch and discuss musicals? As I wondered if we would ever see a live performance again, I learned that these students watched with family members, friends, and roommates, and with great care and attention.

Patterns emerged. Each class had students who performed in musical theater in schools, students who were musical theater fans, students who knew little about musical theater but wanted to learn more, and students who had little or no connection to musical theater. Yet all of them found a way to connect. Students encountering the outrageous stereotypes in Mel Brooks' *The Producers* found it hilarious and were puzzled that any of their classmates were offended. These students wrote and spoke with great passion about the evils of cancel culture. Also, students debated the misogyny and toxic masculinity in *Guys and Dolls*, marginalized groups and capitalism in *Rent*, and gender roles and stereotypes in *West Side Story*. As a Stephen Sondheim fanatic, I was delighted by the how much the students loved *Into the Woods*. One student compared it to chemistry class, explaining that she was told that inorganic chemistry would make sense of all the lies told in general chemistry. She saw *Into the Woods* doing that for fairytales, as the show, "exposes their flaws, and rewrites them to make real sense to us as adults." These students always found relevance to their lives and current times in our musicals.

In the fall of 2021, I was thrilled to be in person with the students in my Aging/Musical Theater class, even though we all wore masks. Like their predecessors, many shared my love of musicals, and others became fans. One student wrote that after watching the original Broadway cast film of *Into the Woods*, she was "inspired to return to the theater again, and even opened a separate tab in search of a local musical I could attend within the coming months. (Let's all go!)" I found this group of first-year students to be particularly discerning. They listened to each other and considered different points of view. They saw nuances. While they acknowledged issues with stereotypes and casting in *West Side Story*, many said that their parents were immigrants, and they recognized the difficult experiences of the immigrant characters in the film. Several students stayed after class to try to organize a class trip to the Spielberg *West Side Story* film. Although the term is over, they are still sending me e-mails about it.

Sitting in the dark and listening for the first notes of an overture always fed my soul. Although it has been over two years since I sat in a theater to watch a Broadway musical, somehow, those students and courses fed my soul even more.

Scott Stein

Excerpt from *The Great American Betrayal* (Chapter One)

Our second case was a real humdinger, which everyone knows is the most challenging variety of dinger. Maybe I'll tell you about it some time, if you have the required security clearance. Right now, however, I'm telling you the story of our third case. It might not have been a humdinger, but it more than made up for that by being a real can of worms.

If this doesn't impress you, it could be that you don't realize just how challenging a can of worms is. Perhaps you assume worms are easy to manage because, as invertebrates, they're generally spineless. You might be thinking, *Nothing to worry about here, just a can of worms.* You might even be saying to anyone who happens to be passing by, "Have no fear, a can of worms is actually pretty easy to handle. It's just worms in a can, after all."[1] And maybe, just maybe, you could be right that a can of worms is really no trouble, but of course that's assuming you kept the lid closed.

"Arjay, what did you do?" famous private detective Frank Harken[2] asked. "Did you take the lid off the can of worms?"

"Yes," I said. It was true. If you're wondering why I had a can of worms in the first place, if you're imagining I'm some kind of insane bot who carries around a can of worms everywhere for no reason at all, you can rest easy. I had a very good reason for carrying a can of worms. We were fishing. Yes, for fish. It was our first time visiting the Great American Lake. It wasn't a naturally occurring body of water—you'd call it a humanmade lake if humans had made it, but they hadn't. As always, many years earlier, bots had done the heavy lifting[3] while people pointed at what they wanted done and where. The lake was twelve acres and shaped like a kidney, which was one of the most popular shapes for a lake. It was encircled[4] by a smooth walking path and enough synthetic grass for people to spread out blankets and enjoy a lovely lakeview picnic. The ceiling didn't look like a ceiling. In the Great American, they often didn't. Projectors and screens created the illusion of drifting cumulus clouds, puffy white against the blue sky above and all around to the treeline on the distant high walls. It was a beautiful spring day at the lake, like every other day of the year.

The rowbot on the floor in the center of our canoe was a squat rectangular chap with two long flexible oarms. One oarm alternated paddling on either side of the boat to propel us through the water; the other oarm stretched back to the rear of the canoe and steered. The canoe was a simulated western red cedar dugout, a perfect plastic wood replica that had an official stamp of authenticity on its side. When the rowbot ceased paddling, we glided another 45.72 feet and came to a rest. A floating breezebot breezed us at a relaxing, moderate setting.

---

1 And they might be wondering what you're talking about, especially if they're carrying a can of not-worms, or a jar, or nothing at all.
2 You've probably heard of him, because that's what *famous* means. If you haven't, don't worry—you can learn all about him in my chronicle of our first case, *The Great American Deception*. However, if you decide to read about it, be warned that even though it wasn't a humdinger, it was quite a doozy.
3 In this case, the heavy lifting was mostly digging.
4 *Enkidneyed* would be more precise, but that isn't a word.

Unfortunately, despite the breeze, Frank Harken was not doing a good job of relaxing. "This is complete chaos—our worms are everywhere!"

This was not literally true. At most, it was partial chaos—there were plenty of places our worms were not. Most places, really. But indeed a few worms had wormed their way to the front of the canoe and others were worming toward the back. So, if it wasn't exactly complete chaos, it wasn't quite perfect order, either.

"Arjay, why'd you take the lid off?"

"I had never met worms before. It seemed only polite to introduce myself."

"Worms don't do introductions," Harken said.

He was right. Rudely, the worms had not said hello nor offered to shake any of my four hands before wriggling every which way out of the can and all around the canoe.

"What are we even doing here, at the lake, of all places?"[5] Harken asked.

"We're fishing," I reminded him. "It's generally preferable to do that near a body of water."

"I know we're fishing." He held up the fishing rod as evidence, in case I'd forgotten that he was a detective. "Why are we fishing?"

"We already talked about this. It's our eight-day-iversary and we're at the Great American Lake to celebrate and get some well-deserved relaxation. I asked you what you did to relax on the outside, and you said you used to fish when you were a boy. So here we are."

"Here we are. And I said I went fishing a couple of times, not that I *used to fish*."

"I'm not seeing a distinction." It's true. I wasn't.

"You badgered me for days to tell you about my childhood outside. 'I want more backstory,' you said. And to get you to give me a moment of peace, I told you about how my father took me to the reservoir they kept stocked with bass, and we fished there. I told you he took me exactly twice, that we caught nothing at all, that it didn't matter anyway because the bass probably weren't safe to eat. Both times, my father didn't say a word to me the whole day. It wasn't some magical bonding experience. I barely remembered it. Somehow you heard all that and concluded that this would be relaxing for me. I swear, this is the last time I let your incessant badgering[6] push me to do something I don't want to do."

---

5 Not to be confused with The Lake of All Places, a water amusement restaurant that could simulate any known location. For example, molk (mall folk) could eat dinner while seeming to cruise across Lake Eerie, Lake Tahoe, Lake Superior, or even through the canals of Venice, New York, or Mars, among many other choices.

6 It was his second mention of badgers even though that species was not known for lake-dwelling and we hadn't seen any at the Great American Lake. We had seen a family of beavers building a dam by a small inlet that led to a filtration system. They were not badgers despite having the same number of syllables and letters and some letters in common. Frank Harken was not much of a taxonomist.

Just then a rainbow trout leapt from the lake and landed in our boat. It flopped around a bit, like a fish out of water, which is an expression but also exactly what it was.

"Good job, Frank Harken. You've caught another one." It was the eleventh trout to jump into our boat. I had set the fishing level to easy.

"This isn't fishing!" Harken said. "Fish aren't supposed to leap at you. Arjay, I've humored you long enough today. First of all, *eight-day-iversary* isn't a thing—"

I stopped him right there. "—It very much is a thing. In the Great American, 68.3% of new couples celebrate their eight-day-iversary. Furthermore, all versaries are a thing if you believe in them. In fifteen more days it will be our twenty-three-day-iversary, and we'll celebrate that as well. The beginning of a partnership as great as ours should be commemorated as often as possible."

Harken looked at me and slowly shook his head. "I wasn't done talking. That's why I started with *First of all*."

I conceded that this was a valid point. "I would be happy to hear your second of all."

He didn't seem to have a second-of-all in mind, hesitated, then found one. "Second of all, we are not a new couple."

"Frank Harken, I know math is not your specialty, but I believe you do know that there are two of us. That's what *a couple* means. And we've only known each other for eight days, which makes us new. Hence, we're a new couple."

"You're being too literal. *New couple* implies a romantic relationship. You know, the kind that usually involves two members of the same species, and not a man and an appliance. You do understand we don't have a romantic relationship, right?"

"Of course I know that," I said, a little insulted that Harken had the temerity to think he was my type. "We're partners. But we can still celebrate our eight-day-iversary. Speaking of which, I got you something."

"What do you mean?"

It was a strange question. What could it mean besides my having got him something? "I mean I got you something."

I held out a wrapped box with a bow on top.

"What's this?"

"It's a wrapped box with a bow on top. It's a gift."

"I can see that," Harken said. "What's in it?"

"That's not how opening gifts works. There's supposed to be the element of surprise. That's why it's wrapped. You have to unwrap it to find out what's in it."

Harken might have been losing patience with me, which I gleaned from his shaking head and his clear articulation of the words, "I'm losing patience with you." We would never have a relaxing eight-day-iversary at the lake with the mood he was in. I handed him a cup of coffee.[7] As always, he received the life-affirming beverage with gratitude and took a sip. And as always, sipping the coffee helped Harken find some of the patience he was losing. He accepted the wrapped box with a bow on top and began the arduous task of removing the striped wrapping paper—I was a thorough gift wrapper, but after one minute and twelve seconds of determined ripping, he succeeded in getting to the box and opening it.

"It's a hat." He was quite perceptive. "Why would I need a hat in the Great American? There's no sun or rain, no weather at all in most locations."

"This isn't just any hat," I said. "It's a fedora."

"I don't see why the kind of hat matters. I still don't need one."

"Frank Harken, you're a private detective. You should wear a hat."

"Detectives don't have to wear hats."

"They don't have to, but the best detectives do. For example, Sherlock Holmes, perhaps the greatest detective of all, was known for wearing a deerstalker. However, since we're not in the woods very often and even when we are there's little chance we'll be stalking deer, that didn't seem like the best choice of hat. A fedora, though, is always in fashion, and some truly great detectives are known for wearing one."

"Please don't list all the detectives who wore fedoras."

"I won't. There are some great ones, of course, like Sam Spade and Dick Tracy. But the fedora has also enhanced the heads of such famous non-detective adventurers as Indiana Jones[8] and Leonard Cohen."

"I know the songwriter but haven't heard of the others. Anyway, I'm not wearing a hat. And don't argue with me—it isn't up for discussion."

Frank Harken could be quite stubborn. I had expected as much, which is why I'd purchased a hat that fit *me*.[9] "Well, I can see there's no use trying to persuade you." And I placed the fedora on my own rounded top—you might call it a head if you insisted that this is where hats had to be worn, though my top didn't look like a head or contain components found in most heads.

"Arjay, what are you doing?"

"I'm wearing a hat."

"You look ridiculous. Coffeemakers don't wear hats."

---

7   This might be a good time to tell you that I'm a coffeemaker. If you already know this because you've read *The Great American Deception*, feel free to ignore this footnote. Use the extra time to do whatever you want. Maybe have a cup of coffee.
8   A fictional archaeologist who hated snakes, Nazis, and anything resembling actual archaeology.
9   A classic Homer Simpson gift-giving tactic. See *The Simpsons* episode "Life on the Fast Lane" (1990). Or don't. I'm not the boss of you.

"Ah, but I'm not just a coffeemaker. I'm also a detective. A detective-in-training, at least."

"You still look ridiculous. But I know how stubborn you can be. You want to wear a hat, wear a hat."

"I will," I said, and I did.

*

Harken was still shaking his head with disapproval at my hat when something caught his eye[10] in the distance. "Arjay, how long has that man been looking at us?"

"The man wearing the military uniform in the red rowboat? The one staring in this direction?"

"Yes."

"Four minutes and twenty-eight seconds, with only two breaks, of five and nine seconds, respectively."

"Were you planning to tell me he was looking at us?"

"No. I assumed he was just admiring my hat." It was clear a moment later this assumption was incorrect.

Its rowbot stroking oars deep and steady, the rowboat conveyed the man in the uniform closer to our canoe. As his boat drew alongside us, we could see that his uniform was festooned with seventeen medals, none of which corresponded to any military in the history of the world. They dangled from colorful ribbons and were shiny just like me. Also dangling but less shiny were the man's jowls, which, like the rest of his flesh, were the color and texture of low-fat cottage cheese that had been left out too long. It was impossible to know his age by looking at him—facial alteration was common in the Great American and usually aesthetically successful, but if taken too far could sometimes leave people resembling a collection of vaguely organic lumps. If I had to guess, I would have said he was a few years older than Harken. Fortunately, age-guessing was not compulsory. His eyes were close-set and dark, his luxurious, shiny black hair smoothed back with some kind of gelatinous concoction composed of exotic ingredients that defied precise analysis at this distance. I'd have to get a strand for testing.

"Detective Frank Harken," the uniformed man in the red rowboat said, his voice sounding like he'd recently gargled with gravel, "I'm sorry to bother you while you're fishing."

"I'm not really fishing," Harken said as another trout leapt from the water into our canoe.

"It looks like you are." He considered the pile of fish at Harken's feet. "You're gonna need a bigger boat."

---

10 Fortunately, not literally, because we were fishing and a hook catching an eye would be unpleasant at best.

"I'm guessing you didn't come all the way over here to give me nautical advice."

"No, I did not. Might I have a moment of your time?"

"You might. Hell, you might have two moments, but after that I start charging." Harken was always a charmer when he met someone new.

The uniformed man didn't smile at Harken's hardboiled wit. "Of course, as you must know, I'm General Major Driver." He waited for the famous detective to acknowledge an equally famous person.

"Of course you are," Harken said. *Must know* notwithstanding, he had no idea who this guy was.

"I'd like to hire you on behalf of my client."

"Your client?"

"Yes, I manage Sannien." He said the word as if he expected the detective to recognize it.

Harken didn't. "Sannien? What is that, some kind of hair product company?"

"Hair product? You haven't heard of Sannien?" General Major Driver couldn't believe his ears.[11]

"No, I haven't. It sounds like a brand of yogurt, the kind that eases digestion. Is it a yogurt?"

"Detective Harken, Sannien is a person, a very important person."

I chimed[12] in. "You might even say Sannien is a VIP if you prefer acronyms."

"That was so helpful." Harken's words weren't dripping with sarcasm, but that's only because of sarcasm's exceptional viscosity.

"You're welcome, partner. Sannien is the third most popular influenceleb in the entire Great American."

General Major Driver was still put off that anyone alive wasn't familiar with him or his star client. "Soon he'll be the second most popular. At least your coffeemaker has heard of him."

"Arjay's heard of most things. Said a lot of them, too. What do you want from me, Mr. Driver?"

He corrected Harken. "It's not *Mister*. It's *General Major*."

"*General Major*? Were you in the war?"

"It's an honorary title."

"Who gave it to you?"

"I gave it to myself," the General Major said with pride.

---

11 Notoriously untrustworthy sensory organs I was fortunate not to possess.
12 I didn't actually chime, but I am shaped like a bell, in case you're curious.

"That's very generous of you. What do you want to hire me for?"

"For my client, Sannien, the third most popular influenceleb in the Great American."

"Yes, yes," Harken said. "We've already established that part. I might need more details."

"Well, Detective Harken, it's very simple, really. Someone is blackmailing Sannien and I want you to find out who it is and put a stop to it."

"Blackmail? That can be tricky. I'll need to know what they have on Sannien. And do they have it on vid?"

"I can't tell you what they have on him because I don't know. He received a message yesterday from someone threatening to reveal damaging information. He didn't know anything about it."

"Didn't know or wouldn't say?"

"Does it matter?"

"Yes, it matters. If he can tell me what they know about him, that could help us narrow down the suspects."

"Well, he said he doesn't know. He only knows that they sent him a message, said they'd expose damaging information if he didn't meet their demands. Then the message disappeared, was wiped away without a trace."

"And what were their demands?"

"They wouldn't tell him that."

"Let me get this straight. He received a message saying that if you don't meet unspecified demands, unspecified information will be exposed?"

"That is correct."

"It doesn't sound like much of a blackmail scheme. Whole thing could be someone just messing around. Has Sannien done anything he doesn't want exposed?"

General Major Driver looked at Harken. "Hasn't everyone?"

"I haven't," I said. It was true. I wasn't afraid of exposure of any kind, didn't even wear clothes, unless you count my new hat.

Harken shook his head at the General Major. "You're not giving me anything to go on. I'll have to talk to Sannien, see what he's leaving out."

"Sannien is booked all day, but he's having a party tonight to celebrate his new scent. Come to the party. When it's over, he'll have a few minutes free to talk."

"I'll need to do some digging.[13] Blackmailers are rarely strangers. Usually it's someone close enough to know something no one else knows. Someone the victim trusts."

13 At least there wouldn't be any heavy lifting.

"All his friends and associates are invited, anyone who might be in a position to take advantage of him. You can be sure whoever's blackmailing him will be there. I'll add you to the guest list. It'll be a good opportunity for you to start digging."

"We'll be there," Harken said.

"I'll bring a shovel," I said, and they both looked at me funny.

Scott Warnock
Yes-More People

Most likely, you know about Simone Biles and the 2021 Olympics. I haven't followed too closely the web scuttlebutt following her decision to withdraw from much of Olympic competition, only partially because I'm shutting myself off from Olympic news so as not to get spoilers every night.

I know that she specifically had the "twisties," and, more importantly, has been inspirational in discussing mental health. Her health, of course, is interlocked with her positioning as one of the greatest athletes ever, but I wonder if, while she is an extraordinary person, that she has something in common with many others: She's one of the *yes-more* people.

It's tough being a *yes-more* person. You always say yes. You always do more.

The lives of *yes-more* people are often engulfed by expectations, accomplishments, roles, titles, and duties. For long stretches of time, they often do get it all done. They brim with pride when someone says, "How do you do it?"

But other times, they're hollowed out, sleep-deprived, disoriented.

I can be a *yes-more* person. I don't know when it all started, but I got in the mode of doing things, saying yes—both in local activities and at work—and increasingly piling on. I got involved, got organized, and wanted to meet the world. I kinda love it most of the time.

But once in a while, it has left me hollowed out, sleep-deprived, disoriented.

It is difficult to escape, because *yes-more* people get a strong sense of identity from these external measures of self. And this can be very difficult to notice.

I had an experience with a very wise counselor once. I had a holiday gift for her, a candle (of course purchased by my wife because I was too busy to get it myself). As I exited my car to deliver the gift, I was not only in a rush (because I was late!), but I also had in my hands too much stuff including a phone, wallet, keys (I mean, why use a pocket?), a book. I tried to then answer a phone call and grab the gift, which was wrapped and in a paper bag, at the same time.

Of course, I dropped the bag on the pavement. I heard the jar around the candle shatter. Damn! I thought, but I brought it to her anyway, so she could see I did have something. I showed her and promised I would take it back and return with a replacement soon.

"Oh no," she said, relieving me of the bag, "I want *this* one." I was puzzled. But she made clear the experience for me by saying, "When you do too many things, something breaks." She kept that candle so she could remind me of that simple fact when I needed such reminding.

You can see that story resonated for me. I don't always succeed in following the advice of the wise counselor. I still often become identified with my *yes-more* self.

Sometimes, world-class athlete or not, you have to say no. Go to one less meeting. Miss a workout. Admit you can't do it.

Make no mistake, there are costs to saying no, missing things. But as I watched Biles' smart interview with Mike Tirico at the end of her Olympic experience, I saw realizing your limits, even for an extraordinary individual, can help you avoid the more serious and sometimes dangerous costs of the *yes-more* person.

Eric A. Zillmer

The Murderer: A Psychological Analysis

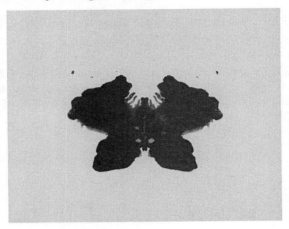

"A smiling face. Eyes. Got badly shot. Four holes."

The jail's occupants are murderers, rapists, robbers and drug dealers who are awaiting trial. The inmates are trying to come to grips with the fact that they have been caught, what they have done, and what awaits them. They are restless and anxious. I have been approved by the Public Defender's (PD) office to probe the mind of a spree killer. To do so, **I** brought with me an arsenal of psychological assessment procedures including: an IQ test, a number of cognitive measures, and a set of Rorschach inkblot cards. As I work my way through security, I **am** being asked to empty the entire contents of my attaché case, including the 10 inkblot cards, each measuring 6.5 by 9.5 inches. "Looks like a butterfly," the security guard offers as he is curiously inspecting Rorschach card number V.

I have been anxious about this evaluation, since spree killers are uncommon for me to interact with. Spree killers embark on a murderous assault of their victims over a short period of time. This differentiates them from a serial killer, who murders intermittently. In most spree killings the perpetrators do not survive, typically either taking their own life or being shot by law enforcement. Tony has been charged with fatally shooting eight people, seven fatally, over a two-day killing spree. "Unimaginable" **the** media summed up the murders. The forensic pictures of the crime scenes were unsettling to look at. While some homicides are planned ahead of time with an attention to details, these murders seemed impulsive and extremely violent. Tony apparently ran out of "ammo" and "finished" one of the victims with a baseball bat.

As a forensic neuropsychologist I was asked to determine whether Tony's police confession occurred as a consequence of a valid waiver of his Miranda rights. Furthermore, I was tasked to uncover any other psychological aspects that would assist in any leniency or diminished capacity for Tony's crimes, should he be found guilty. The precise motivation for this murder spree is unknown and Tony now denies having committed the crimes. My job is not to figure out whether he did it or not, but to assist in his defense. I am certain that the one procedure that will help me the most in terms of providing a glimpse into the mind of an alleged spree **killer** is the Rorschach inkblot method. The inkblot test is a series of ten symmetrical, ambiguous-looking inkblots to which subjects respond to the question, "What might this be?" My experience has been that murderers are often unable or vague in articulating a psychological explanation for their killings. The District Attorney (DA) agreed stating in the newspaper that, "one can't explain or understand it." As a psychologist, I think of the act of murder as a behavior, even a problem-solving task, illegal, but a set of behaviors, nevertheless. But what cognitive and psychological operations are set in motion when humans engage in murder?

At this moment Tony is being brought down the hallway dressed in an orange prison jump suit. Although his chin was tinged with a thin goatee, Tony's boyish face, and slight build, betrays his current age of 17. "Tony, it is good to see you. I am Dr. Eric Zillmer, I hope you remember me, we met about three weeks ago when the PD introduced me to you." "Yeah," he answers without making eye contact. I thank the guard, excuse him, and show Tony where I want him to sit. I can tell right away that Tony dislikes sitting in a chair. His attention wanders as he slouches over. "Tony, please sit straight, this morning we will do some work together and it will be important that you try your best." Tony became "overnight" a notorious killer. Tony was 16, a minor, when he committed the crimes and when he was interrogated. The prosecution is planning to charge him as an adult in exchange for waiving the death penalty. I was able to ascertain that Tony was alone with two veteran police interrogators, having waived his right to be with an adult or have a lawyer present. As a forensic psychological expert, I have to establish whether Tony provided this waiver of representation knowingly and intelligently.

"Tony, pay attention. What does the following mean? Anything you say may be used against you in a court of law." "If I say something it will be used against me in court," Tony responds without hesitation. "If you do not have an attorney available, you have the right to remain silent until you have an opportunity to consult one." "I can be quiet until I get a lawyer, right?" He told me that the interrogation lasted from 6 pm to the early morning hours. "I wasn't listening," he summarized his experience that evening. An hour of cognitive testing demonstrates that Tony has a rudimentary appreciation of the Miranda rights, which were introduced in 1966 via a United States Supreme Court decision in the case of Miranda v. Arizona as a way of protecting a criminal suspect's fifth amendment constitutional right for due process. I reviewed the psychological research on this topic and know that in many cases, and especially with minors, there is a motivation to tell the interrogator what they want to hear, even if it is not true. Because of a juvenile's developmental and emotional immaturity, they are especially at risk for misunderstanding the situation and being "tricked" into a false confession, that is, admitting to a crime that they did not commit. So, is there probable cause that Tony did not have the cognitive capability to withstand the police interrogation?

As a neuropsychologist I would think that a teenager like Tony would have difficulty matching wits with seasoned interrogators and understanding the legal consequences of his testimony. There is a neurodevelopmental reason why Tony would have been too young to drive a car or not be of age to legally drink. But he is able to represent himself vis-à-vis two experienced interrogators? I have to stay objective. I know that psychology and the law often don't mix. My focus as a forensic psychological expert is to establish whether Tony provided this waiver knowingly and intelligently. Keeping emotions and facts separate is a professional requirement for a forensic expert. As such, my role is very different than the point of view of a psychotherapist, who tries to "help" people. I am not trained as a lawyer but given that a confession remains the most compelling type of evidence in United States criminal law, I would imagine that it would be quite difficult to ignore Tony's 100-page signed statement. In addition, I gathered from reading about the case that Tony's fingerprints are on the murder weapon and that there are eyewitnesses. But I soldier on knowing that the legal process often involves a lot of behind-the-scenes horse-trading.

"What is the greatest stress being in here?" I ask Tony to provide a break from the testing procedures. "The glass when I have visitors. I can't be with them, which hurts a lot. My bail was set at 5 mill, don't you think that is a lot ... 5 mill, I bet you, you **have** a mill, but who has 5 mill?" Tony may be street smart, but the testing reveals that his psychometric intelligence corresponded to the 2nd percentile, which means that 98% of his peers score higher. Not a surprise given his record of poor academic achievements and class absenteeism. Tony is not a brilliant criminal. Can one plead not guilty in the court of universal justice just because of low IQ? Probably not.

I gauge Tony's attention and decide to start with the Rorschach inkblot procedure. I present card number I to him. "What might this be?" "A smiling face. Eyes. Got badly shot. 4 holes" Tony responds immediately and without any affect. I am taken aback by this chilling and psychological strained response. The emotional incongruence between "smiling" and being "badly shot," is very odd. Eerily, I remember many eyewitness accounts and security videos from spree killings, which often show the shooter as smiling. Smiling in this case may be a psychological defense mechanism of self-deception and reality distortion, given the seriousness of the situation. There is a lot going on in Tony's first inkblot response as I take a deep breath and continue.

While the first card is achromatic, five of the ten Rorschach cards have color in them, and this is true for card number II, which is red and black. "What might this be?" "I can't see anything," Tony shoots back as he pushes the card away visibly upset with the inkblot. I noticed that within one second his demeanor has suddenly changed. I remind Tony that most people can see something in every inkblot, trying to encourage him. "I don't know about that red stuff." He shoots back, glaring at me. Tony for the first time is becoming upset today. The intensity of his affect is quite remarkable. I remember reading in the legal records that he once sucker-punched a high-school principal in the face. Tony can't integrate a response that has the color red in it, which demonstrates **significant** constraints in his ability to express emotions and modulate affect appropriately. I am hypothesizing that this may be the root of his **problems**.

Card V: "That's it! This is the wings and stuff. Like a butterfly." Tony is thankful to have found something in this, the easiest of inkblots, that he can identify and lets out a big sigh, since he pretty much made a psychological mess of the preceding cards. Card VII: "Two people looking at each other. Looks like nobody I know." Seeing humans in inkblots is often a good sign. And since they are looking at each other the response almost qualifies for what we consider a Cooperative response, which would show that Tony has some emotional depth. But Tony adds to the response that he does not know the people, a personalization suggesting he is a loner.

Card X is the last card of the Rorschach procedure. "A spinning top. Up here spinning," ... spinning out of control, I add in my thought. "You know you could make it in here" he spontaneously offers. "You would be alright. There are many bald guys in here with glasses. You would be OK. Just keep to yourself and out of the way, and they will respect you," he offers with a smirk. I interpret Tony's willingness to chat as a sign that he does not want me to leave. But it is time, after nearly six hours of testing I **am** finished. I summon the guard to pick him up. In the hallway I hear Tony bitterly complain since he insists that he could find his way upstairs alone. To no avail. The guard slams shut an ominous-looking metal sliding door and Tony is out of sight.

My findings suggested that Tony has a rudimentary appreciation of the Miranda verbiage, legally speaking. This would be my expert opinion. Not every forced interrogation results in **a** false confession. While his IQ was low, which corresponds to his poor academic record, his verbal comprehension and social understanding of the world suggested that he knows right from wrong. The findings from the Rorschach showed that Tony has problems developing and mobilizing appropriate cognitive strategies. His emotional life is in turmoil. Having been abandoned by his parents and raised by relatives, it appears that he never formed close attachment to other people. In fact, Tony sees himself very much as a **victim** of circumstances. This is very similar to other perpetrators, especially those with childhood histories of abuse and trauma. They feel that life provided them with very few choices. It is not surprising Tony's biggest deficits are emotional. He has severe difficulties in modulating emotions, is very oppositional even defiant, and resents authority. Tony is very much at risk for inappropriate social behavior and impulsivity. I have not been asked to write a threat assessment on Tony, but I would think that in certain emotionally confusing situations that he could become extremely violent; dangerous **too**. Mitigating factors, to be sure, but probably not enough that would allow for his confession to be overturned. I sit back in the chair in my office. It is now midnight.

The next week I meet with the PD to discuss my findings. Not pleased with my conclusions that Tony most likely "understood" his waiver of Miranda, the public defender's office asked me to withhold from writing a report and terminated me from the case. The public defender was hoping for even more impairment in Tony that could provide a stronger case for his defense. Better to be accurate than tell the lawyer what he wants to hear. Most of the time counselors appreciate my professional honesty since it saves them time and money. Not in this case. A week later another psychology expert was hired and flown in from Los Angeles to examine Tony.

Five years later I read in the newspapers that, Tony, now age 22, was sentenced to 350 years in a state prison for his deadly shooting spree. He will be eligible for parole in 268 years.

Based on true events. Specific details, including name and location, have been changed.

Inkblot courtesy of Molly Harrower.

Contributors

Jennifer Britton joined Drexel's professional staff in 2002 and has coordinated multi-stakeholder programs like the International Area Studies major and the Drexel Engineering Cities Initiative. Since 2012 she has been with the Office of University and Community Partnerships and as part of that team was the founding director of the Dornsife Center for Neighborhood Partnerships. Most recently Jen has brought the experience of connecting Drexel with its neighbors and designing mission-driven initiatives to developing Drexel's climate and sustainability strategy. She has published research about wild horse governance and institutional anchor mission development.

Claire Brown (she/her) is a writer, musician, and English student at Drexel University. She has written for websites such as *The Hard Times, Points in Case, and Spill Magazine*. Her music spans many genres and has received positive reviews on websites such as Instagram and *RateYourMusic*. She is a transgender pansexual woman and hopes to create art that speaks accurately and humorously to the queer experience. She wants you to know that if you're reading this, you're also transgender and you just don't know it yet.

Madeline Burger is a Drexel student majoring in Computer Science. She is the president and founder of the Drexel University Book Club. In her free time, she enjoys reading, writing, coding, snowboarding, and listening to music.

Grace Carson is a sophomore Economics and Data Science major at Drexel University. In her field, she seeks to leverage beneficial outcomes for businesses by applying economic insight to the utilization of skills practiced by data scientists. An underlying passion of hers is exploring how data science can be applied to solve problems at the forefront of the music industry. Creating enjoyable experiences for individuals, especially involving music, is the catalyst which drives her to pursue a minor in interactive digital media.

Upoma Chakraborty is a fifth-year English major with minors in Writing and Legal Studies. She hopes to attend law school in the future for immigration law. Upoma has been featured in *The 33rd* before, along with publications in *Maya Literary Magazine* and *The Paper Dragon*. When she is not reading and writing, she likes photography, spending too much money on food, travel, and memes.

Paula Marantz Cohen is Distinguished Professor of English and Dean of the Pennoni Honors College at Drexel University in Philadelphia. She is the author of 12 books, including scholarly and nonfiction works on literature and film, and a half dozen novels, some spin-offs on Jane Austen and Shakespeare, a YA novel, and a thriller involving the James family and Jack the Ripper. She is a frequent contributor to *The Wall Street Journal, The Times Literary Supplement, The Yale Review, and The American Scholar*, and the host of the nationally distributed television interview show, The Civil Discourse (formerly The Drexel InterView), which also produced her documentary film, *Two Universities and the Future of China*. Her latest book, *Of Human Kindness: What Shakespeare Teaches Us About Empathy*, has just been published by Yale UP, and her book *Talking Cure: An Essay on the Civilizing Power of Conversation* is forthcoming from Princeton UP.

Qwuacii Cousins is a 4th year Civil Engineering Major. Playing on her Caribbean heritage, her writing is designed to give a glimpse into the inner workings of the culture, the storytelling style and colourful language, reminiscent of all the fireside stories she grew up on. A hesitant writer, you'll be hard pressed to find pieces outside of academia. When she takes the occasional flutter, you notice the subtle details; a trickle of moonlight here and there to paint the scene, as it were, and no piece is complete without the gentle mockery of the characters and the still small voice of reason that shines though.

Lily DeSimone is an English major with a concentration in Writing and in the Pennoni Honors College. Her inspiration for her piece was because she wanted the opportunity to explore the ideas of rhetoric and the structure of grammar in English after taking Issues in Modern Grammar. Lily hopes to continue further research with topics relating to the structure of the English language and its social implications which surround the grammatical structure. Outside her interests in English, Lily is an athlete and races sprint triathlons and is a member of the Club Swim Team, and as many other college students, she thoroughly enjoys an iced coffee.

Noah Entz is a Biology major and plans to return home to California to attend veterinary school after graduating. Writing has been his hobby of choice and he has been writing in his free time since elementary school. Noah enjoys being able to intertwine these two interests and found this to be a wonderful opportunity to do so while deepening his own understanding of the topic.

Ebubechukwu Donatus Enwerem is a first-year Computer Science undergraduate student. He is captivated by the incredible concepts that exist in the world of computing. He is no stranger to writing, having published his first book when he was ten years old. He believes in the philosophy of "beauty in the struggle, ugliness in the success," and views every challenge that life throws at him as an opportunity to grow.

Arthur Fink is a first-year Biological Sciences major with a passion for animals and entomology. He plans to work as a Veterinary doctor for exotic animals, like big cats and other zoo animals. In addition to his passion for racial and LGBT justice, his interests include nature walks, drawing, and just taking life one day at a time.

Grace Fisher is a second-year student double-majoring in English and Dance. She enjoys writing poetry as well as analysis of language and literature. When she's not reading, writing, or dancing, she enjoys playing the piano and knitting, although not simultaneously.

Tim Fitts teaches in the First-Year Writing Program at Drexel University and is a faculty member of The Curtis Institute of Music. He has published over fifty short stories, along with two short story collections. His novel, *The Soju Club*, was published in Korea as a Korean translation, by Loupe, an imprint of Munhakdongne.

Valerie Fox's books include *The Rorschach Factory, The Glass Book, and Insomniatic*. She's published prose in *Cleaver, The Ekphrastic Review, Juked, Reflex, The Cafe Irreal, Ellipsis Zine, The A3 Review,* and other journals. A story she wrote is included in *The Group of Seven Reimagined: Contemporary Stories Inspired by Historic Canadian Paintings*, edited by Karen Schauber. Recently,

Valerie published *The Real Sky*, a handmade artist's book (sketches, words) in an edition of 26, with artist Jacklynn Niemiec.

Max Gallagher starts every day with a beautiful bowl of oatmeal, complete with a large spoonful of peanut butter and a healthy sprinkling of cinnamon. When they're not eating oatmeal, they enjoy living their life, singing, writing, smiling. At Drexel University, they've studied a blend of mathematics, philosophy, and playwriting, plus whatever else they could stuff into their bloated plan of study. Knitting sure is fun. Max enjoys knitting, and they also enjoy you.

Geneva R. Gigliati is an undergraduate student at Drexel majoring in Philosophy, Politics and Economics. She works at a local animal hospital full-time in addition to being a full-time student. In her free time, Geneva enjoys spending time at home with her partner Lino and their dog Xena. Geneva has a background in art and creative writing.

Kathleen R. Grillo is a senior in the College of Arts and Sciences majoring in Chemistry with a minor in English. She loves anything to do with reading and writing and has a personal collection of over 300 books. She has written over fifty academic essays spanning an array of topics, including culture, STEM, and literature, two of which have been published in an online journal.

Henry Israeli is the author of four collections of poetry, most recently *Our Age of Anxiety*, winner of the 2019 White Pine Poetry Prize. He is the founder of Saturnalia Books and runs the annual Drexel Writing Festival and the Jewish Studies program.

Kirsten Kaschock was, until recently, Faculty Director with Writers Room and Associate Teaching Professor at Drexel. She is a writer with degrees in dance and literature and believes that art is an essential part of being human. She is the mother of three sons and the author of five poetry books and a novel.

Miriam N. Kotzin writes fiction, poetry, and occasional creative nonfiction. Her novel *Right This Way* will be published by Spuyten Duyvil Press in 2022. It joins *Country Music* (Spuyten Duyvil Press 2017), a novel, *The Real Deal* (Brick House Press 2012), and a collection of flash fiction. She is the author of five collections of poetry, most recently, *Debris Field* (David Robert Books 2017). Her fiction and poetry has been published in a number of anthologies and publications such as *Shenandoah, Boulevard, Eclectica, Goliad Review, Mezzo Cammin, Offcourse, and Valparaiso Poetry Review*. Her micros have been published in or are forthcoming in *Blink Ink, 50-Word Stories, and Five Minutes*. She teaches creative writing and literature at Drexel University.

Dylan Lam is a recent graduate of the Film and Television major at Drexel. Since he's mostly useless with a paintbrush, he uses a camera as his artistic medium of choice, searching for moments of unison and harmony out in the world. Currently, he works as Lead Editor at Dream Machine Creative, a full-service creative studio based in New York City. More of Dylan's work can be found at iamdylanlam.com.

Lynn Levin is a poet, writer, translator, and member of Drexel's Department of English and Philosophy. Her fiction, essays, and poetry have been published in *The Saturday Evening Post, Cleaver, The Satirist, Hawaii Pacific Review, Michigan*

Quarterly Review, Boulevard, Rattle, and other places. She is the author of five collections of poems. House Parties, her debut collection of short fiction, is forthcoming from Spuyten Duyvil.

Allison Lord is a first-year Film and Television major with a minor in Sports Management. She is on the Women's Club Rugby Team and Drexel's Mock Trial team. She enjoys writing argumentative and research essays, as it channels her inner high school debate kid. She also enjoys writing humor pieces. She has been published once previously, for a poem she wrote in the second grade.

Tanya Lulla is a Biology major as part of the BS/MD program at Drexel University. While her academic interests revolve around the sciences and the medical field, outside of school, she loves the arts, whether it be performing arts, visual arts, or even makeup artistry. To share this passion, she holds art classes for children and parents in her local community. In her free time, Tanya enjoys watching movies, spending quality time with her family and friends, and exploring new dessert shops in the city.

Tiffany Mai (she/hers) is a first-year student at the Lebow College of Business, majoring in Management Information Systems. She has enjoyed reading ever since she was little. When she is not studying or reading, Tiffany enjoys spending time with her friends and family, watching shows and k-dramas on Netflix, listening to music, eating, and playing video games in her free time.

Carol Richardson McCullough is a retired language arts teacher by trade and a poet/memoirist at heart. A founding member of Writers Room, she has served as its Cultural Liaison, connecting the multi-generational writing community with arts institutions throughout the city. She has been a TRIPOD Writer-in-Residence since 2017, fashioning photographic and written images that honor the past and the present, preserving them for the future. She has also conducted research on combating gentrification through cooperative living strategies in her surrounding community, sponsored by AmeriCorps and the Drexel School of Education. This Mountain Mama-turned-Philly Jawn is learning to embrace her newly acquired Auntie Life status while taking a lesson from Ecclesiastes 3: As seasons change, she adjusts.

Leah Mele-Bazaz is the author of *Laila: Held for a Moment.* She earned her MFA in Creative Writing at Drexel University, where she also teaches rhetoric and composition. In 2022, she was shortlisted for the Eunice Williams Nonfiction Prize.

Victoria Faith Miller is a first-year Entrepreneurship and Innovation major with a concentration in Social Entrepreneurship, inspired by her growing interest in girls' education and gender equality advocacy. She is a Theatre Performance Scholar, Student Ambassador, and Pennoni Honors College Student. Victoria is passionate about singing, songwriting, playing the ukulele, and acting for film and television. She is an avid lover of the outdoors and exploring the curiosities of the world, where she finds much of the inspiration for her creative pursuits.

Maya Micci Morrison is a senior Music Industry student in Drexel University's Westphal College of Media Arts and Design. She is currently studying to become an A&R executive and artist manager. Since she joined a creative writing club at her high school in 2016, Maya has always expressed herself through her lyrics, poetry and short stories. After college, she wishes to support artists throughout their careers in telling their own stories through music.

Iris Nguyen Ho was a first-year Physics student at Drexel at the time of this work. She enjoys the arts and finds herself capable of drawing, painting, and creating things. Writing has not been one of her strengths, but she loves using words to paint pictures of her mind.

Gwen Ottinger is Associate Professor at Drexel University, in the Department of Politics and the Center for Science, Technology, and Society. They direct the Fair Tech Collective, a research group that uses social science theory and methods to promote social justice in science and technology. They have received a CAREER award from the U.S. National Science Foundation for their research on "Environmental Justice and the Ethics of Science and Technology," and the 2015 Rachel Carson Prize from the Society for Social Studies of Science for their book, *Refining Expertise: How Responsible Engineers Subvert Environmental Justice Challenges.* Ottinger has been an ACLS-Burkhardt Fellow, Fellow at the Center for Advanced Study in the Behavioral Sciences (CASBS) at Stanford University, and Fulbright Research Chair in Science and Society at the University of Ottawa.

Shraddha Pandya is a current Biomedical Engineering major at Drexel University from Maryland. She plans to pursue further education in the biomedical/neuroscience fields and wants to go into research. She enjoys reading, photography, and creative writing, and is in the process of writing a novel.

Sarah Phan has passions that run deep when it comes to anything of the arts: music, dancing, drawing, acting; you name it. She grew up reading (and being a big fan of) romance stories, always finding them to be anomalies because they never reflected reality. Thus came her research piece, "Love As a Pessimist," in which she explores how others have asked and answered the same questions to not only understand the world around her, but herself more.

Anh Quach is a junior majoring in Biology with a minor in Food Science. She hopes to become a microbiologist to explore the fascinating freakiness of bacteria and help tackle the antibiotic resistance crisis. When she is not running experiments in the lab, doing homework, or napping, she enjoys experimenting with her hair color, cooking, playing the piano and violin (albeit badly), and going on long walks in the city. An international student from Ho Chi Minh City, Vietnam, Anh's creative writing is inspired by her upbringing in urban Vietnam. Through her previous work, "Tales from Quarantine" published in the 2021 edition of *The 33rd,* as well as "Home and Away," she hopes to portray the monumental impacts of COVID-19 on the lives of fellow Vietnamese people as well as retell their stories of struggle, resilience, and hope.

Sanjana Ramanathan is an undergraduate English major at Drexel University with a concentration in Writing. She enjoys writing poetry, essays, and fictional short stories. Her hobbies include reading and playing video games. Her essay previously published by *The 33rd,* "An End to Sexism in Gaming Communities," has been included in the newest edition of W.W. Norton's textbook *They Say / I Say.*

Cosmo Randazzo ('24, Chemical Engineering) from a young age and now at 20, has a passion for reaching the hearts and minds of others that extends across mediums such as STEM work, food, illustration, music, mental health advocacy, and writing. With empathy and self-truth as fuel, they use poetry, psychological fiction/nonfiction, and spoken word as vessels through which they can connect with the world in a deeply personal way.

Don Riggs (he, him, his) studied Medieval French, Latin, and English at the University of North Carolina Chapel Hill, focusing on the Troubadours, translation, and the Arthurian literatures. He has published poems in various places, and now places a fresh one each day on Facebook. He has also co-translated Francois Cheng's *Chinese Poetic Writing* (1982 and new expanded edition 2017). His previous Arthurian publication was on Marie de France and Marion Zimmer Bradley in the *Journal of the Fantastic in the Arts*, special issue on The Goddess.

Gail Davida Rosen is a teaching professor at Drexel University in the department of English and Philosophy. She has been editor of *The 33rd* since 2017. She teaches in the First-Year Writing and Literature programs, as well as in the Pennoni Honors College.

Katelynn Rudolph is an undergraduate Psychology major with a minor in Neuroscience at Drexel University. She was born in Modesto, California and has a strong passion for self-expression through means of writing. On campus, she is involved with several organizations and plans to pursue neuropsychology after her studies. Outside academia, she enjoys modeling, inline skating, and reading.

Lucy Song is an undergraduate Health Sciences student at Drexel University on the physician assistant track. She has always been fascinated by how the human body functions and how every piece must work together. She enjoys writing as a hobby, as well as playing sports like volleyball and figure skating, volunteering, and traveling. Lucy is passionate about helping others and developing meaningful relationships with people, which is why she is interested in working in healthcare.

Scott Stein is the author of four novels: *The Great American Betrayal, The Great American Deception, Mean Martin Manning, and Lost.* His writing has appeared in *The Oxford University Press Humor Reader, McSweeney's, Points in Case, Philadelphia Inquirer, National Review, Reason, Art Times, Liberty, The G.W. Review,* and *New York Magazine.* He is a teaching professor of English at Drexel University.

Malea Troy is a Nursing major from Worcester, Massachusetts. She is very interested in the exploration and analysis of diversity and equity dynamics in different social and cultural climates. While she claims writing is not usually her forte, she found her piece easy to write because of how important and pertinent she finds this topic.

Roger Vitek is a Product Design major who has an interest in human interaction and behavior. He enjoys the research process and hopes to apply psychological research towards the design field. Roger enjoys playing piano and bicycling.

Scott Warnock is a professor of English and Associate Dean of Undergraduate Education in the College of Arts and Sciences at Drexel. He teaches a variety of courses and is widely published in the areas of online writing instruction, computers and composition, and education technology. Dr. Warnock is immediate past president of the Global Society of Online Literacy Educators. He is president of the Palmyra High School Foundation for Educational Excellence and has coached youth sports in his community since 2005. He writes the blog/column "Virtual Children" for the website *When Falls the Coliseum*.

Maddie White is currently pursuing her bachelor's degree in Mechanical Engineering with a concentration in Aerospace. She is in her second year at Drexel and is a member of the Division 1 Women's Lacrosse team. In her free time, Maddie enjoys playing lacrosse and spending time with friends and family. Both of her parents were Dragons; her father competed on the baseball team and her mother on the field hockey and lacrosse teams. Maddie is very close with her two sisters. Her twin sister, Lily, attends Northeastern University, and her little sister, Natalie, will be attending the University of Florida in the fall.

Eric A. Zillmer is the Carl R. Pacifico Professor of Neuropsychology and a Licensed Clinical Psychologist in the Department of Psychological and Brain Sciences at Drexel University in Philadelphia. He is the author of the texts The Quest for the Nazi Personality (Routledge) and Military Psychology (Guilford) as well as two psychological assessment procedures: The d2 Test of Attention (Hogrefe) and The Tower of London Test (MHS Assessments). Dr. Zillmer is a Fellow of the College of Physicians of Philadelphia, The American Psychological Association, and the National Academy of Neuropsychology, for which he also served as President. At Drexel he teaches courses on Neuropsychological Assessment and was the 2019 recipient of the Outstanding Faculty Award in the Pennoni Honors College.

Want to appear in the 2023 edition of *The 33rd?*

All Drexel students and faculty are eligible

For more information, visit **drexelpublishing.com**